STITCHES

A PATCHWORK OF FEMINIST HUMOR AND SATIRE

Edited By
Gloria Kaufman

Indiana University Press
Bloomington and Indianapolis

© 1991 by Indiana University Press
All rights reserved

The paper used in this publication meets the minimum requirements of American
National Standard for Information Sciences—Permanence of Paper for Printed
Library Materials, ANSI Z39.48–1984.

(∞)™

Manufactured in the United States of America

Library of Congress Cataloging-in-Publication Data

In stitches : a patchwork of feminist humor and satire / edited by
    Gloria Kaufman.
        p.   cm.
    Includes index.
    ISBN 0-253-33141-2 (alk. paper). — ISBN 0-253-20641-3 (pbk. :
alk. paper)
    1. Feminism—Humor.   2. Women—Humor.   I. Kaufman, Gloria J., date.
PN6231.F44I5   1991
305.42'0207—dc20   90-47553
                                                              CIP

2 3 4 5   95 94 93 92

Contents

Older and Bolder   51

If Clothes MAKE the Man, Do Clothes UN-make the Woman?   67

> **"On Freezing Embryos: Defrosting a human being when they can't even get a *Pizza* to come out right?"**
>
> **Elayne Boosler**

That Three-Letter Word

"No chivalry prevents men from getting women at the very lowest possible wages."

Elizabeth Robins

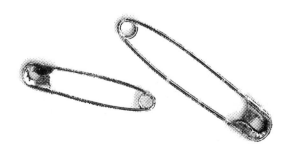

Snooking & Snaffling Snools

Grabasket

" . . . we whose hands have rocked the cradle are now using our heads to rock the boat . . . "

Wilma Scott Heide

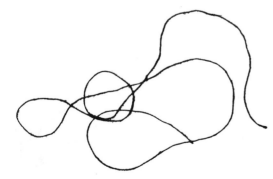

Zap!

Witty Women

"Here the melting pot stands open—if you're willing to get bleached first."

Buffy Sainte-Marie

INTRODUCTION
Humor and Power
Gloria Kaufman

Humor is empowering.

Oppressed peoples deliberately use humor to lighten the burdens of daily life so that they can survive. Feminist humor, however, is not merely (or even primarily) survival humor. It grows out of a conviction that the assigning of power on the basis of genitalia is both ludicrous and unacceptable. Feminist humor clarifies vision with the satiric intent of inspiring change. It is therefore essentially hopeful rather than resigned or bitter, as mainstream women's humor often is. In contrast to feminist humor, *nonfeminist* women's humor is frequently survival humor. It accepts a status quo regarded as inevitable.[1] The empowerment derived from such humor is far less than that of revolutionary humor, which points toward change.

Feminist humor, insofar as it indicates (or inspires) change, is obviously concerned with the transfer of power from those who have it overwhelmingly to those who have too little. But feminist humor is much more. To indicate its overt political dimension is like describing a dolphin only in terms of the magnificent muscle that propels her flamboyantly into the air. If feminist humor is our dolphin, we must also describe her sleek body, her rich language, her subtle smile. The subtleties are immense.

Why, then, attempt to define feminist humor? Because an editor has some obligation to explain to readers interested in such matters why some of the items in the book have been included. "That's amusing, but how is it feminist?" was a constant challenge I received from Leslie Viktora, whom I used as a sounding board in compiling *In Stitches*.

All definitions are of course partial, for as soon as a person or an idea can be defined, it is dead. But the world of ideas and people is richly alive. What eludes definition? Perhaps it is their possibilities that are the most important aspects of concepts and of creatures, and we don't define a person or an idea by its potential. Understanding, then, that my quixotic sallies into definition are incomplete, let me add to my initial description of feminist humor, our graceful dolphin. Her spectacular leaps are the self-conscious political aspects of feminist humor I have described in the opening paragraph, but there is more to say about her life under water. If a contributor is a proclaimed feminist (such as Mary Kay Blakely and Barbara Ehrenreich), then her feminist vision informs all aspects of living, and it is reflected in her humor, not only in overt but also in quite subtle ways. If an artist is *sub*consciously or *un*consciously feminist, that too is expressed in complex and oblique ways that are far less discernible. Furthermore, feminism so pervades our culture today that feminist humor is sometimes produced by consciously nonfeminist people—and even occasionally by antifeminists. When the "message" of a piece is overtly political, it is of course easy to label. That is the dolphin leaping. Under water, I am disposed to quote Dorothy Parker (as Nancy A. Walker did in introducing her book on women's humor):

> I had thought, on starting this composition [*The Most of S. J. Perelman*] that I should define what humor means to me. However, every time I tried to, I had to go and lie down with a cold wet cloth on my head. [p. xii]

I, like Dorothy Parker and countless others, am undone by the task at hand. Much of the humor of *In Stitches* is not brazenly political, and is thus "under water." For example, the feminist aspects of Bambara's "My Man Bovanne," a poignant work of art, are less obvious than many of the story's other important meanings. But when we think about how painfully typical it is that United States culture devalues or ignores the humane wisdom of older women and how painfully typical it is for mothers to be treated with disrespect by their children, we see profoundly feminist perspectives.

Under water, we must acknowledge that the sleek body of feminist humor has an end-

DIRECTION FOR USE

1. Purchase: 1 designer gun per child; 1-2 designer guns per adult.
2. Usage: The designer gun can be used anywhere and everywhere. Please choose those you love or hate. Choose colors and materials to enhance your specific environment.
3. Method: when angry just reach for the designer gun, put finger on trigger and say, "Bang, bang." Join those who "Shoot to Laugh."
4. Warning: This product has been determined to be harmless to your health and those you shoot.

less variety of subtleties, as shown in Bambara's fiction. Under water, we must realize that our dolphin's rich language has multileveled meanings (as in Virginia Maksymowicz's "The History of Art," p. 169) that make critics' current comments on subtexts seem inadequate, simplistic, and reductive. Under water, we can suppose that our dolphin's enigmatic smile asserts that she is totally beyond definition and that she tolerantly chides our attempts to describe her and that she wants us to know she is not even who she is but also who she will become, that her soul is her as-yet-unrealized and never-to-be-described potential.

The only sense, then, in which I am willing to define my vision of feminist humor is to assert that the entire volume of *In Stitches* is an instance of definition by example. The contents taken totally define the dolphin to the extent that definition is possible. The reader's imagination is then free to discover subtleties other than those that I see, to disagree with my selections, to ponder, and to meander where it will. (I particularly invite disagreement because my choices and analyses of feminist humor reflect my own bias toward what is positive.)

The humor that people create is a strong indicator of who they are and what they value. Feminist humor celebrates modes of power quite different from masculine societal norms. Indeed, it regularly satirizes as puerile or illogical the common equation of force and power. In the feminist view, the man with the gun, lacking persuasive power, lacking imagination, insecure in himself, is weak, not powerful. Molly's Designer Guns (p. 70) are a delightful burlesque, comically suggesting that men have failed to appreciate the best potential in firearms. Pat Oleszko's walking poster (p. 69) shows us the multiple powers of art, of pleasure, and of visual delight. Jane Wagner's "The Suicide Note" (p. 128) is a brilliant and subtle demonstration of how a mere feeling for the connectedness of human beings can charge us with another kind of less conscious but vividly felt understanding—an understanding that is both exhilarating and deeply empowering.

Feminism is committed to the idea that knowledge and understanding themselves convey strength (far more than guns and force), and that they can be put to use to enhance their powers still further. In a general sense, therefore, everything we know empowers us. In the "Zap!" section, all the street actions bringing information to the general public express (in complex ways) both the power of words and the power of actions. In another sense, our learning that such actions took place, as, for example, that the Ladies Against Women held a bake sale at the Republican National Convention (p. 154), gives us greater knowledge of our history of protest, and that knowledge strengthens us. In contrast to mainstream masculinist humor, feminist humor often and consciously presents information that can empower people.

Mainstream attack humor is not salutary in the way that feminist humor is. The laughter that a put-down elicits smears a smile over someone's pain and leaves its victim hurting. Perhaps it even damages the teller, who certainly knows he or she has provided more pain than mirth. The smirk of the superior is not a positive thing. Feminist humor, in contrast, invites its "victims" to change their wrong behaviors and join the laughter. Thus in "Psychic Economics" (p. 137), Mary Kay Blakely allows the unnamed administrator to share with us the folly of his "psychic income." Her purpose is not to hurt him (or to ridicule him to elicit a cheap laugh) but rather to educate him so that he can make intelligent changes. The intent of the humor is to improve rather than to damage its object. Where mainstream humor strives to hurt the weak to maintain hierarchy and the status quo, feminist humor strives to educate both weak and powerful in order to stimulate change in the direction of equity or justice.

Some of the most imaginatively rebellious feminist humor comes from the art world. *In Stitches* deliberately attempts to suggest the variety of feminist humor in artistic productions—Glenna Park's Texas Marching Band (p. 155), Virginia Maksymowicz's "The History of Art" (p. 169), Elizabeth Layton's self-portrait (p. 53), Pat Oleszko's numerous "spectacles of herself," Susan Mogul's incursion into stand-up performance (p. 142), Evi Seidman's environmental art (p. 128), and so on. If I have partially succeeded in suggesting the variety of humorous art by feminist artists, I have in no way been able to suggest the enormous quantity of such art.

Humor and power are related in highly complex ways. On the one hand society has recognized the expression (or creation) of humor as an exercise of power and has reacted negatively to women humorists. (Things are changing.) On the other hand women (and other suppressed groups) have privately and regularly used humor to empower themselves in order to survive oppression or subversively to resist it. No one doubts that humor is empowering. It is especially positive in dispelling fear. Laughing at our enemies diminishes them and emboldens us. When they hear our impertinent, fearless humor, it additionally discomfits or angers them; sometimes it nourishes their self-doubts. But they also grudgingly admire our wit, if only subconsciously, and that somewhat weakens their will to oppress us.

Power dynamics are visible in joke telling, and a few comments are in order to explain why there are no jokes in *In Stitches*. Jokes are not a favored form of humor with feminists—not only because so many jokes are based on stereotypes and feminism tends to be sharply critical of stereotypical thinking. And not only because some jokes are aggressively destructive. Freudians explain such jokes as a healthy mechanism for the release of repressed hostilities, a convenient catharsis beneficial to the joker. Surprisingly (since they are therapists), they fail to consider the negative psychological impacts on victims of such jokes. Feminists do. Where catharsis for an aggressor leads to trauma for a victim, feminism sees no benefit.

The above reasons, however, do not sufficiently explain the dearth of feminist jokes and jokebooks. As feminists we are more likely to enjoy or to collect the jokes of other groups than to create our own. Our preferences are toward spontaneous wit, amusing real-life anecdotes, clever dialogue, and other forms of humor that are participatory. Jokes involve tellers and listeners. The teller is the active one at the center of attention, and the listeners are relatively passive. While the joke is being performed, conversation is closed off. Even when one joke teller does not monopolize attention and allows others in the group to tell their favorite jokes, spontaneous human interaction is largely absent. The group listens to performances that are predetermined and often unrelated to the lives of the listeners. (The truly artful joke teller, of course, knows when to joke and when to be silent.)

In dialogue, feminists generally prefer wit to jokes. The witticism grows out of the conversation: it is spontaneous, integrated, and integrating. Witty remarks contribute to dialogue, while jokes interrupt and distract from it. Jokes interjected into lively colloquy often seem, therefore, less creative and less meaningful than integrated witticisms. Feminists are far more likely than others to regard jokes as artificial, as old hat, or as inhibiting community, and to prefer humor forms more spontaneous, unpredictable, participatory, and lively. (For these reasons, I often advise social scientists measuring the reception of humor according to gender to use forms other than jokes in their studies.)

Finally, the joke teller often exerts a kind of control that feminists find unpleasant, particularly in social situations. The performer is safe. He is in control. He disallows the egalitarian risks of dialogue. That is one reason that Ronald Reagan told so many jokes. As Eileen Bender has pointed out to me, Reagan's joke telling gave him access to a power he could not have achieved in any other way. It allowed him to sidestep uncomfortable questions. It allowed him to defuse anger. It allowed him to take control from interrogators armed with far more information than he. Ronald Reagan's success is, indeed, one of the best illustrations of the power humor gives to those who know how to use it. Reagan validated his position as leader by his use of humor.

Because establishment patriarchal culture recognizes that humor is empowering, it has sought to deny women, children, and other "inferior" groups the capacity for humor. While society has failed to convince us that we women are humorless, it has succeeded in using mainstream humor to denigrate and to divide us. Mainstream humor has created a rich palette of negative stereotypes as devices for maintaining and increasing senses of inadequacy in oppressed groups. Think of all those mother-in-law jokes (by contrast, there are *no* father-in-law jokes). Mother-in-law jokes cause women to bond with men against other women (the mothers-in-law) and finally against themselves; for in patriarchal normative society, every woman will become a mother-in-law—nagging, unattractive, unpleasant at best, and nasty at her usual worst. The oppressive stereotype is so harped upon that mother-in-law humor causes the new young wife to look upon herself as exceptional, as unlike other (nasty) women. It teaches her to dislike and to separate from members of her own gender group. Negative stereotypes, a mainstay of patriarchal culture, are thus effective politically in maintaining the rule of "superior" white males over stereotypically conceived women, children, and minorities.

Feminist humor does not use power in such a way. It avoids stereotypes. A major purpose of feminist humor is, indeed, to build people up rather than to break them down. In the Introduction to the first collection of feminist humor and satire, *Pulling Our Own Strings* (1980),[2] I described feminist humor as largely pick-up in contrast to the huge quantity of put-down mainstream humor. Hostility humor is ultimately unattractive. We want something more, and we find it in other kinds of laughter—in humor that restores, in humor that renews, in humor that creates. The scholarship focusing on positive aspects of humor seems to me much more valuable and profound than the relatively monotonous work emphasizing humor as aggressively destructive.[3] Perhaps that is inevitable in a culture still dominated by Freudian ideas. Yet humor is surely striking for its positive effects, not only in stimulating laughter and pleasure but also for restoring perspective and enhancing clarity of vision.

Notwithstanding my personal preference for the positive, there is feminist humor that is angry or despairing or bitter. In general, the greater the perceived possibility for change, the more cheerful the humor. The less the likelihood of change, the grimmer or the angrier the humor. Much medical humor tends to be bitter because most people (feminists included) see little chance of significantly changing a profession so extravagantly worshipful of money and prestige. Of course, the other professions also cherish money and status, but none so deliberately train their practitioners to be arrogant (see *Getting Doctored* by Martin Shapiro, M.D.). More important, no other profession has established the unique control that places physicians almost entirely beyond reach of the law: i. e., almost nothing pernicious or even homicidal that a physician does is subject to criminal investigation or penalty. Currently, the medical profession is seeking further to diminish liability for its consciously harmful acts and devices (such as the Dalkon Shield). It reasons that compensating people who have been proven permanently harmed is too expensive. Logic, of course, dictates that medicine should stop the known harm. Physicians, however, use a special form of thinking which guarantees their blamelessness. Hazel Houlihingle explores that thinking in "Medical Logic" (p. 122), a piece that is more cheerful than much feminist medical humor because of its hilarious analogies.

A sense of humor is requisite for twentieth-century living. Today we are daily bombarded (through mass media) with more of the wrongs, miseries, and evils of the world than sensitive people can endure. Humor saves us; it preserves sanity. It insists that in the persistent darkness, there is also light. Its insistence is not a delusion but an important part of truth—a part too easily trivialized, a part too rarely prized.

The clarity of vision gifted to us by feminist humor should be emphasized in any comments on humor and power. The purpose of feminist theory is to strengthen us through analysis that leads to understanding. Feminist humor, however, often conveys understanding without leading us through jungles of abstraction. Thus, for example, Glenna Park's Texas Art Band marching down the streets of San Antonio, combined with relatively short news coverage, was able to convey a rich understanding of government priorities vis-à-vis budgets for the Department of Defense and the National Endowment for the Arts. The Band effectively dramatized national values. Humor, thus, often visits us with instant understanding. It is a valuable (and sometimes necessary) supplement to theory.

In Stitches intends to reaffirm our positive directions, to restore flagging feminist energies, to demonstrate the progress of the past decade, to cherish our artists who through humor achieve clarity and insight, to demonstrate and to reaffirm that in diversity there is strength. Feminist humor has a salutary social function. It brings us an abundance of nonmalicious laughter. It encourages playfulness. It puts our problems at laughing distance, restoring our perspective and sharpening our insight. It allows us to share our deep and serious commitments in joyful ways. Feminist humor renews in the mysterious way that great comedy renews—by putting its finger on the hugely positive potential of human beings and by reminding us of our rejuvenating choices.

Indiana University at South Bend
January 1991

NOTES

1. For a somewhat different view of feminist humor, see Nancy A. Walker, *A Very Serious Thing: Women's Humor and American Culture* (Minneapolis: University of Minnesota Press, 1988), esp. p. 13 and chapter 5.

2. *Pulling Our Own Strings: Feminist Humor and Satire,* edited by Gloria Kaufman and Mary Kay Blakely (Bloomington: Indiana University Press, 1980).

3. Uninformed readers can get a sense of the variety, volume, and solidity of humor scholarship from Patricia Keith-Spiegel, "Early Conceptions of Humor: Varieties & Issues," in *The Psychology of Humor,* edited by J. F. Goldstein and P. E. McGhee (New York: Academic Press, 1972), pp. 3–39; and from Paul E. McGhee and Jeffrey H. Goldstein, eds., *Handbook of Humor Research,* 2 vols. (New York: Springer Verlag, 1983). They might also consult publications of the International Society for Humor Studies, which are rich and various. A new interdisciplinary journal, *HUMOR: International Journal of Humor Research,* is edited by Victor Raskin at Purdue University, West Lafayette, IN 47907.

WHERE THE BOYS ARE

Barbara Ehrenreich

"I've never been married, but I say I'm divorced so people won't think there's something wrong with me."

Elayne Boosler

The other day I said something critical about men. "Pshaw, men!" would have been my exact words if I knew how to pronounce *pshaw*, but the point is, it was an altogether mild statement, considering that I was talking about the sex that invented antiballistic missiles and that grows hair in its ears. "Shh," said my friend—who will be called Claire—looking around anxiously, "don't you know there's a man *shortage*?" I was mystified. Why worry about offending them if we've got them outnumbered?

Of course, I already knew about the man shortage from reading *Cosmo, Mademoiselle, and Glamour,* where, along with the possibility of a breakthrough in bronze-tone lipsticks, it has been the only news for six months. My first reaction was to demand a recount. Everywhere *I* look there seems to be a shocking man *excess.* Take the U.S. Senate, with 98 men and 2 women—a man excess of 96. Or if you can't take the U.S. Senate as presently constituted, try taking the 6:00 P.M. Eastern shuttle out of Washington, and you'll risk being trampled by 200 massed males in three-piece suits stampeding for the aisle seats.

Once you start looking for it, you'll see the man excess everywhere—for example, in the table of contents of the *New Republic,* which routinely gathers together "Fred," "Stanley," "Joseph," "Mickey," and other like-named fellows. Or there's the tenured faculty at Harvard: 853 men and 45 women, for a man excess of 808. It's even possible to be alone in a room with one's husband, lover, or boss and discover, subjectively speaking, that there's a man excess of exactly one.

Claire was not impressed by my theory of a man excess. She had just read a scientific study showing that her chances, at age 34, of finding a man to marry were about the same as the probability of being struck dead in midtown Manhattan by a 747 piloted by a Croatian terrorist. Not one to mope, she took action. First, a Reticence Training seminar to "smooth out those rough edges caused by too much assertiveness training," as the brochure put it. Then a refresher course in home economics, with a focus on Sock Ironing and Football Appreciation to give it contemporary relevance. Finally, she purged her bookshelves of emasculating titles like *Sisterhood Is Powerful* and replaced them with more comforting fare like *How to Make Love to a Man* and *The American Heritage Cookbook.*

It must have worked, because she called me not long ago to say, in the hushed and proud tone of someone who has just acquired a thoroughbred ocelot at a discount, "I've got one! Would you like to come over and see him?" When I got there, she waved excitedly toward a pudgy figure sprawled on the living room couch, listening to something that might have been music or might have been Led Zeppelin—it was hard to tell at that volume. He had a two-day stubble and a look of extreme emotional inaccessibility on his face; otherwise he bore no resemblance to Don Johnson. "Well," I said, as politely as possible, "he's, uh, certainly cute." "Forget it!" Claire snarled. "I'm not into sharing!"

I couldn't help wondering, as she rushed off to freshen up his Diet Coke, whether there might not be more humane solutions to the man shortage. For example, men could be imported from the Third World, many parts of which are suffering from a man excess, at least when measured in terms of the local food supply. Or, if there is a premium on English-speaking men, we might be able to find some way to tap into the U.S. prison system, which presently houses 500,000 adult males, many of whom are single and only a minority of whom are rapists or serial killers. Or perhaps desperate singles like Claire should be retrained for man-rich work settings such as oil rigs or cocaine freighters—or missile-bearing nuclear submarines, which go underwater for months at a time and may represent the closest thing we have to canned men.

Otherwise, sooner or later, some smart editor or talk-show guest is going to realize that the problem isn't a man shortage, but a *woman* excess. Historically, societies have dealt with preponderances of women by clumsy methods such as female infanticide and witch-burnings. In our Information Age, though, the techniques would be more civilized. We'd start seeing *Cosmo* covers like "Rotten Beauty Advice to Give Your Girlfriends (Tee-Hee!)," with before and after pictures of lovelies destroyed by false eyeliner tips; or "A Wife in Your Way? Easy-to-fix Herbal Remedies That Leave *No* Trace!"

Needless to say, men are taking full advantage of the situation. On a first or second date, just when things are warming up enough for a woman to begin inquiring about her date's history of sexually transmitted diseases and the whereabouts of a photocopy of his latest blood-test results, it's now common for the fellow to snap back with: "Are you now or have you ever been a member of a feminist conciousness-raising group, or of NOW, or any similar coven of twisted, man-hating wretches?" (The correct answer is "Nooo!" with a dainty shudder.)

It would be a sickening irony if feminism were to be defeated, not by men, but by a shortage of them. And we women would have only ourselves to blame. I mean, we must be suffering from a terminal case of "fear of success" if we're going to let a numerical advantage for our side turn into a reason for full-scale retreat. Instead, we ought to be figuring out how to beat them while we still outnum-

> **"How many people know what it's like to be the only person in a relationship? *That's* solidarity!"**
>
> **Linda Moakes**

"Go! Go! Go! Go!"

(Drawing by C. Barsotti; © 1973 The New Yorker Magazine, Inc.)

ber them. Here's our chance, for example, to mobilize to get pay equity, strict child-support laws, subsidized child care, paid parental leave, and a few other items that have been of only incidental interest to the minority sex. As for husbands: Well, I say, let those petted darlings among the dwindling supply of single males aged 25 to 45 learn to fetch their own Diet Coke.

A GLOSSARY

Nancy Linn-Desmond

DATING is the process of spending enormous amounts of money, time, and energy to get better acquainted with a person whom you don't especially like now but will learn to like a lot less.

DIVORCE is an event that occurs when a man and woman have been married long enough to forget what dating was like.

GEOGRAPHICALLY UNDESIRABLE is a term used by a man to describe a woman who is not a good dating prospect because she is either more than a 15-minute drive away or else lives near enough to see what time he comes home and with whom.

INDIFFERENCE is a woman's feeling toward a man, which is referred to by the man as "playing hard to get."

INTERESTING is a word a man uses to describe a woman who lets him do all the talking.

LEFT HAND is the hand that every married man in a singles bar keeps in his pocket.

LOVE is a feeling for another person, meaning that you would rather be treated rotten by him than by anyone else.

RELATIONSHIP is the process of giving up those people who share

> " **We don't believe in rheumatism and true love until after the first attack.** "
>
> **Maria Ebner von Eschenbach**

your interests, humor, and habits in order to spend more time with someone who doesn't.

YOUNG is an adjective used by men to describe a woman who is under 18 or a man who is under 80.

(From *Dating*, ©1988, Citadel Press.)

GONE WITH THE WIMP

On New Sensitive Males (NSMs)

Alice Kahn

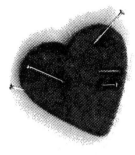

Pity the NSM.
He has worked so hard to educate himself, to be correct, to purify even the slightest sleazy thought. Now he finds himself the object of ridicule, not only from his unrepentant brothers (*Real Men Don't Eat Quiche*), but, worse yet, from the very sisters he has tried so hard to understand and empathize with. There are even some women who doubt his absolute sincerity, who consider his proclamations of feminist principles yet another subterfuge to get under the covers—a kind of missionary impossible, Clint Eastwood in Alan Alda's clothing. My feeling (and I know you care about my feelings) is that NSMs are not made; their sensitivity is born out of pain. Frequently there is a history of unrequited love, performance anxiety, or a deep longing to be morally superior that few women are sensitive enough to understand. It is this callous streak in women that drives the NSM mad. He can't tolerate cruelty or ambiguity. He has gone to great lengths to please, to be correct, and now feels hurt by what he perceives as the double message women seem to be sending.

This quest for miso and macho in one man was driven home to me some years ago while driving home from a feminist conference with a woman who called herself Shanti Litvok (not her real name). Shanti, a sensitive soul if ever there was one, had done time in every ashram from here to Delhi. Yet it turns out she had finally

"How many of you ever started dating someone 'cause you were too lazy to commit suicide?"

Judy Tenuta

(Reprinted by permission of Jules Feiffer.)

achieved Perfect Bliss with a simple flesh and blood man, an artist, a sculptor who possessed "magic fingers." Not only could he cook up a mean bowl of tofu but he would often pause in the middle to grab Shanti, throw her over his shoulder, and carry her up to the bedroom. "You know," she said, pausing to cast a glance towards Mecca, "sometimes you really need that male energy."

Of course, not every man is capable of achieving such sex-role centeredness (SRC). Thus we have at one extreme the NSM, the man who has sought through pain and guilt, or sheer lack of humor, to drive all assertiveness from his behavior. His quest is for real moral macho, and like all martyrs, he fails to understand why his effort is not appreciated, or better yet, rewarded. . . .

. . . Is there no end in sight to the battle of the sexes? Must it be wimps and tough guys and bitches to the bitter end? Can't we declare a truce? Perhaps women in search of men could send clearer messages. How about: Make Love and Breakfast. And men in search of women must work on their sex-role centeredness. It will be necessary for these men to undergo A Sex-role Self-Assessment (ASSA). Part One: Are you a tough guy? Hey, loosen up. See, this is easy. No mess, no fuss, and godforbid, no therapy. Just *loosen up*, let yourself go, the camera's not running and John Wayne is dead. Now, for the hard part. Part Two: complete the following test.

The Test: Are You an NSM?

1. Do you watch football? (Score 10 points if you said no; 5 if you watched only when the 49ers were champions because you thought Joe Montana had NSM role model potential.)

2. Are you now or have you ever been married? (Score 10 points if you said no. NSMs don't marry; they prefer to struggle with a relationship until they're really sure.)

3. If you were married and had children would you change diapers? (Score 10 points if you said yes; 5 if you said only the pee-pee ones.)

4. Are you comfortable with words like "flow," "vagina," "tampons," "areola," and "placenta?" (Give yourself 2 points for each word you're comfortable with.)

5. How about "pussy?" (Deduct 10 points.)

6. Are you able to hug and kiss other men? (Give yourself 5 points for hugging, 5 more for kissing, but 0 if you find it an erotic experience. NSMs aren't latent or blatant. The otherwise totally sensitive NSM feels absolutely nothing in this situation. They really don't.)

7. What drugs do you use? (Score 10 points if you said herb tea. Deduct 10 if you said cocaine. Deduct 20 if you said Wild Turkey.)

8. What do you do for exercise? (Score 10 points for dance, Jazzercise, or co-ed volleyball; 5 points for jogging, skiing, or swimming. If you play team sports with men only or lift weights give yourself one point because you care about your body.)

9. Do you believe in God? (10 points if you answered: Do you?)

10. You hear a woman call another woman "girl." What do you do? (5 points if you correct her; 10 points if you know it's wrong but say nothing.)

11. Would you work as a nurse, secretary, or day-care teacher? (10 points if you said yes; 5 points if you said you'd be afraid to take these jobs away from women.)

12. A guy on your construction crew asks if you want to take in

"PSSST! WOULD YOU LIKE A MARRIAGE MADE IN HEAVEN?"

Campbell

an adult cinema and have a couple of beers. What do you do? (10 points if you explain that pornography exploits and perverts normal sexual feelings; 5 points if you shanghai him and force him to attend a Men's Awareness Workshop; 0 if you go along with it but are totally disgusted by the experience. Deduct 10 if you dig the blonde with the cute ass.)

Scoring: Need I say it? NSMs are *not* into scoring. But for the rest of you here's the breakdown:

0–40 He Man. Move to Oklahoma or seek professional help.

40–80 Normal. If you don't have a mate it's time to look elsewhere for answers. Your breath, your clothes, perhaps arch supports would help. You may be one of those people who actually *needs* a Mercedes.

80+ NSM. Is it lonely at the top?

LOVE

Zora Neale Hurston

Perhaps the oath of Hercules shall always defeat me in love. Once when I was small and first coming upon the story of the Choice of Hercules, I was so impressed that I swore an oath to leave all pleasure and take the hard road of labor. Perhaps God heard me and wrote down my words in His book. I have thought so at times. Be that as it may, I know about the major courses in love. However, there are some minor courses which I have not grasped so well, and would be thankful for some coaching and advice.

First is the number of men who pant in my ear on short acquaintance, "You passionate thing! I can see you are just *burning* up! Most men would be disappointing to you. It takes a man like me for you. Ahhh! I know that you will just wreck me! Your eyes and your lips tell me a lot. You are a walking furnace!" This amazes me sometimes. Often when this is whispered gustily into my ear I am feeling no more amorous than a charter member of the Union

Dear Ellen written by Shirley Milgrom and Bonnie Dickel and illustrated by Jackie Urbanovic.

© 1988 Shirley Milgrom, Bonnie Dickel, Jackie Urbanovic

League Club. I may be thinking of turnip greens with dumplings, or more royalty checks, and here is a man who visualizes me on a divan sending the world up in smoke. It has happened so often that I have come to expect it. There must be something about me that looks sort of couchy. Maybe it's a birthmark. My mother could have been frightened by a bed.

Number two is a man may lose interest in me and go where his fancy leads him, and we can still meet as friends. But if I get tired and let on about it, he is certain to become an enemy of mine. That forces me to lie like the crossties from New York to Key West. I have learned to frame it so that I can claim to be deserted and devastated by him. Then he goes off with a sort of twilight tenderness for me, wondering what it is that he's got that brings so many women down! I do not even have to show real tears. All I need to do is show my stricken face and dash away from him to hide my supposed heartbreak and renunciation. He understands that I am fleeing before his allure so that I can be firm in my resolution to save

(Reprinted from *Dykes to Watch Out For*, © 1986 by Alison Bechdel, Firebrand Books.)

the pieces. He knew all along that he was a hard man to resist, so he visualized my dampened pillow. It is a good thing that some of them have sent roses as a poultice and stayed away. Otherwise, they might have found the poor, heartbroken wreck of a thing all dressed to kill and gone out for a high-heel time with the new interest, who has the new interesting things to say and do. Now, how to break off without acting deceitful and still keep a friend?

Number three is kin to number two in a way. Under the spell of moonlight, music, flowers, or the cut and smell of good tweed, I sometimes feel the divine urge for an hour, a day, or maybe a week. Then it is gone, and my interest returns to corn pone and mustard greens, or rubbing a paragraph with a soft cloth. Then my ex-sharer of a mood calls up in a fevered voice and reminds me of every silly thing I said, and eggs me on to say them all over again. It is the third presentation of turkey hash after Christmas. It is asking me to be a seven-sided liar. Accuses me of being faithless and inconsistent if I don't. There is no inconsistency there. I was sincere for the moment in which I said the things. It is strictly a matter of time. It was true for the moment, but the next day or the next week is not that moment. . . .

So the great difficulty lies in trying to transpose last night's moment to a day which has no knowledge of it. That look, that tender touch, was issued by the mint of the richest of all kingdoms. That same expression of today is utter counterfeit, or at best the wildest of inflation. What could be more zestless than passing out canceled checks?

But pay no attention to what I say about love, for as I said before it may not mean a thing. It is my own bathtub singing. Just because my mouth opens up like a prayer book it does not just have to flap like a Bible.

(Excerpt from *Dust Tracks on a Road.* Copyright 1942 by Zora Neale Hurston, renewed © 1970 by John C. Hurston. Reprinted by permission of Harper & Row.)

TALKING WANT AD

a talking blues

Janet Smith

Oh, I'm lookin' for a man to wash my clothes,
Iron my shirts and blow my nose,
Sweep the floor and wax the kitchen
While I sit around playin' guitar an' bitchin'!
Mud all over my boots,
Feet upon the table,
—Just doin' my thing.

I'm lookin' for a man to cook my meals,
Wash the dishes and take the peels
Off my bananas with a grin,
And ask me how my work day's been—
*Insufferable, as usual,
Playing music is such a struggle.

Well, I'm lookin' for a guy with curly hair
And great big muscles and a nice derrière
Who'll get up nights and feed the baby
An' bring my coffee when I'm ready—
I gotta feel good in the morning—
That's when I make my best music.

So if you feel you'd like to apply,
Just send a photo or drop on by,
And I'll let you shine my shoes today,
'N if you do that good, I'll let you stay
And cook my dinner
And after you've cleaned up after yourself
(If you're lucky—)
I *might* let you listen to me practice my guitar!

PERSONAL HABITS

Gail Sausser

When I moved in with her bringing only a guitar, chest and clothes she looked at me in horror and said, "That's it?! No dishes? No furniture? No stuff? . . ." To a devout packrat my lack of possessions was unbelievable. I, on the other hand, sell or give away anything I am not currently using. She looked at me with tears in her eyes and asked if I would get rid of her the way I rid myself of possessions. Packrats take my way of living personally.

That was only the beginning of many things we were to discover about one another while living together. Regardless of what you would like her to believe about you while you are dating, living together eventually brings out your less attractive side.

She and I grew up in different generations. I grew up in an age of cheap energy, in the shadow of Hanford's reactor. She grew up in an age of conservation and concern over shortages. I turn on all the lights in the house and leave them on until I go to bed. In one household I was followed by conservers from room to room. If I went upstairs to the bathroom I would find the entire house blackened upon my descent. "I wasn't done down here," I would scream, clawing at the wall for a light switch. I also despise being cold and have had the misfortune of living with people who camp in igloos for fun and fresh air. I have had to beg (or sneak) the thermostat above 55 degrees. I cannot relax in a living room in which I must wear mittens and ear muffs.

People of my generation, I am told, also waste water. It is not unusual for me to begin brushing my teeth, turn the water on and roam around combing my hair, starting the coffee and putting on a sock before I finally take the toothbrush out of my mouth and shut off the water. If anyone else turns off the water during my meanderings I yell, "I wasn't done yet!" My lover, however, runs only enough water to dampen the toothbrush, shuts off the faucet, brushes, stays over the sink, briefly rinses her mouth and is done. She takes five minute showers. I don't believe I'm clean until my skin puckers.

Our differences in personal habits don't end with our attitudes on conservation. She doesn't watch T.V. I turn it on for company and background noise. I also watch it while bathing. I eat with the refrigerator door open, munching from a half dozen ready to eat foods. She actually cooks. I dislike doing dishes so I drink from cartons, prefer finger food, and if I must, use a single fork or spoon. I have learned to eat leftovers cold and like them. What she eats, she prepares. A full complement of dishes and utensils are used. Even if she only eats a cookie it goes on a plate to catch crumbs—I figure crumb removal is what the cats are for.

It's amazing how many illusions you try to sustain while dating. When you first get together she may pretend to be a morning person too, till one morning you find her slumped in her cornflakes. She may pretend not to watch T.V. (which is how I ended up installing a T.V. in the bathroom and taking two hour baths during prime time). She pretended not to be a sugar junkie till I found two pounds of frosted animal crackers hidden in the cereal cupboard.

My first impression of her was that she dressed very tastefully. I have since found out that she wears a twenty year old bathrobe of faded blue with a large hole in the rear end.

When you first fall in love nature has a way of insulating you from reacting to these discoveries. This is known as "phase one" of a relationship, wherein everything she does is cute and wonderful. Phase two is when you finally realize that some things have been driving you crazy for the last three months.

(From *Lesbian Etiquette*, copyright © 1986 by Gail Sausser, The Crossing Press.)

HEARTBREAK HOTEL

Jean Gonick

I t isn't fair.
I was just beginning to recover from divorcing Dr. Infidel when I inadvertently became the proprietress of Heartbreak Hotel. He ran off one year ago with Nurse Vivacious, leaving me the three-bedroom house and Paisano, the old, tired, golden retriever.

I have to admit I did not cope well. I spent six months wallowing in self-pity, revenge fantasies, and varying degrees of alienation. I dated inappropriate men, I watched too much TV, I even poured Chianti into Paisano's water dish one night because I didn't want to drink alone.

But I got better. I emerged from my stupor and enrolled in a French literature class and intermediate aerobics. I was on the fourth volume of Proust's *Remembrance of Things Past* (in French, thank you) and I could run in place for fifteen minutes without passing out. I apologized to Paisano for trying to turn him into a co-alcoholic. In short, I got off self-destruct. Then Elaine called.

"Eddie's left me," she sobbed into the phone. "He left me for our tax consultant. I hate professional women."

It wasn't much of a surprise. Eddie was the kind of man who always tried to get the waitress's phone number while Elaine was in the ladies' room.

"I hate him, I hate our apartment, and most of all I hate being alone. Could I stay with you and Paisano for a while? Until I feel stronger?"

What could I say to a woman who had given me the name of the best vet in the city when Paisano had mange? "My home is your home," I said. After all, I had stayed with my mother the first three weeks after the disclosure of Dr. Infidel's infidelity. Elaine's mother lived in Florida, so I would fill in.

I was putting fresh sheets on Elaine's bed when the phone rang again. It was uncannily synchronistic, which synchronicity always is.

It was my friend Pam. She was leaving Howard. "I finally decided to cut my losses," she said. Her voice did not have the hysteria of Elaine's, just the flat tone of the resigned. "The thing is, in order to leave him, I have to go somewhere. Can I stay with you?"

That's when I heard Elvis Presley singing the sad words of "Heartbreak Hotel."

"Why are everyone's marriages going belly up at the same time?" I asked her, explaining about Elaine and Eddie and the tax consultant.

Pam pretended not to be comforted by the news. "I guess the warranties ran out," she said.

"Misery loves company," I offered lamely.

"Party hearty," she deadpanned, and hung up.

They arrived at my door at the same time, Elaine dressed defiantly in cheerful white, Pam, who had defiantly left her husband, in a bathrobe and slippers. Paisano, teeming with boisterous canine sympathy, lunged for Pam, licking her face. This made her cry.

"Why doesn't he feel sorry for *me*?" Elaine asked. "I'm the one who got left."

"You're dressed too well," I said.

"The dumped have to dress well," she explained. "We have to have *some* dignity. Sorry about this particular outfit, though," she apologized.

During my Negative Phase I had forbidden my friends to wear white in my presence—it was too medical. "I'm sane now," I said. "You can wear stethoscopes around your neck and it won't bother me. I don't have hatred in my heart any more." I knew how inane I sounded, but it was a necessary part of the Positive Phase.

"Don't worry," said Elaine, "I have enough hatred in my heart for both of us."

She did, too. The first thing she did when she got inside was mount a homemade Eddie dart board on my living-room wall. Instead of risking a miss by throwing the darts, she stood six inches away from his photo and thrust them into his nostrils and eyeballs. "I wish they made dart boards that bleed," she said. "Hey, maybe I should patent that idea and make a million dollars. Then I can hire a hit man to kill Eddie and that heinous tax bitch."

Pam looked at the dart board incredulously and said, "You are really sick."

"Me? Sick? If Howard had left *you*, you'd be just as sick!"

They looked to me as if I, their proprietress of Heartbreak Hotel, should decide who was sick and who wasn't. "It's a harmless ventilation of hostile feelings," I said idiotically. I was glad Paisano couldn't speak, as only he knew about the Dr. Infidel and Nurse Vivacious voodoo dolls that I'd made and then murdered with my own hostile hands.

"It's already seven," Elaine said, turning from the pockmarked Eddie. "Why don't we go out to dinner?"

"Fine," I said. "There's a good Japanese place down the street." Along with Proust and exercise, I had discovered the calming effects of raw fish and rice. Food for the serenely positive.

"I am far too upset for gentle yin-yang cuisine," said Elaine. "I need carbohydrates and spices. I need spaghetti in marinara sauce and lots of drinks." As she spoke, visions of my Negative Phase menu flashed before me: mountains of pasta and gallons of wine, resulting in a ten-pound weight gain. I knew there was a reason I'd taken up aerobics.

"I can't go out," Pam whimpered. "I'm wearing a bathrobe."

"So take it off," Elaine said, impatiently.

"Why should I? I think I'll wear it the rest of my life. You two go without me—I'm too depressed to eat anyway."

"Too depressed to eat?" Elaine blurted. "Food's the only dependable thing in life. It never betrays you!" Paisano, a voracious and indiscriminate eater, barked affirmatively. "See? Paisano knows," she said, throwing her arms around his furry, overweight neck. He was thrilled by the attention. "Wonderful Paisano. I wish I'd married a dog, at least they're faithful."

"Now I *really* can't eat," Pam said, disgusted at this display.

"What if we order in?" I asked Pam, and she brightened. Aha. It wasn't lack of appetite; it was post-breakup agoraphobia. When I'd stayed with my mother for those first three weeks, I left her house

"I want a man in my life but not in my house. . . . "

Joy Behar

She: I DON'T KNOW WHETHER I WANT TO GO BACK OR NOT

(From *Life*, 1919. Reprinted by permission of Paul Petticrew.)

maybe twice. I felt as if a neon sign saying MY HUSBAND LEFT ME FOR ANOTHER WOMAN was growing out of my head. I was also afraid of the very real possibility of running into Dr. Infidel and Nurse Vivacious somewhere. And I harbored, for that time, a sincere hatred for all humanity and didn't see why I should interact with any of it. Nor did Pam; even though she was the one leaving Howard, she felt stigmatized by a failed marriage.

"Okay, let's order pizza," Elaine said, grabbing the phone. She ordered a jumbo giant with everything on it plus double on the pepperoni and two bottles of red wine.

"Couldn't we get salads too?" I suggested gently after she hung up.

"What's the point?" she yelled, scaring Paisano. "What's the point of eating fresh greens and trying to be healthy? I steamed broccoli and broiled chicken breasts for Eddie for years! I made a fresh green salad every night! I never used anything from a can or a package and there was always fresh fruit on the table! And where did it get me? He left me for a tax consultant! Well, forget it! I've had it with good health and following the rules—I'm eating nitrites from now on!" She burst into tears. Pam did too, then padded over to the couch in her furry slippers and put her arms around Elaine. Paisano, unable to cry, drooled consolingly on Elaine's knees. And I, who hadn't cried in six months, suddenly remembered that was all I did in my Negative Phase and bawled like a baby.

Great, I thought, dropping a box of Kleenex on the coffee table. Just great.

I woke up with my first hangover since entering my Positive Phase. We'd stayed up until two, drinking wine and philosophizing on the death of love. I staggered out of my bedroom and tried to open the bathroom door.

"I'm taking a bath," came Pam's muffled voice.

Defeated, I went to the kitchen to make tea. Elaine was still sleeping, as was Paisano, who'd thrown up a slice of pepperoni pizza at midnight. I drank tea, ate toast, and tried the bathroom again.

"It's so warm in here," came Pam's voice. "Like the womb."

I turned on the TV to see how Jane Pauley and Maria Shriver were doing. I'd give Pam five more minutes. At the commercial, I knocked on the door again.

"Hydrotherapy," she said.

I remembered now that I was not only afraid of leaving the house after Dr. Infidel left me, I'd been afraid to leave the bathtub. I used to drink steaming mugs of hot water, brandy, and lemon while I sat in the bubbles, enveloping myself inside and out in warm, lulling liquid. It *was* therapy. But why did she have to do it at 7:30 in the morning? Probably because she couldn't sleep, another post-breakup problem.

I sighed and dressed. Just this once I'd be Saint Heartbreak and go to work dirty.

I called home at noon to see how my guests were faring. Elaine answered.

"Did you find your house keys?" I asked. "I left a set on the coffee table."

"Thanks. I was going to make another set for Pam, but she's never leaving the house, so she doesn't need them."

"Is she still in the tub?"

" Hmmm, I suppose you <u>could</u> be my first husband. Do something annoying."

"She came out to watch *The Young and the Restless* and then went back in. She has quite a capacity for suffering, considering she's the one who left."

"What are you doing?"

"I went out to breakfast and gave the short-order cook my phone number. I mean, your phone number."

Right—the inappropriate man syndrome. A date with the doorknob, as long as it raises the damaged self-esteem. At least it was better than digging through the old boyfriend file and trying to rekindle long-dead flames.

"How's Paisano?"

"Better. He stopped throwing up."

"Good. I'm going to my exercise class and I'll be home at seven. Want me to bring you anything?"

"Is heroin on special anywhere?"

WANDA, SMITTEN WITH THE SECOND BASEWOMAN, DISGRACES HER TEAM BY FORGETTING TO RUN

(Reprinted from *WomaNews*, 1984, by permission of Alison Bechdel.)

It wasn't, so I brought home a chicken, carrots, onions, a bottle of Chablis and three boxes of Kleenex. Pam, Elaine, and Paisano were waiting for me in the living room, which was beginning to feel like the lobby. Pam had switched from her bathrobe to one of mine and sat in an armchair looking pale and very clean. She was reading *People* magazine. Elaine wore a red dress and seven pounds of eye makeup and was reading Lana Turner's autobiography.

"I always read dumb magazines when I'm upset," Pam said defensively.

"Lana Turner is the only person whose love life is stupider than mine," said Elaine.

I thought of Proust and how much I hadn't read last night. "I'm making chicken soup for dinner," I said. "It will make us all feel better."

"I have a date," Elaine said. "Thanks anyway."

"I'm not hungry," whimpered Pam.

"Well, I'm not making soup for one," I said. This meant dining on English muffins and tuna fish, a depressing habit I'd tried to get rid of. Pizza and tuna—these were bad signs.

"The bathroom's free now," Pam offered apologetically. I raced in to take my shower. When I came back Elaine had left on her date with the short-order cook, and Pam was watching *Valley of the Dolls* on cablevision. I thought of Proust; I thought of a documentary on the war in Vietnam that was on the public broadcasting station.

"It helps to watch movies about people whose lives are more wrecked than your own," Pam felt the need to explain.

Didn't I know it. "Tuna fish?" I offered, heading for the kitchen, knowing I was too undisciplined to go to my room and read Proust. My response to trashy TV was Pavlovian—I couldn't wait to see Patty Duke.

"No thanks," she said. "I would like a glass of wine, though. A big one."

Elaine checked back into Heartbreak Hotel at seven in the morning. "That was a very big mistake," she said, stepping over the sleeping Paisano, entering her bedroom and closing the door.

I decided to skip my French class that night because I'd lost two nights' reading and was embarrassingly behind. I wanted to go home and catch up, but was afraid of being lured into another evening of depressed bathrobe inactivity: drink, gossip, and TV. But maybe I could get around to making the chicken soup. And I was curious about Elaine's date.

They were arguing about her date when I got home.

"What did you expect?" Pam chided. "How could you even think of seeing another man five seconds after Eddie left?"

"I thought it would cheer me up."

They were drinking martinis straight up. I couldn't believe they'd found the ancient shaker that Dr. Infidel had left behind in the bowels of our kitchen. Actually, the martinis looked rather elegant in their chilled glasses. I poured one for myself.

"Really, Elaine," Pam continued. "I don't know how you can even think about men. I don't think I'll ever date again."

"You won't if you keep wearing that bathrobe," Elaine warned.

"What was wrong with the short-order cook?" I asked, eating my olive. "Aside from his being a total stranger who might have been an axe murderer with AIDS?"

"He had a copy of *Hustler* in his living room."

Pam almost lost her martini.

"And that's not the worst part," Elaine said, hurling a dart with her free hand into her husband's forehead. "His name was Edward."

We shared a superstitious silence.

"What about you?" Pam said, turning to me. "Do you think you'll ever date again?"

"What makes you think I don't date now?" I asked. I looked at Paisano, again relieved that he could not tell them that since I'd stopped dating inappropriate men, I'd stopped, period.

"I think I need a cigarette," I said, suddenly panicked. Damn. Proust and aerobics had kept me free of panic for a while, and I had made a point of never thinking about love or the future.

Elaine held out her Marlboros, but I waved them away and took one of Pam's unfiltered Camels instead. "These are worse for you," I explained.

The chicken remained uncooked in the refrigerator, and we smoked and drank the night away, ordering another pizza at ten. It sounds implausible, but I think Paisano was sending me rueful looks.

If he wasn't, he should have been; I was in sad shape. I went to aerobics the next night but was too tired to keep up. The rest of my French class had moved on to volume five. My lungs hurt from smoking Camels. The rotting chicken had to be thrown into the garbage. I started using the Eddie dart board, pretending it was Dr. Infidel and Nurse Vivacious in alternate rounds. I realized I still hated them, that beneath my positive veneer was a morass of maladjustment. I became snappy, irritable; I pounded on the bathroom door and told Pam to get out of the tub so I could get into it myself.

I think they call it a relapse.

I awoke to find Pam actually wearing a skirt and blouse and Elaine with a normal amount of eye makeup. They had set the kitchen table and cooked a sane breakfast.

"Poached eggs," Elaine said soothingly, putting two in front of me.

Pam poured my tea solicitously, then buttered my toast.

"It was so cold I almost got married."

Shelley Winters

"Staying here has been great for us, but not too healthy for you," Elaine said. "So we've made some decisions. Pam can't go back to her place because Howard insists on staying there paying millions of dollars in rent and being wounded. I don't want to go back to my apartment because it's too much memory lane."

Memory lane: maybe that was why I'd had this relapse. Was it wise to remain in the house where I'd lived happily and then unhappily with Dr. Infidel? Jane Austen said something to the effect that one should not love a place the less for having suffered in it, but then she'd never been married. Or divorced.

"So we're getting a new place and rooming together," Elaine said.

I tried not to look surprised. I didn't think Pam and Elaine got along all that well. But misery is bonding.

"We're getting a place with two bathrooms," Pam said quickly. "Anyway, we're too poor to live alone."

"What if you reconcile with your husbands?"

"That would only happen if I killed that tax bitch and if Howard got a brain transplant," Elaine assured me.

"What if one of you gets a lover and the other one gets cranky?"

They looked at me as if I was crazy. "I've had my short-order cook for the year," Elaine said.

"I can buy my own *Hustler* if I want to," said Pam.

They looked as though they had taken care of everything. They'd packed their suitcases, laundered their sheets and towels, and were on their way.

"You run a great hotel," they shouted to me from Elaine's Honda.

I have to say, their manners improved with their moods. When I got home that night a dozen red roses with a profuse thank-you note were waiting. My house was back to normal: no more overflowing ashtrays or overturned wineglasses, no empty pizza boxes smeared with tomato sauce, no Eddie dart board.

Paisano and I settled on the couch to read Proust, my French-English dictionary at my side. Then the phone rang. It was Brian, a math genius I've known since college. His marriage had just exploded into a million pieces.

"I ran into Pam and Elaine today," he said, "and they told me you were running sort of a Heartbreak Hotel, a halfway house for the romantically displaced. Lots of room, good water pressure. Do you allow male guests?"

Oh, sure. I'd be in the Betty Ford Center in a month.

"Sorry, Brian, but I don't think I'm really cut out for the hotel business." He sighed. I sighed. Then I remembered that Brian was a man, and not an entirely inappropriate one. I knew the newly separated are almost disfunctional, but it wouldn't hurt to see him. If he'd ask.

"That's too bad," he said. "But God, I'm miserable. If I took you to dinner, would you let me tell you how miserable I am?"

"Of course!" I said gaily, shoving Proust aside. "Just don't bring any dart boards." He promised he wouldn't if I promised to explain over dinner what that meant. I promised, hung up, kissed Paisano and dressed for dinner.

(From *Mostly True Confessions: Looking for Love in the Eighties.* Copyright © 1986 by Jean Gonick. Reprinted by permission of Random House.)

" Any gal is gonna go out of her mind when she looks at her husband one day and realizes that she is not living with a man any longer. She is living with a reclining chair that burps."

Roseanne Barr

LOU ANN ON MEN

Barbara Kingsolver

one time when I was working in this motel one of the toilets leaked and I had to replace the flapper ball. Here's what it said on the package; I kept it till I knew it by heart: "Please Note. Parts are included for all installations, but no installation requires all of the parts." That's kind of my philosophy about men. I don't think there's an installation out there that could use all of my parts.

(From *The Bean Trees*, copyright © 1988 by Barbara Kingsolver, Harper & Row.)

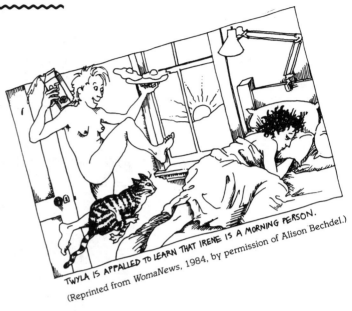

TWYLA IS APPALLED TO LEARN THAT IRENE IS A MORNING PERSON.

(Reprinted from *WomaNews*, 1984, by permission of Alison Bechdel.)

ICE CREAM AND MARRIAGE

Mary Kay Blakely

In a recent cover story in Ms. magazine about "over 30" marriages, several of America's most successful women smile out from behind gossamer white veils, wearing happily-ever-after expressions on their faces. What I hoped would be a rational discussion of marriage turned out to be a blushing illustration that even feminists can lose their marbles on the subject of love.

Brides are so happy they haven't noticed yet that the institution of marriage is designed to hold only one and a half persons. They don't immediately comprehend the multiple implications behind Norman Mailer's suggestion that the whole question of liberation boils down to one: "Who will do the dishes?" The same one who does the dishes also gets to be the half person.

In the case of "nontraditional" marriages, it can take a woman even longer to comprehend that she is the half person. Many intelligent couples like to believe they can balance the equation to an even three-quarters apiece. With a few liberating amendments—she gets to keep her job, maybe even her name, he helps with the dishes—they hope to even things out. So subtle is the shift from "bride" to "wife" that a woman convinced of her independence can miss it altogether.

I would certainly have remained oblivious to the myriad assumptions hidden in the institution of marriage had it not been for a woman named Agnes who rudely interrupted my bliss only six months after I became a bride.

I ran into Agnes at Hemingway's Moveable Feast, our neighborhood delicatessen in Chicago. We were returning from the bike paths along the lakefront, tennis sweaters draped cavalierly over our shoulders, looking like a couple who had just passed the screen test for an Erich Segal movie. We stopped at Hemingway's to find a

> **"Blessed is the man who, having nothing to say, abstains from giving wordy evidence of the fact."**
>
> **George Eliot**

treat to bring home. Newlyweds are fond of treats. After some deliberation, I selected a high-quality brand of butter-pecan ice cream and handed it to the man who was carrying our money in his wallet.

He looked at the price, something that had not occurred to me. He handed it back, explaining that $1.95 was exorbitant for any ice cream, and besides, he didn't like butter-pecan. I gave it back to him, because what was $1.95 between friends and besides, he didn't have to eat any. We stood there for some time, passing the pint back and forth, straining for patience, he refusing to indulge an irresponsible purchase, I insisting it was none of his business. His

patience was melting with the ice cream when he delivered his final opinion: There was no way he was going to pay $1.95 for a pint of ice cream just because it said on the bottom of the carton "Hand packed by Agnes." He was starting to hate Agnes.

We rode home in stony silence. Only six months before I had been the kind of self-actualized woman who could walk into just about any delicatessen and order whatever I wanted. Dimly, I realized that this sudden loss in opportunity had something to do with the vows I had taken. I didn't remember ever saying, "And I defer all ice cream judgments to you." That's when I first became aware that love is not only blind, it is also deaf. A woman in love can't possibly hear the varied assumptions packed between the promises and the vows. The "I do" that took approximately 10 minutes to pronounce will be followed by 10 incredulous years of asking, "I did?"

The next day, on the way home from work, I stopped at Hemingway's and bought six pints of butter-pecan ice cream, all hand packed by Agnes. I had to get rid of the status of half wife, and it was the first step to becoming an unwife. My success as an unwife depended largely on the cooperation of an unhusband, and I knew that undoing our unspoken vows could well result in an unmarriage. For better or worse, I packed our small freezer full of butter-pecan ice cream.

The young woman who asks whether she should get married is not really interested in hearing about the laborious journey from "bride" to "wife" to "unwife." The story would bore her, since she's in love and love is impatient with long explanations.

I would tell her about Agnes, who packs a lot of information about the institution of marriage between the pecans and the sweet cream. I would tell her simply, go ask Agnes.

(From *The New York Times*, April 16, 1981. Reprinted by permission of Mary Kay Blakely.)

"Once Galen has equated male and female genitals, he insists that the internal location of woman's genitals can only be explained by an arrested development. Fully concocted genitals, the 'true' form of genitals, are, of course, the penis and testicles. Woman remains, so to speak, half-baked."

Nancy Tuana

MY HUSBAND'S VIEW OF HOUSEWORK

Margery Eliscu

My husband is seeing housework from a little closer up this summer while I work and he plays househusband.

"I just cleaned the faucets," he reports to me on the phone. (I am at the newspaper office.)

"What faucets?" I ask.

"The ones with all the crud on them. Don't you ever wash the backs of the faucets?"

"Larry," I say, "forget the faucets. Did you wash the dishes?"

"I had to use a mirror to see back there."

"Back where?" I ask.

"I just told you," he answers, sounding almost enthusiastic. "Back of the faucets. They shine now. You'll love them."

" Repeat after me,
'I'm leaving you, Margaret.'"

"How about the dishes?"

"What dishes?" he asks.

"The ones that were in the sink after breakfast," I say.

"You have nothing to worry about."

"You washed them."

"No," he says, "but I moved them to the table before I scrubbed the faucets. I scoured the sink too."

"Did you put the dirty dishes on top of the *clean* tablecloth?"

"Huh?"

"The dishes. They were all wet and sloppy. Did you just set them that way on the table?"

"I don't know," he says. "I think they're on some papers."

"What papers?" I ask.

"Maybe the mail."

"You put the dirty dishes on the mail?"

"No," he says. "No. Stop worrying. I just remembered. They're on top of the laundry. They're okay."

"Is the laundry on the table?"

"I think so," he says.

"You put the clean laundry on the table with the dirty dishes from the sink?"

"Of course not!" he says. "I wouldn't do that. I put the dirty laundry on the table. Everything there is dirty. You've got nothing to worry about."

"Why didn't you at least remove the tablecloth first?"

"It seemed foolish what with the spilled stuff."

"What spilled stuff?"

"The can of insect repellent. It leaked."

"What was the can of insect repellent doing on the table?"

He doesn't answer. Then, "Do you have any red nail polish?"

"My God!" I say.

"The insect stuff removed the red color from that tray you keep on the table. I'm through with the faucets now, so I thought I'd put the red back on."

"No," I say. "Don't."

"I don't mind," he says. "I feel bad about the insect stuff."

"No," I say. "Don't."

"Well then," he says, "I guess I'll just get back to sweeping up the vacuum bag."

"I didn't hear that."

"The vacuum bag broke when I was changing it."

"Did the dirt go all over the floor?"

"Yes," he says, "and all over the—"

"Don't tell me," I say into the phone. My voice is rising. People are watching. Then I whisper, "Anything else?"

"Yes," he says. "One of your bridge friends called. She said you sure are lucky to have maid service this summer."

"Larry," I say, "did you take her name?"

"She asked me what I was making an hour." He chuckles. "I think she wants to steal me."

"Did you take her name?"

"Sure, it's right here."

"Good," I say. "Hang on to it. I'll write you a reference immediately."

(From *Russell Baker, Erma Bombeck & Me*, © 1987 by Lance Tapley, Publisher [Yankee Books].)

" "Sometimes the only thing left to hang onto is letting go."

Linda Moakes

A SOLUTION TO HOUSEWORK

Dave Barry

Almost all housework is hard and dangerous, involving the insides of ovens and toilets and the cracks between bathroom tiles, where plague germs fester. The only housework that is easy and satisfying is the kind where you spray chemicals on wooden furniture and smear them around until the wood looks shiny. This is the kind of housework they show on television commercials: A professional actress, posing as the Cheerful Housewife (IQ 43), dances around her house, smearing and shining, smearing and shining, until before she knows it her housework is done and she is free to spend the rest of the afternoon reading the bust-development ads in *Cosmopolitan* magazine. She never cleans her toilets. When they get dirty, she just gets another house. Lord knows they pay her enough.

Most of us would rather smear and shine than actually clean anything. For example, our house has a semifinished basement, which means it looks too much like a finished room to store old tires in, but too much like a basement to actually live in. Our semifinished basement has a semibathroom, and one time, several years ago, a small woodland creature crept into the house in the middle of the night and died in the shower stall. This is common behavior in the animal world: many animals, when in danger, are driven by instinct to seek refuge in shower stalls.

Since we hardly ever go down to our semifinished basement, we didn't discover the dead woodland creature until several weeks after it crept in, at which time it was getting fairly ripe. Now obviously, the correct thing to do was clean it up, but this is the hard kind of housework. So instead we stayed upstairs and went into an absolute frenzy of smearing and shining, until you could not walk into our living room without wearing sunglasses, for fear of being blinded by the glare off the woodwork. Eventually, we managed to block the woodland creature out of our minds.

Several months later, our friend Rob, who is a doctor, came to visit. He stayed in our semifinished basement, but we noticed that he came upstairs to take showers. One of the first things they teach you in medical school is never to take a shower with a dead woodland creature. We were so embarrassed that we went down and cleaned up the shower stall, with a shovel and acid. But I doubt we'd have done it if Rob hadn't been there.

Our behavior is not unique. People have been avoiding housework for millions of years. Primitive man would stay in one cave until the floor was littered with stegosaurus bones and the walls were covered with primitive drawings, which were drawn by primitive children when their parents went out to dinner, and then the family would move to a new cave, to avoid cleaning the old one. That's how primitive man eventually got to North America.

In North America, primitive man started running out of clean caves, and he realized that *somebody* was going to have to start doing housework. He thought about it long and hard, and finally settled on primitive woman. But he needed an excuse to get himself

> **"I will clean house when Sears comes out with a riding vacuum cleaner."**
>
> **Roseanne Barr**

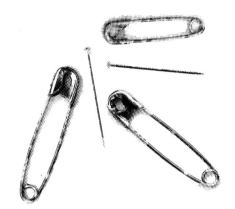

out of doing the housework, so he invented civilization. Primitive woman would say: "How about staying in the cave and helping with the housework today?" And primitive man would say: "I can't, dear: I have to invent fire." Or: "I'd love to, dear, but I think it's more important that I devise some form of written language." And off he'd go, leaving the woman with the real work.

Over the years, men came up with thousands of excuses for not doing housework—wars, religion, pyramids, the United States Senate—until finally they hit on the ultimate excuse: business. They built thousands of offices and factories, and every day, all over the country, they'd get up, eat breakfast, and announce: "Well, I'm off to my office or factory now." Then they'd just *leave,* and they wouldn't return until the house was all cleaned up and dinner was ready.

But then men made a stupid mistake. They started to believe that "business" really *was* hard work, and they started talking about it when they came home. They'd come in the door looking exhausted, and they'd say things like "Boy, I sure had a tough meeting today."

You can imagine how a woman who had spent the day doing housework would react to this kind of statement. She'd say to herself: "Meeting? He had a tough *meeting?* I've been on my hands and knees all day cleaning toilets and scraping congealed spider eggs off the underside of the refrigerator, and he tells me he had a tough *meeting?*"

That was the beginning of the end. Women began to look into "business," and they discovered that all you do is go to an office and answer the phone and do various things with pieces of paper and have meetings. So women began going to work, and now nobody does housework, other than smearing and shining, and before long there's going to be so much crud and bacteria under the nation's refrigerators that we're all going to get diseases and die.

The obvious and fair solution to this problem is to let men do the housework for, say, the next six thousand years, to even things up. The trouble is that men, over the years, have developed an inflated notion of the importance of everything they do, so that before long they would turn housework into just as much of a charade as business is now. They would hire secretaries and buy computers and fly off to housework conferences in Bermuda, but they'd never clean anything. So men are out.

But there is a solution; there is a way to get people to willingly do housework. I discovered this by watching household-cleanser commercials on television. What I discovered is that many people who seem otherwise normal will do virtually any idiot thing *if they think they will be featured in a commercial.* They figure if they get on a commercial, they'll make a lot of money, like the Cheerful Housewife, and they'll be able to buy cleaner houses. So they'll do *anything.*

For example, if I walked up to you in the middle of a supermarket and asked you to get down and scrub the floor with two different cleansers, just so I could see which one worked better, you would punch me in the mouth. But if I had guys with cameras and microphones with me, and I asked you to do the same thing, you'd probably do it. Not only that, but you'd make lots of serious, earnest comments about the cleansers. You'd say: "I frankly believe that New Miracle Swipe, with its combination of grease fighters and wax shiners, is a more effective cleanser, I honestly do. Really. I mean it." You'd say this in the same solemn tone of voice you might use to discuss the question of whether the United States should deploy Cruise missiles in Western Europe. You'd have no shame at all.

So here's my plan: I'm going to get some old cameras and microphones and position them around my house. I figure that before long I'll have dozens of people just *dying* to do housework in front of my cameras. Sure, most of them will eventually figure out that they're not going to be in a commercial, but new ones will come along to replace them. Meanwhile, I'll be at work.

MARRIAGE AND COOKING

Margaret Atwood

In my opinion, most women made one basic mistake: they expected their husbands to understand them. They spent much precious time explaining themselves, serving up their emotions and reactions, their love and anger and sensitivities, their demands and inadequacies, as if the mere relating of these things would get results. Arthur's friends tended to be married to women like this, and these women, I knew, thought of me as placid, sloppy and rather stupid. They themselves made it from crisis to crisis, with running commentaries, on a combination of nerve ends, cigarettes, bludgeoning honesty and what used to be called nagging. Because I didn't do this, Arthur's friends envied him a bit and confided to me in the kitchen. They were beleaguered and exhausted; their wives had a touch of the shrill self-righteousness familiar to me from my mother.

But I didn't want Arthur to understand me: I went to great lengths to prevent this. Though I was tempted sometimes, I resisted the impulse to confess. Arthur's tastes were Spartan, and my early life and innermost self would have appalled him. It would be like asking for a steak and getting a slaughtered cow. I think he suspected this; he certainly headed off my few tentative attempts at self-revelation.

The other wives, too, wanted their husbands to live up to their own fantasy lives, which except for the costumes weren't that different from my own. They didn't put it in quite these terms, but I could tell from their expectations. They wanted their men to be strong, lustful, passionate and exciting, with hard rapacious mouths, but also tender and worshipful. They wanted men in mysterious cloaks who would rescue them from balconies, but they also wanted meaningful in-depth relationships and total openness. (The Scarlet Pimpernel, I would tell them silently, does not have time for meaningful in-depth relationships.) They wanted multiple orgasms, they wanted the earth to move, but they also wanted help with the dishes.

. . . for Arthur's sake I would try anything, though cooking wasn't as simple as I'd thought. I was always running out of staples such

> **"There is a woman who swam around Manhattan, and I asked her, why? She said, it hadn't ever been done before. Well, she didn't have to do that. If she wanted to do something no one had ever done before, all she had to do was vacuum my apartment."**
>
> **Rita Rudner**

as butter or salt and making flying trips to the corner store, and there were never enough clean dishes, since I hated washing them; but Arthur didn't like eating in restaurants. He seemed to prefer my inedible food: the Swiss fondue which would turn to lymph and balls of chewing gum from too high a heat, the poached eggs which disintegrated like mucous membranes and the roast chickens which bled when cut; the bread that refused to rise, lying like quicksand in the bowl; the flaccid pancakes with centers of uncooked ooze; the rubbery pies. I seldom wept over these failures, as to me they were not failures but successes, they were secret triumphs over the notion of food itself. I wanted to prove that I didn't really care about it.

Occasionally I neglected to produce any food at all because I had forgotten completely about it. I would wander into the kitchen at midnight to find Arthur making himself a peanut-butter sandwich and be overwhelmed with guilt at the implication that I'd been starving him. But though he criticized my cooking, he always ate it, and he resented its absence. The unpredictability kept him diverted; it was like mutations, or gambling. It reassured him, too. His view of the world featured swift disasters set against a background of lurking doom, and my cooking did nothing to contradict it. Whereas for me these mounds of dough, these lumps burning at the edges, this untransformed blood, represented something quite different. Each meal was a crisis, but a crisis out of which a comfortable resolution could be forced to emerge, by the addition of something . . . a little pepper, some vanilla . . . At heart I was an optimist, with a lust for happy endings.

It took me a while to realize that Arthur enjoyed my defeats. They cheered him up. He loved hearing the crash as I dropped a red-hot

platter on the floor, having forgotten to put on my oven mitt; he liked to hear me swearing in the kitchen; and when I would emerge sweaty-faced and disheveled after one of my battles, he would greet me with a smile and a little joke, or perhaps even a kiss, which was as much for the display, the energy I'd wasted, as for the food. My frustration and anger were real, but I wasn't that bad a cook. My failure was a performance and Arthur was the audience. His applause kept me going.

(Reprinted by permission of Margaret Atwood, from *Lady Oracle* published by Simon & Schuster © 1976.)

TWO, THREE, MANY HUSBANDS

Barbara Ehrenreich

It is midsummer and a soft sound of concupiscent lip-smacking rises from the Potomac valley, for it is all right, once again, for important men to talk about The Family, and especially its most fascinating and recalcitrant form, The Black Family. Not so long ago poverty was believed to be the result of unemployment, discrimination, low wages, and other dreary economic factors, the mere reciting of which would cause a whole seminar full of modern-day social thinkers to slump forward in profound slumber. It was further thought, in the old days, to be impolite to blame poverty on the sleeping arrangements of the poor, just as no one would have thought of blaming plant closings on the personal hygiene of America's blue-collar workers. In those days, white men felt inhibited about castigating the black family, more or less as they hesitated to approach a random young man of color with amusing speculations about the sexual proclivities of his mama.

But, hey, this is the '80s and it sure is fun to reflect on what the poor are doing in the privacy of their tenements or street-side cardboard shelters, as the case may be. Are they married, single, promiscuous, underage, depraved? Whole books, conferences. and sonorous speeches are now devoted to these questions, which some believe may hold the key to every social problem from infant malnutrition to subway graffiti. If you wish to appear *au courant* in the postliberal set, just cast your eyes downward and mutter knowingly about The Black Family. White folks should still be a little circumspect when in mixed company, perhaps adding modestly, "It's up to *you people* to do something about it, of course . . ."

Actually, the problem is not a new one. It's been tossed back and forth like a hot potato between Daniel Patrick Moynihan and various members of the black intelligentsia for over 20 years now. When he first suggested that black poverty was caused by black "matriarchy"—i.e., that the very existence of so many single mothers was "emasculating" black men—the intelligentsia wisely suggested that his mouth be washed out with soap. But time passed. Moynihan transmogrified himself from a liberal into a neoconservative and finally into a neoliberal. The black intelligentsia mellowed too, produced their own crop of neoconservatives, and

"Many think they have a kind heart who only have weak nerves."

Marie Ebner von Eschenbach

perhaps—sensing that a righteous distance had at last grown up between themselves and the wretched underclass—decided to reclaim The Problem of The Black Family for themselves. And recently, with just the tiniest trace of a smirk on his face, Moynihan has come out with a book (*Family and Nation*) reminding everyone that he thought of the whole thing first.

So what is The Problem of The Black Family, now that you have surely grasped that it is not someone's idea of a catchy title for a *Cosby Show* spin-off? The problem, to simplify volumes of sociological folderol, is that the black family does not have enough grown-ups in it. Almost half of all black families—43 percent—contain only one grown-up, the mother; and the fact that so many black female-headed families—over 50 percent—are poor, is taken as prima facie evidence that a mother is not enough. That, plus the wisdom of 7,000 years of patriarchy, 70 years of Freudian psychology, and 40 years of Parsonian sociology, establishes conclusively that the black family is short one person, and that person should be an adult male.

Or so the experts think. But I have come to believe that this formulation seriously understates the problem. Most of us would agree that a family consisting of *zero* grown-ups—say a 15-year-old girl and her baby—is probably not viable either as an economic unit or as a fundamental building block of civilization. Add one grown-up—the closest one at hand usually being an adult mother—and all we get is the feminization of poverty. But can we assume that adding a husband will solve the problem? And this is really the most challenging question that the black family confronts us with: Are two parents really enough?

It takes just a few simple calculations to reveal the inadequacy of the two-parent black family. First we observe that the median black male income is $9,448, which is approximately $1,000 less than the official poverty level for a family of four. So adding one median-type black male to a preformed family unit consisting of a mother and two children leaves us with a black family that still has a problem, namely, poverty. Adding two black males is still not much of an improvement; only by adding three can we hope to clear the median U.S. family income, which is $26,433. If our hypothetical black family is to enter the middle-class mainstream, which means home ownership, it will need at least $36,596— or four black men.

I can hear the objections already. The morally squeamish will point out that polyandry contradicts the policies of Judaism, Islam, and even Mormonism. The overly sensitive will fret about the possibilities of "intimacy" and "commitment" in a five-way relationship involving at least four heterosexual males. The nit-pickers will say I have neglected certain diseconomies of scale—e.g., that each man we add will take up a certain amount of spending money and space—so that it may actually take six or seven husbands to produce the problem-free black family.

But I am convinced that upper-middle-class whites (the politically pivotal group in our society) are already warming to the notion of the six-parent black family. Just days ago, at a wine-and-brie reception for some worthy cause, I overheard a young blond woman in linen suit and Reeboks opine, to general mutters of approval, that "blacks really haven't gone anywhere, considering all that's been *done* for them. Why, just look at the Orientals—but of course they have these really wonderful big extended families!"

This is not the place to take on the myth of the Oriental family, which, as the story goes, escaped from Saigon with only a suitcase full of bullion from the national treasury, a few keys of heroin, and a dozen hardworking aunts and grandmothers, set up a modest asparagus and kiwi dealership on Sunset Boulevard, and now has six sons at MIT. The point is that—just as we have learned to look to the East for clues about how to run corporations, assemble VCRs, and manufacture automobiles—we have begun to look to the Orient for the model family, especially the model poor-but-striving family. It must have been easier for the black family when the model for comparison was the two-parent European immigrant family. But standards are rising. Implicitly, the upper middle class has come to believe that a family that is *really* trying will include a half-dozen or more breadwinners, all willing to work at least 12 hours a day at the minimum wage.

There is another solution, one that may not go down quite so well with the wine-and-brie set. It occurred to me only after many hours of poring over the dour statistics made available by the U.S. Census Bureau, when I came across a fact so striking, so curious, that it is hard to believe that it has escaped the notice of all those worthy scholars who muse about The Problem of The Black Family. The fact is that the number of white *single* men who have never married and earn more than the median *family* income (i.e., the number of really *prime* bachelors) is almost the same, give or take a 100,000 or so, as the number of poor, black single mothers!

Could this be a coincidence, a meaningless convergence of unrelated digits? I very much doubt it. To all those single white males earning far more than they need, we must say firmly, "Shape up. fellas, for demography is destiny! Go forth to the welfare hotels, the

(Reprinted from *More Dykes to Watch Out For,* © 1988 by Alison Bechdel, Firebrand Books.)

day-old bread shops, the emergency rooms of the public hospitals, and find a single mom to woo!''

Some will find this an unfeeling solution, a heavy-handed attempt to reduce a complex issue to mere dollars and cents. After all, a family income does not a family make.

Just look at that other great sociological conundrum—The Problem of The White Family. Even when it is not poor (and space does not permit us to deal with the doleful fact that white poverty is numerically still a far greater problem than black poverty), The White Family has long been a nesting place for social ills too numerous to list: alcoholism, incest, organized crime, abuse of the elderly, pediatric stress diseases—not to mention, in many cases, national chauvinism, racism, and militant religious intolerance. No wonder that white families by the millions have turned to the black gentry, represented by Bill Cosby and the Huxtables, to learn the elementary principles of domestic nonviolence.

But if economics isn't everything, neither should it be forgotten in our search for a solution to poverty. Money helps, and it is especially helpful to those who have very little of it. In the absence of all the old-fashioned ways of redistributing wealth—progressive taxation, jobs programs, adequate welfare, social services, and other pernicious manifestations of pre-Reaganite "big government"—the rich will just have to marry the poor.

(Excerpted with permission from *Mother Jones* magazine, © 1986, Foundation for National Progress.)

WHEN YOUR HUSBAND FORNICATES WITH YOUR BIRTH INSTRUCTOR

Kathleen Rockwell Lawrence

Maud left with nothing. Not even a fine-toothed comb. But before taking leave of her drunken husband, she dumped the contents of the Chuckle Bag over him, carefully emptying the vial of sand into one of his huge ears. She kicked him once in the balls and contemplated murder. It would have been justified. If Thomas Aquinas could carry on about the notion of a just war, he would have approved the murder of Jack Devlin that night. The *Post* headline would read: DAD-TO-BE FOUND WITH BIRTH INSTRUCTOR; SLAIN, WIFE WALKS. She would walk in any court in the land. St. Augustine would defend her. The Heavenly Host (her peers) would be her jury. None of this fifteen-years-to-life stuff—Jack was damned for sure.

Maud's thin wool cape, the only article of outerwear capable of covering her bulk, was flapping wildly in the freezing bursts from the East River. A neat trick to get a cab at 3:00 A.M. She would have

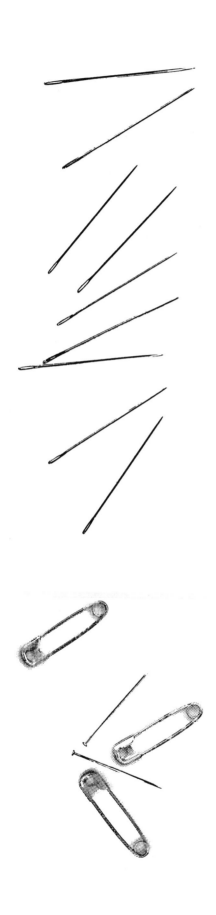

to walk from Stuyvesant Oval to 14th Street. It was slow going, though the winds helped to push her along. As she picked her way past mirrors of ice, she felt the baby go into her salute. Just as she reached 14th, the nerve kicked in, and her right leg stiffened with a cramp. She leaned against a nearby lamppost and began massaging it. She looked, and felt, like an aging, knocked-up match girl.

"Hey-yy, Mama! I do mean *mama*! Whatchu doin' out tonight, girl? You got no sense in your mind, woman?" The voice came from a pink Lincoln double-parked in front of Pete's-A-Place.

The leg would not come around. The tears began again, uncontrolled. "Leave me alone. Just go away, please."

A tall black man in a beige felt hat emerged from the car. "Listen here, woman, you need help. You got to get to a hospital? Get your fanny into that car right now, hear? I'll take you wherever you want to go."

Maud considered the car. Pepto Bismol pink it was, with heavy chrome and white-walled tires that glistened ominously in the sodium vapor lighting. The New Jersey vanity plate proclaimed "SERGE R." Even in her dazed state, there could be no questioning what sort of car it was. Jack had his names for such vehicles: a Pimpmobile, a Ho Hauler, a Drug Abuse Center, a Perpetrator's Palace. But who gave a shit what Jack called anything? Deirdre, though, would have taken herself immediately to confession if she had seen this car. It was a car that, under normal circumstances, Maud would never enter. Not that, under normal circumstances, a woman like Maud would have given a passing thought to such a possibility. "Get *in*, girl!" Maud hobbled over to the car. The night's events could not be called normal. Besides, her belly made her brave. Maud climbed into the front seat.

She asked Serge R. to take her to Jane Street. Johanna's was the only place she could go. . . .

Maud had known Johanna for fifteen years, but sometimes she was still surprised by her. "What's doin'?"—as casual as if Maud weren't due momentarily, as if it weren't four in the morning, as if she weren't accompanied by a tall black man wearing star-studded leather pants. "Let me in, will ya?" Because Johanna had not made a move. She was still standing in the doorway, eyeing Serge with more than a little interest. Maud was annoyed, but stopped to note what apparently Johanna had seen immediately. Serge R. was a beautiful man. A really gorgeous specimen of fine-boned male, with deep-set sorrowful island eyes and skin as dark and smooth and delicious as the Chocolate Flavor Packet in the Duncan Hines Double Fudge Brownie Mix. Johanna would not have failed to appreciate a man with Serge's endowments if Maud had already given birth and were standing there with a bloody newborn in her arms, the umbilical cord still uncut. Because, the truth was, Maud's friend Johanna was a manizer.

. . . Johanna was able to summon, quite genuinely, the requisite righteousness at Maud's recounting of Jack's transgression. Screwing priests was one thing; screwing the birth instructor, quite another. Her "What a motherfucker!" had a solidity to it, a resonance that brought great comfort to Maud just then, at six in the morning, when her water broke.

As the warm gray-speckled fluid began running down Maud's leg, Johanna paused in her tirade against Jack the Motherfucker to ask a question that had been in the back of her mind since Maud's arrival:

"Who was that guy who brought you here?" But Maud was already off in search of paper towels. It was a question that was not to be answered just yet.

Maud took Kate to Johanna's apartment because she had no place to take her. Johanna was bewildered but gracious about Maud's decision, though she had not invited Maud, though it meant rearranging her apartment and her life, though her experience with infants was limited to their birthing. It was what you did for friends. It was what you did for anyone with a small child and no place to go. If Maud said she had no place to go, then it was good enough for Johanna. And if she was going to do it, she would do it right. She went to the most elegant baby store in the city and purchased a bassinet resplendent with eyelet and lace. She came to pick up Maud and her baby the morning they left Jefferson Hospital. She did not count on the scene with Jack.

He, too, had come to the hospital. He had clothes for the baby and clothes for Maud and a bottle of pink Lake Champlain Champagne. He explained his choice, a little sheepishly, by saying that he had wanted pink for a girl, and that was the only bottle of pink in the liquor store. "And the only champagne that sells for $2.99," Maud added scornfully. The cheap bastard, she thought, as Jack grinned. Even he knew he had deep pockets. Maud took the clothes and told him, for the sixth time that week, that she was not coming home with him.

"You have to come with me. You have no place else to go. I'm the only one that'll have you." He strutted as he said it, and then was instantly sorry. You jerk, Devlin, he told himself. You're supposed to be good today, remember? You want her back, don't you? God, he did. He wanted her back. "Maud, I'm sorry . . . I don't know why I said that."

But his reminder of her need infuriated her. Some reason. Live with him because there was no one else. She walked slowly about the room, putting what little she had with her in the shopping bag Jack had brought. She was grateful for a basket of baby items, a sort of Welcome Wagon for the new baby provided by manufacturers. "Welcome, babies! Goo-goo ga-ga spoken here. Get on the wagon! Buy our products for life!" A tiny bottle of Johnson's Baby Oil, a tube of Desitin diaper cream, a box of newborn Pampers. She hoped Jack didn't know it had come in a pack. Maybe he thought she had had the foresight to purchase them beforehand. She ostentatiously displayed each item before dropping it in the shopping bag and then ignored her husband as she dressed the baby in the ridiculous outfit he had gotten for her, probably in Job Lot or from a street vendor: a long-sleeved chartreuse Banlon turtleneck with the legend, "The kid's got class!!" Two exclamations points, not one. This was accompanied by matching chartreuse Banlon leggings so long that they had to be folded back up to the waist and pinned.

"She looks beautiful," Jack exulted. She looks crazy, Maud thought resentfully. He gets his own clothes at Brooks Brothers but shops for his daughter at some flea hole on Chambers Street and thinks he's terrific for shopping for her at all. It hurt her to pull "The kid's got class!!" over Kate's tiny head, but it was ten degrees outside and so she did, taking care to help the material over the ears. Fortunately some friends from work had brought a pastel quilt which would hide the idiotic ensemble. . . .

The nurse escorted them out the door to the sidewalk before she relinquished the babe to its mother. Hospital policy, Maud knew. Jefferson Hospital was afraid mothers would drop babies' new heads on the green line that led to the exit. Let them drop 'em on city sidewalks. Jefferson wanted no-fault babies.

"Maud, we've always loved each other. This is a big day for us . . . Jesus, Maud, come home with me, please!"

His plaint was so piteous it found its mark at the base of her spine and reverberated off each vertebra. She wavered. It was the fresh air making her dizzy, she decided. She had to be strong.

The nurse solemnly handed the bundle to Maud under the green awning, making motherhood official. She smiled crisply and was gone. Had Maud heard her click her heels? Maud tenderly kissed a piece of the quilt and turned to the street as Jack began a new assault. But he closed his mouth as Maud opened hers, stunned by the sight of a waiting pink Lincoln with New Jersey vanity plates.

"Johanna!" Maud blurted, laughing. "What's been doin', Johanna? I've only been gone a couple of days, girl. You been busy."

"I have been busy," Johanna agreed, smiling quietly, her eyes never leaving the tall figure leaning against the DOCTOR'S PARKING ONLY sign.

"What's going on?" asked Jack.

Serge kissed Johanna, then Maud. "You know, lady, you don't look pregnant from the front now, either. Let's see that pretty little daughter. Come on, come on . . . get in the car. I know the way now. I know the way just fine." Serge's slight of Jack was perhaps intentional, perhaps not, though Jack hung so closely and so abjectly and so ferociously to the little group as to leave no doubts about his paternal interest in the pastel quilt.

Jack sure thought it was intentional. Who was this guy and where had he gotten that jumpsuit? It had the longest zipper Jack had ever seen. And why was this guy kissing Maud and Johanna and taking his baby away? He banged on the window to Maud in the backseat. "Get out of there now, Maud. This car is danger. This man is a baby seller. You don't know. It's the painkiller they gave you that's doing it to you. You still have drugs in your bloodstream."

This was too much. She couldn't ignore him anymore. She had suffered natural childbirth and she damn well wanted credit for it. She pushed the window button forward. "I didn't have any drugs, remember? I had Painless Birth, remember?" She pushed the window button back.

"Bye, Jack," said Johanna blithely, and hopped in next to Serge.

As she closed the door, Jack tried one last pathetic feint: "They'll think you're lesbians!" he screamed.

Siblings & Sublings (parents)

Photo by Gloria Kaufman

"If the kids are still alive when my husband comes home, I've done my job."

Roseanne Barr

CALLING ALL WORKING FATHERS:

A Homespun Idea for Revolutionary Change

Mary Kay Blakely

> **"There's a time when you have to explain to your children why they're born, and it's a marvelous thing if you know by then."**
>
> **Hazel Scott**

"Hello, Tony? This is Ryan's mom. Is your father there?" It's 7:30 on a Wednesday evening, I am sitting at my desk, my son's class list of 22 names and telephone numbers in front of me. I am only on the D's. "Nobody kept answering," as Holden Caulfield once said.

"He's watching TV," Tony replied.

"Great." I said, making a check mark next to his name. "Tell him I want to talk to him."

While Tony notifies his dad, I scan the list and look up at the clock. I still have work to do this evening, on a deadline that should have been mailed Express two hours ago.

Tony's dad is taking his time. I try to recall what programs are on the air at 7:30 P.M., but the last one I remember watching was "Marcus Welby, M.D." Leisure time has disappeared from my life, which is how I became a Room Mother in the first place. I couldn't volunteer to be a Field Trip Mother or a Cafeteria Mother, because those required daytime hours, but Room Mothers can make their phone calls at night.

I still try to do my share of PTA-type tasks, because I don't want to fuel the current flames between mothers who work at home and mothers who work outside. Mrs. Laura L. Luteri, of Mt. Prospect, Illinois, just fired a tiny grenade into my camp, in a letter to the editor of *Better Homes and Gardens.* She wrote that she was sick of hearing the excuse, "I can't, I work," from women like me.

Mrs. Luteri resents me for depending on women like her to fill in. In fact, I am depending on school administrations to recognize that Room Mother and Cafeteria Mother and Field Trip Mother should all become paid positions.

"Hello?" A male voice interrupts my thoughts with a touch of boredom. The voice doesn't sound as if it's dressed in a suit and tie; it has a sweatshirt and jeans on, but it manages to talk down to me nevertheless. Perhaps I have been referred to as "Ryan's mom," and so I sit up a little straighter and introduce myself.

"Hello, Mr. D., this is Mary Kay Blakely. I'm the Room Mother for Mr. Baldino's sixth-grade class," I begin in my most professional voice.

"Hold on," he interrupts, "I'll get my wife." The professional disguise fails. "Room Mother" gives me away—he recognizes this as a woman's call.

"No, wait," I reply instantly, keeping him attached to the receiver. "I've already spoken to your wife several times this year. . . ."

A mental image of Mrs. D. flashes into my mind—like all the mothers of the children in Mr. Baldino's class, she is making dinner. I call during dinner to save myself time dialing repeats—working mothers are usually home at dinner-time. "Oh, God," they sigh when I mention my name, "let me get a pencil." Four times this year, I have made requests on their time and heard their fatigue. The cumulative guilt of 22 sighs repeated four times made me revise the message I'm sending out. I've only changed one word.

"We're asking the sixth-grade fathers . . ." I begin, and falter slightly. It is an editorial "we," but in fact I have no authority behind me. The other Room Mothers are not asking for fathers tonight. It is a "we" to make me bigger than "I," a "we" representing the plurality of motherhood, a "we" to give some power to the request I'm about to make.

"We're asking the fathers," I repeat, "to make brownies for the class party next Wednesday. Will you send a dozen to school with Tony?" I stop, to let the request sink in. I imagine Mr. D.'s eyebrows rising up on his forehead.

"Me?" he asks incredulously. After 12 years of fatherhood, Mr. D. has apparently never been asked to make brownies, never been a Room Mother. Perhaps he is a father who spends "quality time" with his children on weekends and evenings, but he did not sound like a man who knew his way around the kitchen. That's where mothers generally conduct their "quality time," helping children with homework while making dinner and taking phone calls.

"Oh, I don't know, I've never made brownies." Mr. D. chuckles, as if I were teasing him. But I'm not.

"It's easy. All you have to do is read the box." I'm prepared to give him detailed intructions, over the phone, on how to make brownies. Fudge brownies, brownies with nuts, blondie brownies . . . suddenly, Mr. D. has 12 years of knowing nothing about

" DID SHE KNOW ABOUT PRINCE CHARMINGS PREVIOUS MARRIAGE TO CINDERELLA?"

(From *Down the Street*, © 1988 by Lynda Barry, Harper & Row.)

38

brownies to make up for with me. I realize I'm getting worked up. I pretend that I'm late on my deadline because I've been making brownies all day.

Be patient, I caution myself—if he's never been asked to help out, how can I expect him to know? He could know from watching Mrs. D.'s fatigue, by observing the diminishing "quality" of her time in the kitchen. He does not see her exhaustion, perhaps, because "exhausted" is the way women in kitchens have always looked. Maybe he thinks "exhausted" is a normal state for us. The mothers in Mr. Baldino's class have been forgiving fathers on "how could he know" grounds for 12 years. Mr. D.'s "learning" time has just expired.

"I'll see what I can do," he says, taking me for a fool. "I'll see" is not the same as "I will." Those two words and their lack of commitment are why "working father" is still unfamiliar to the culture; why men and their newspapers fill up the early morning commuter trains, in time for "power breakfasts," while women catch the later ones, after junior high carpools; why executive mothers are telling the press they are leaving their jobs because they "can't do both," while their executive husbands are never even interviewed. "I'll see" is just inches above "I won't"—the phrase given up, with reluctance, in the seventies.

"We need a commitment tonight," I insist, keeping him on the phone. I am speaking to Mr. D., but I am thinking of the man in the study next to mine, the one I argued with last night, the one who's also working under a crushing deadline. He hates these arguments, as do I, because we both "understand" the pressures of work and family. We both understand, but I am the one who meets them. His deadline meant a month of 60-hour weeks at his office, a month of brief appearances at home. "I have no *choice*," he would say, apologetically, listing the emergencies, "I have to work."

"Tell that to Laura L. Luteri," I reply, although he'd never recognize the *Better Homes and Gardens* reader, or have any inkling of why she hates me.

"You *see* no choice," I amend, naming others. He could quit his job, I suggested last night, but didn't mean it. I couldn't argue persuasively for that choice, since my salary wasn't close to meeting our expenses. He made more money, and making more bread is partly why men are exempted from making the brownies.

Or he could quit the family, I offered as a second alternative, although I didn't mean that either. They were the kinds of statements that get blown out heatedly during arguments, born of injury or jealousy. But he *had* temporarily quit the family, and by empathizing with his deadlines I lost ground on my own. What good did it do us to "think" equality if we didn't get to live it?

Or finally, he could introduce his boss to the term "working father" and the phrase "I'm running late." That's the "choice" I campaigned for heavily. It would diminish his considerable esteem at work, and wouldn't be easily accepted. There is no plurality of working fathers, and he would undoubtedly have to run late alone. But in a month of 60-hour workweeks, the subject of home responsibilities had never come up at his office. How could his boss know he needs time for his family if he didn't ask? His boss could know, of course, if he chose to "see" the family portrait on his desk and consider for a moment how such pictures are developed. Faces of affection don't just happen, he would have to conclude. They take

"Children use up the same part of my head as poetry does."

Libby Houston

time and care.

"You have to ask to change your hours," I pressed. "Our lives have to catch up with our heads."

"I'll see," he said.

"Mr. D., we need to know tonight," I repeat, asking for brownies but wishing for a revolution in the priorities of men. "If you can't bake them yourself, Sara Lee offers a good alternative." While I wait for his answer, I think about opening a new business, a consulting firm to help fathers "see," to discuss the many options to "I can't, I work."

"Okay," he says, recognizing the only answer that will return him to his TV program. "A dozen brownies, next Wednesday."

I then dial the number for Mr. F., repeating my message, then Misters L. and M. I am thrilled to raise the eyebrows of the fathers in Mr. Baldino's class. I imagine I am healing some tensions among women, between the mothers at home and outside it.

I have begun with brownies, but I plan to ask for day care and field trips next. I want fathers to absorb some of the home pressures they leave to mothers. When working fathers have the same needs as working mothers, corporations will begin to "see" the need for day care, flextime, sick days for family. The truth: when working fathers need the same benefits as working mothers, we will have them.

My deadline is still ahead of me when I finish the last call. But I feel successful, having pledges for 144 brownies, all from fathers. I can't be certain Mr. D. or Mr. F. did not immediately delegate the responsibility to their wives: "Tony needs a dozen brownies." Or that their wives did not reply, "I don't do brownies." But I realize, this evening, that I was through excusing fathers who "understood," but "had no choice." Understanding is fine, but now I want fathers to put their brownies where their mouths are.

(From *MS.* magazine, December 1986. Reprinted by permission of Mary Kay Blakely.)

ON HYPERACTIVE TWINS

Jane Wagner

You don't know what it's like!
Hyperactive twins!
When they turned three, my doctor prescribed Ritalin—
I wouldn't dream of giving drugs to my children,
but it does help when I take it myself.
I can't keep up with them.
At some point, they looked at one another,
realized there were two of them
and only *one* of me. Sometimes it gets so bad, I brew up some
Sleepytime herb tea, pour it over ice, serve it in Spiderman
glasses and
tell them it's a new-flavor
Kool-Aid.

I feel so guilty as I watch their little heads nod out.

> "Children ask better questions than do adults. 'May I have a cookie?' 'Why is the sky blue?' and 'What does a cow say?' are far more likely to elicit a cheerful response than 'Where's your manuscript?' 'Why haven't you called?' and 'Who's your lawyer?'"
>
> **Fran Lebowitz**

Remember that rainy day last month I stayed home from the office, sick?
They were unusually hyper. That day, I was desperate.
I said, "Do you want Mommy to teach you a new game?"

And I actually dragged them out to my car in the pouring rain, put them in the backseat and told them,

"Stay there and play car wash."

NECESSARY INFORMATION ABOUT MOTHERS AND SLEEP

Teresa Bloomingdale

Parents are funny people. When I was a baby, my father sang to me so I would go to sleep by seven o'clock. When I was in grade school, my mother let me "stay up" till eight-thirty. In my teenage years, both parents spent half of every evening asking:
"Good heavens, aren't you in bed yet? You've got to get more sleep!"
They sent me to college where the dorm rules demanded "Lights Out at 10:00" and God help the girl who disobeyed and studied her history notes by penlite.
Yet, oddly enough, my parents and the good nuns all claimed to be preparing me for motherhood. This is a preparation for motherhood? Teaching us to get some sleep? They should have been teaching us to stay awake.
A new mother might as well forget everything she learned about sleep. From the very moment that Number One bundle of joy joins the family, your nights are shot. The new baby wakes for feedings at two and five, and a pox on the pediatrician who will try to tell you that a baby who sleeps till 5 A.M. has "slept through the night." The night is not through at 5 A.M. Mother may be through, but the night isn't.
So after falling into bed at midnight, a new mother can expect to be up at one-thirty or two o'clock for feeding, changing, and burping (which, depending on your degree of success or failure, may necessitate more changing). With any luck at all, you can get back to bed by three-thirty only to get up again in an hour or so for the five-o'clock feeding, after which you won't get back to bed at all because by then it's breakfast time for the Cause of it all.
In your innocence and exhaustion, you may tell yourself that things will get back to normal when Baby gets a little older, but

> " I'm going home next week. It's kind of an emergency: my parents are coming here. "
>
> **Rita Rudner**

you're wrong. Things won't get back to normal until Baby gets married. For as Baby gets older, you merely progress from the nighttime feedings to nighttime earaches, and kicking-off the covers, and better-check-to see-if-he's-breathing.

By the time he is old enough to convince you that he can breathe without supervision, he will be into the terrible twos, which is always accompanied by a terrible thirst. For the next year or two you will have to get up several times each night to get him a drink of water, and since he is still a little-bitty guy and can't hold all that water (you were the one who wanted him out of diapers, Dum-Dum), you will have to get up again to take him to the potty.

Baby will outgrow this at about three or four, but by that time he will undoubtedly have a little brother or sister requesting the pleasure of your company at 2 A.M. and 5 A.M., and there you go all over again.

Eventually, of course, you will stop having babies. (Even I quit having babies) and you will think:

"At last! I can get some sleep!"

Forget it. You have just begun to wake. For just about the time your youngest baby begins sleeping through the night, your oldest baby begins to stay out half the night, and you will be back to walking the floor and wondering if you are *ever* going to get some sleep.

As I was thirty-nine when Patrick was born, I figure I will be sixty before I can count on getting a good night's sleep.

Maybe.

I just read an article which said that women over sixty often have difficulty sleeping. I'm not surprised. By that time they have forgotten how.

(From *I Should Have Seen It Coming When the Rabbit Died,* copyright © 1979 by Teresa Bloomingdale. Used by permission of Doubleday, a division of Bantam, Doubleday, Dell Publishing Group, Inc.)

PARENT ABUSE

Karen Williams

Everyone talks about child abuse, but what about parent abuse? I have a theory: I don't think parents and children should live together. No, really . . . after all, I pay the rent for the apartment; can't I smoke a cigarette in there every now and then? NOOOOOOO!

My oldest son dances around me chanting, "Go on, Mom, admit it. . . . You're addicted, you're addicted, you're addicted." The seven-year-old comes right to the point, "Mom, you're gonna die."

It's like, give me a break. So I'm back in the bathroom stuffing towels under the bathroom door, burning incense, and smoking out of the bathroom window.

SEVEN: THE AGE OF REASON

Gina Cascone

Going to Church became increasingly important during my second grade year. Until now, I had only attended church as an observer. Soon, I would be indoctrinated as an active participant. According to the rules of the Church, I had come of age. Seven. The age of reason. I wasn't allowed to cross the street yet—but I was made to understand that now I was totally accountable for my sins. What sins? At seven you can't even understand most of the commandments, much less break any of them. No dogmatic problem! There was the Catholic door prize, Original Sin. Since you hadn't time or the opportunity to accumulate any of your own, they gave you a starter sin—Original. Actually I think it was only a cheap reproduction and it was sort of hard to feel genuine guilt over it. But with a little time and conditioning, you began to feel as though you were the original perpetrator—a real trick, since at seven you didn't even know what Original Sin was. As a matter of fact I'm not too clear on it to this day.

That apple story is terrible PR for God. It makes Him look really petty; I mean, one lousy apple. He had a whole treeful. If a friend broke one of my toys; my mother would say, "Now come on, don't be angry, you've got a whole roomful of toys." You mean to tell me that I was supposed to be more forgiving than God? And the extent of my retaliation would have been, at most, a smack or refusing to play with him for the rest of the day. I certainly wouldn't have exiled him and cursed his progeny for all time.

The whole Adam and Eve story is a tremendous embarrassment to the human race. Not only do we have Adam and Eve, the original sinners, but they have two kids, Cain and Abel. Cain kills Abel, his own brother. The only decent member of the family gets iced. This is from whence we come? You can't help but feel ashamed to be human. Now you've got it—Original Sin. You still can't quite put your finger on it, but you're feeling miserable and that's enough. You can't wait to get into that confessional and purge your soul of this smirch. We didn't even mind coming in early from recess to learn confessional etiquette.

That spring while the other kids were outside playing jump rope, we were inside playing confession. First we had to make believe that Sister Michael was Father Joseph. That was a cinch; she did, after all, have a mustache and we all suspected that she was as bald as he was too. It would have been a lot more fun if we could have practiced with Father Joseph, which is exactly why the nuns did their best to keep us away from him. He was a real sucker for little girls. He used to call us "sweet souls," and put his hand on our heads and bless us like this: "May God bless you and keep you. And don't forget to say a prayer for me," and then he'd wink. He made us believe that God loved us like crazy. And that's why he was no good for teaching confession. To Father Joseph, we were sweet souls, not tarnished ones.

" Mom, it's time we had a man-to-man talk about jock itch."

Sister Michael, on the other hand, was perfect for the job. It was her attitude that it was a sin for a kid even to be alive. And she made *you* sorry for it too. The idea must have been, if you could confess to Sister Michael, you could confess to any priest. In the nine years I spent in Catholic school, I never saw Sister Michael enjoy herself more than when we played confession. The sight of so many penitent children must have warmed the cockles of her heart.

Making up sins is a lot tougher than committing them and not nearly as much fun. You really had to be careful to make up a good confession for Sister Michael; too few sins and she knew that you were going to lie in confession, too many and she was going to keep an eye on you for the rest of the year. You had to be careful about the kinds of sins you made up. "I ate meat on Friday," or "I missed mass on Sunday," were definitely out. You didn't even want her to know that such things entered your mind. That would have offered her the opening for an unendurable lecture. It was better to stick to sins that she herself had accused us of committing—like being disrespectful, disobedient, and inconsiderate. That was the format we all stuck to. Except Dianne Luca. I'd already done my confession and gotten my penance—say the rosary every day for a week—and was back in my seat when Dianne got to the front of the line.

She went up to the desk and knelt down next to Sister Michael. "Bless me, Sister, for I have sinned."

"Father," Sister corrected her.

"Oh, yeah, right. Anyway, this is my first confession."

"Dianne, I think you should do it again."

"Bless me, Father, for I have sinned. This is my first confession."

"That's better. Now, Father may say something to you or he may not. So just pause a minute and if he doesn't say anything, go ahead with your sins." Sister must have thought that we were either idiots or hard of hearing; she went over the same thing with every single kid.

"Okay. Well, I have graven idols, I committed murder, and I coveted my neighbor's wife."

(From *Pagan Babies*, © 1982, St. Martin's Press.)

THE LESSON

Toni Cade Bambara

Back in the days when everyone was old and stupid or young and foolish and me and Sugar were the only ones just right, this lady moved on our block with nappy hair and proper speech and no makeup. And quite naturally we laughed at her, laughed the way we did at the junk man who went about his business like he was some big-time president and his sorry-ass horse his secretary. And we kinda hated her too, hated the way we did the winos who cluttered up our parks and pissed on our handball walls and stank up our hallways and stairs so you couldn't halfway play hide-and-seek without a goddamn gas mask. Miss Moore was her name. The only woman on the block with no first name. And she was black as hell, cept for her feet, which were fish-white and spooky. And she was always planning these boring-ass things for us to do, us being my cousin, mostly, who lived on the block cause we all moved North the same time and to the same apartment then spread out gradual to breathe. And our parents would yank our heads into some kinda shape and crisp up our clothes so we'd be presentable for travel with Miss Moore, who always looked like she was going to church, though she never did. Which is just one of the things the grownups talked about when they talked behind her back like a dog. But when she came calling with some sachet she'd sewed up or some gingerbread she'd made or some book, why then they'd all be too embarrassed to turn her down and we'd get handed over all spruced up. She'd been to college and said it was only right that she should take responsibility for the young ones' education, and she not even related by marriage or blood. So they'd go for it. Specially Aunt Gretchen. She was the main gofer in the family. You got some ole dumb shit foolishness you want somebody to go for, you send for Aunt Gretchen. She been screwed into the go-along for so long, it's a blood-deep natural thing with her. Which is how she got saddled with me and Sugar and Junior in the first place while our mothers

"I want to have children while my parents are still young enough to take care of them."

Rita Rudner

(Reprinted by permission of Lynn Johnston from *Do They Ever Grow Up?* Meadowbrook, Inc., © 1978.)

were in a la-de-da apartment up the block having a good ole time.

So this one day Miss Moore rounds us all up at the mailbox and it's puredee hot and she's knockin herself out about arithmetic. And school suppose to let up in summer I heard, but she don't never let up. And the starch in my pinafore scratching the shit outta me and I'm really hating this nappy-head bitch and her goddamn college degree.

. . . Miss Moore asking us do we know what money is, like we a bunch of retards. I mean real money, she say, like it's only poker chips or monopoly papers we lay on the grocer. So right away I'm tired of this and say so. And would much rather snatch Sugar and go to the Sunset and terrorize the West Indian kids and take their hair ribbons and their money too. And Miss Moore files that remark away for next week's lesson on brotherhood, I can tell. And finally I say we oughta get to the subway cause it's cooler and besides we might meet some cute boys. Sugar done swiped her mama's lipstick, so we ready.

So we heading down the street and she's boring us silly about what things cost and what our parents make and how much goes for rent and how money ain't divided up right in this country. And then she gets to the part about we all poor and live in the slums, which I don't feature. And I'm ready to speak on that, but she steps out in the street and hails two cabs just like that. Then she hustles half the crew in with her and hands me a five-dollar bill and tells me to calculate 10 percent tip for the driver. And we're off. Me and Sugar and Junebug and Flyboy hangin out the window and hollering to everybody, putting lipstick on each other cause Flyboy a faggot anyway, and making farts with our sweaty armpits. But I'm mostly trying to figure how to spend this money. . . . the driver tells us to get the hell out cause we there already. And the meter reads eighty-five cents. And I'm stalling to figure out the tip and Sugar say give him a dime. And I decide he don't need it bad as I do, so later for him. But then he tries to take off with Junebug foot still in the door so we talk about his mama something ferocious. Then we check out that we on Fifth Avenue and everybody dressed up in stockings. One lady in a fur coat, hot as it is. White folks crazy.

"Will you look at this sailboat, please," say Flyboy, cuttin her off and pointin to the thing like it was his. So once again we tumble all over each other to gaze at this magnificent thing in the toy store which is just big enough to maybe sail two kittens across the pond if you strap them to the posts tight. We all start reciting the price tag like we in assembly. "Hand-crafted sailboat of fiberglass at one thousand one hundred ninety-five dollars."

"Unbelievable," I hear myself say and am really stunned. I read it again for myself just in case the group recitation put me in a trance. Same thing. For some reason this pisses me off. We look at Miss Moore and she lookin at us, waiting for I dunno what.

"Who'd pay all that when you can buy a sailboat set for a quarter at Pop's, a tube of glue for a dime, and a ball of string for eight cents? It must have a motor and a whole lot else besides," I say. "My sailboat cost me about fifty cents."

"What I want to know is," I says to Miss Moore though I never talk to her, I wouldn't give the bitch that satisfaction, "is how much a real boat costs? I figure a thousand'd get you a yacht any day."

"Why don't you check that out," she says, "and report back to the group?" Which really pains my ass. If you gonna mess up a perfectly good swim day least you could do is have some answers. "Let's go in," she say like she got something up her sleeve. Only she don't lead the way. So me and Sugar turn the corner to where the entrance is, but when we get there I kinda hang back. Not that I'm scared, what's there to be afraid of, just a toy store. But I feel funny, shame. But what I got to be shamed about? Got as much right to go in as anybody. But somehow I can't seem to get hold of the door, so I step away for Sugar to lead. But she hangs back too. And I look at her and she looks at me and this is ridiculous. I mean, damn, I have never ever been shy about doing nothing or going nowhere. But then Mercedes steps up and then Rosie Giraffe and Big Butt crowd in behind and shove, and next thing we all stuffed into the doorway with only Mercedes squeezing past us, smoothing out her jumper and walking right down the aisle. Then the rest of us tumble in like a glued-together jigsaw done all wrong. And people lookin at us. And it's like the time me and Sugar crashed into the Catholic church on a dare. But once we got in there and everything so hushed and holy and the candles and the bowin and the handkerchiefs on all the drooping heads, I just couldn't go through with the plan. Which was for me to run up to the altar and do a tap dance while Sugar played the nose flute and messed around in the holy water. And Sugar kept givin me the elbow. Then later teased me so bad I tied her up in the shower and turned it on and locked her in. And she'd be there till this day if Aunt Gretchen hadn't finally figured I was lyin about the boarder takin a shower.

Same thing in the store. We all walkin on tiptoe and hardly touchin the games and puzzles and things. And I watched Miss Moore who is steady watchin us like she waitin for a sign. Like Mama Drewery watches the sky and sniffs the air and takes note of just how much slant is in the bird formation. Then me and Sugar bump smack into each other, so busy gazing at the toys, 'specially the sailboat. But we don't laugh and go into our fat-lady bump-stomach routine. We just stare at that price tag. Then Sugar run a finger over the whole boat. And I'm jealous and want to hit her. Maybe not her, but I sure want to punch somebody in the mouth.

Me and Sugar at the back of the train watchin the tracks whizzin by large then small then gettin gobbled up in the dark. I'm thinkin about this tricky toy I saw in the store. A clown that somersaults on a bar then does chin-ups just cause you yank lightly at his leg. Cost $35. I could see me askin my mother for a $35 birthday clown. "You wanna know what costs what?" she'd say, cocking her head to the side to get a better view of the hole in my head. Thirty-five dollars could buy new bunk beds for Junior and Gretchen's boy. Thirty-five dollars and the whole household could go visit Granddaddy Nelson in the country. Thirty-five dollars would pay for the rent and the piano bill too. Who are these people that spend that much for performing clowns and $1000 for toy sailboats? What kinda work they do and how they live and how come we ain't in on it? Where we are is who we are, Miss Moore always pointin out. But it don't necessarily have to be that way, she always adds then waits for somebody to say that poor people have to wake up and demand their share of the pie and don't none of us know what kind of pie she talkin about in the first damn place. But she ain't so smart cause I still got her four dollars from the taxi and she sure ain't gettin it. Messin up my day with this shit. Sugar nudges me in my

I gotta go to the bathroom...

(Reprinted by permission of Lynn Johnston from *Do They Ever Grow Up?* Meadowbrook, Inc., © 1978.)

pocket and winks.

Miss Moore lines us up in front of the mailbox where we started from, seem like years ago, and I got a headache for thinkin so hard. And we lean all over each other so we can hold up under the draggy-ass lecture she always finishes us off with at the end before we thank her for borin us to tears. But she just looks at us like she readin tea leaves. Finally she say, "Well, what did you think of F. A. O. Schwarz?"

. . . Rosie Giraffe mumbles, "White folks crazy."

Then Sugar surprises me by sayin, "You know, Miss Moore, I don't think all of us here put together eat in a year what that sailboat costs." And Miss Moore lights up like somebody goosed her. "And?" she say, urging Sugar on. Only I'm standin on her foot so she don't continue.

"Imagine for a minute what kind of society it is in which some people can spend on a toy what it would cost to feed a family of six or seven. What do you think?"

"I think," say Sugar pushing me off her feet like she never done before, cause I whip her ass in a minute, "that this is not much of a democracy if you ask me. Equal chance to pursue happiness means an equal crack at the dough, don't it?" Miss Moore is besides herself and I am disgusted with Sugar's treachery. So I stand on her foot one more time to see if she'll shove me. She shuts up, and Miss Moore looks at me, sorrowfully I'm thinkin. And somethin weird is goin on, I can feel it in my chest.

"Anybody else learn anything today?" lookin dead at me. I walk away and Sugar has to run to catch up and don't even seem to notice when I shrug her arm off my shoulder.

"Well, we got four dollars anyway," she says.

"Uh hunh."

"We could go to Hascombs and get half a chocolate layer and then go to the Sunset and still have plenty money for potato chips and ice cream sodas."

"Uh hunh."

"Race you to Hascombs," she say.

We start down the block and she gets ahead which is O.K. by me cause I'm going to the West End and then over to the Drive to think this day through. She can run if she want to and even run faster. But ain't nobody gonna beat me at nuthin.

> **"Breakfast cereals that come in the same colors as polyester leisure suits make oversleeping a virtue."**
>
> **Fran Lebowitz**

ON SINGING OFF-KEY— SAFELY

Faye Moskowitz

The year I was in sixth grade, one of my teachers decided to put together a school program on the concept of "America as the Melting Pot." She pounced on me eagerly, of course. "Won't you contribute something to the program?" she asked. My stomach lurched in misery. I didn't want to be different, no matter what my mother believed.

I received no sympathy at home. My mother stared at me incredulously when I told her of my reluctance to be singled out. "For five thousand years the Jews have been persecuted because of their faith, and you want to hide your heritage," she scolded. "Go to school and sing the Hatikvoh and be proud of what you are."

"Mama," I said. "What if I sing off key? You know what happens when I get nervous."

She looked at me for a long moment and then she laughed. "How many people in your school know the Hebrew National Anthem?"

"No one," I said.

Triumphantly she pushed the bangs off my worried forehead. "Then who will know if you sing off key?"

(From *A Leak in the Heart*, © 1985 by Faye Moskowitz, David Godine, Publisher.)

A CHILD'S VIEW OF THEOLOGY

Gina Cascone

"I WOULDN'T HAVE THIS PROBLEM WITH A SPERM BANK FATHER."

As I got older, I began to realize that those movies we were seeing were meant to be Catholic training films. That realization turned me off to my favorite movie, *Quo Vadis*. That's the one where Deborah Kerr falls in love with Robert Taylor. After a really steamy romance, their love conquers the Roman Empire and they ride off into the sunset together. But according to the nuns, I missed the main thrust—the persecution of the Christians. They were crucified, burned, eaten by lions, and thereby transformed into martyrs. I suppose the reason that didn't impress me as the central theme was because I had my eyes closed during most of those parts. I'm funny that way; I'm not crazy about watching people get mutilated. That wasn't the point that the nuns were trying to make either. But you did have to watch the people being martyred in order to see that they were doing it with smiles on their faces. While I thought that was nuts, Sister thought it was not only noble but required.

I hadn't even begun to live when they hit us with the news that we were supposed to be willing to die for our religion. And the way

WOULD YOU SHUT UP AND LISTEN! ... AND, NO – I DON'T KNOW WHY THE DISH RAN AWAY WITH THE SPOON...!!!

(Reprinted by permission of Lynn Johnston from *Do They Ever Grow Up?* Meadowbrook, Inc., © 1978.)

they told the story, they made it sound as though it were a definite possibility for each and every one of us. Another reason for me to feel guilty. Nonetheless, I determined early on that if someone decided to start rounding up Catholics with the intention of doing away with them, they weren't going to get me. I knew exactly how I would play it.

"Are you a Catholic?"

"No. I'm a kid."

"A Catholic kid?"

"No. An American kid."

"A Catholic American kid?"

"No. A cute American kid."

If they pushed it any further, or if they managed to get a copy of my baptism certificate before I had a chance to get out of the country, they were going to have to take me kicking and screaming. Dignity was out and so were smiling and singing. If I was going to be an hors d'oeuvre for a lion just because somebody threw water on me without my consent, I wasn't going to pretend to be happy about it.

Staying away from lions wasn't enough to guarantee safety, though. Certainly Circus Maximus and the lions were all the rage for a while there. But there were audiences who preferred the more subdued show, or who could not afford to import lions. In which case, there were crucifixions; also burning at the stake, beheading, disembowelment, dismemberment, and a multitude of other imaginative means to the same end. We heard about each and every one in explicit detail. I couldn't even smile through the explanation of these things and that proved to me beyond a shadow of a doubt that I wouldn't be smiling if it really happened.

While I was busy trying to keep my lunch down through these rather grim fairy tales, Sandra Minelli egged Sister on. That girl was determined to be a card-carrying saint by hook or by crook and martyrdom looked like the quickest way for her to get there.

. . . in order to go straight to heaven, you also had to sing, preferably some snappy Gregorian chant tune. I was sure that, given the chance, Sandra could pull it off.

As if listening to these stories didn't have enough impact on kids, there were pictures on the walls to illustrate the stories. While kids in public school were looking at Picasso prints, we had pictures of Jesus with his heart in his hand, or being crucified, Joan of Arc smiling through the flames, and others meeting similar ends. This did give us an edge in one area, though. On Saturday afternoons while Pauli was hiding under the theater seat, making foul noises and spitting jujubes, I was enjoying the picture. Frankenstein, Dracula, the Wolfman, and their peers were rather docile and likeable fellows compared to the persecuting pagans we'd been hearing about. Horror movies scared the life out of Pauli, but for me they were happy-go-lucky entertainment. Let's face it, what's so frightening about being bitten on the neck by a vampire compared with being disemboweled?

(From *Pagan Babies*, © 1982, St. Martin's Press.)

Older and Bolder

The Wink. 1977

(Reprinted from *Through the Looking Glass: Drawings by Elizabeth Layton.*
© 1984 by Mid-America Arts Alliance.)

MARLEY'S MOTHER

Tama Janowitz

(From *The Whole Enchilada,* copyright © 1986 by Nicole Hollander, St. Martin's Press.)

When I got back to my building, my mother was waiting in the lobby. More overweight than ever, if such a thing was possible. From the top of head to ankles, one piece of flesh, indisposable. Without joints—nor did I believe there were bones underneath that skin. Then beneath, the tiny feet, little figgys. "I told you yesterday I was coming to visit," she said. "Do you know how long I've been waiting? Where've you been?"

"Aw, Ma," I said. I gave her a smack on the cheek to placate.

So we went upstairs. To distract her from the mess I took her around and showed her the latest frescoes on the wall and ceilings, which I started when I ran out of canvas: goddess and nymph and semitropical vegetation. The God of Baseball, playing a game of billiards with Bacchus. I was proud of the God of Baseball, in his Yankees cap, chipmunk cheek filled with a plump throb of chewing tobacco. One hand fiddling with his crotch. But my mother barely seemed to notice. "How can you live in this pigsty?" she said. "You're twenty-nine years old, Marley. A person can't go on this way. I was hoping you'd be able to support me in my old age."

Listen, with remarks like this I was titled to my irritation. Old Vinnie van Gogh never sold a painting in his life, but at least his brother was there with support. My mother, of all people, should have worshiped the ground I walked on. "A pigsty?" I said. "You call this a pigsty? Who did I learn my housekeeping habits from if not you?"

"Not like this, though," she said.

"Oh, yes," I said. "Like this. Listen, Ma, all your life you've lived in a dream. You haven't had it easy, I'm willing to admit that. This perpetual fog that surrounds you can't be much fun to be in."

"I had a hard life," my mother said.

"That's true," I said, without feeling sorry for her, "Grandfather disowning you when you got knocked up with me. That so-called husband of yours, Marco, running around the world to play the violin, then all of a sudden dying. It wasn't much of a marriage, I guess. But for all these years you've basically ignored me. Now you show up, a stranger—I'm nearly thirty years old—and tell me I live in a pigsty!"

My mother didn't even look surprised. "Yes, yes . . ." she muttered. "It's true." She sat heavily on the couch. I noticed she wasn't making any effort to clean the place up, either. Well, at her great weight it took a lot out of her just to rest.

"You were brought up to expect one thing," I told her. "You were a rich little girl, no one told you life wasn't going to be chipped beef on toast forever. If you had married someone from your own background, Grandfather wouldn't have disowned you and things would be different for me today. But you've always done exactly as you pleased. Well, why don't you sell those stocks in Marvel Comics"— for I had discovered this secret wealth she had managed to squirrel away the last time I went home and was looking through some of her papers—"and use the money to help me out?"

"Oh, I don't know, Marley," my mother said. "At one time I

MARLEY'S MOTHER

thought you'd make these paintings, which seems to be all you're capable of, and make some money, and in this way things would work out for you. A boy like you, from an unknown background, without connections—what choice did I have but to encourage you? But let's face it, other, younger artists have come along who are by now a big success. Your shows don't even get reviewed. I wish you'd get out of this business, which is making you neither rich nor happy. It's not too late, you could still change. There are schools to learn the computer—''

''I have my own goals, Mother. If you don't want to help me, then say so. But let's not pretend you couldn't do it if you wanted to.''

My mother, however, wasn't listening. Yet even though I was mad, I still adored her. I happen to think my mother is a brilliant woman who has not let modern civilization or the twentieth century disturb her in any way. That mass of Valkyrien hair, mostly gray. Those washed-out blue eyes, always looking at a person who wasn't in the room. The thin lines just beginning to form around her mouth.

It gave me an idea for painting Athena after she reached middle age.

(From *Slaves of New York,* copyright © 1986 by Tama Janowitz. Reprinted by permission of Crown Publishers, Inc.)

SOMETHING TO LOOK FORWARD TO

Marge Piercy

〰〰〰〰〰〰〰〰〰〰〰〰〰〰〰〰〰〰〰〰〰〰〰

Menopause—word used as an insult:
a menopausal woman, mind or poem
as if not to leak regularly or on the caprice
of the moon, the collision of egg and sperm,
were the curse we first learned to call that blood.

I have twisted myself to praise that bright splash.
When my womb opens its lips on the full
or dark of the moon, that connection
aligns me as it does the sea. I quiver,
a compass needle thrilling with magnetism.

Yet for every celebration there's the time
it starts on a jet with the seatbelt sign on.
Consider the trail of red amoebae
crawling onto hostess' sheets to signal
my body's disregard of calendar, clock.

How often halfway up the side of a mountain,
during a demonstration with the tactical police
force drawn up in tanks between me and a toilet;
during an endless wind machine panel with four males
I the token woman and they with iron bladders,

Self-Portrait (with Glenn) as Phyllis Schlafly, 1981. Elizabeth Layton.

I have felt that wetness and wanted to strangle
my womb like a mouse. Sometimes it feels cosmic
and sometimes it feels like mud. Yes, I have prayed
to my blood on my knees in toilet stalls
simply to show its rainbow of deliverance.

My friend Penny at twelve, being handed a napkin
the size of an ironing board cover, cried out
Do I have to do this from now till I die?
No, said her mother, it stops in middle age.
Good, said Penny, there's something to look forward to.

Today supine, groaning with demon crab claws
gouging my belly, I tell you I will secretly dance
and pour out a cup of wine on the earth
when time stops that leak permanently;
I will burn my last tampons as votive candles.

THAT WARM FEELING HELPING LITTLE OLD LADIES

Margery Eliscu

There is nothing that gives me a warmer inner glow than helping a sweet elderly lady in her time of need.

That's what I tell my friend, Miriam, as she picks me up in her car and asks me to do her a favor.

"Of course I'll take your mother shopping for an hour while you go to your business appointment," I say. "It'll give me an inner glow of warm . . ."

"She can really take care of herself," says my friend. "It's just that when you're in your eighties and the streets are full of ice, it's easy to fall."

"I won't let her out of my sight for a minute!"

"You won't have to hover. Nothing like that. You'll find Mother is pretty independent, but I'll certainly feel a lot better knowing you have her by the arm out there in the city traffic."

I've never met her mother before and she turns out to fit a storybook image—a cross between Mrs. Santa Claus and Whistler's Mother. I feel protective just looking at her.

Miriam jumps out of the car and runs around to help her mother into the front passenger seat. I am in the seat behind her.

Miriam says: "Mother, this is Marge. She's going shopping with you until we meet for lunch."

"How do you do, Mrs. . . ." I start.

"Just call me Ethel, Marge!" she says.

When my friend pulls up at a curb in the city, I start out of the back seat to give Ethel a hand. But before I can get my door open, she's pulling on it from the outside to help me.

"Right there, Ethel," I call as I stumble out the back door and almost knock her over.

I wave good-bye to Miriam and then I turn to take her mother's arm. "I'm going to help you . . ."

Ethel is already on the other side of the street waiting for me. So I feel my way across the slippery street while Ethel holds out her hand to me. "I'm coming to help you, Ethel!" I cry as I grab for her hand and skid across the gutter.

"Now listen," Ethel says when I'm on the sidewalk, "we've only got an hour." She starts up the sidewalk, which is rutted with ice.

"Ethel," I say, reprimandingly, "I promised Miriam I would take your arm."

"Well, here," she says, tucking my hand under her sleeve, "just walk slowly and lean a little toward me and you won't stumble again."

She takes off at a clip and heads into the street. She races along the gutter. "Less snow out here!" she says to me as I still try to hold her arm.

"Ethel," I say, "slow down. You just beat a pickup truck to the corner. There's a lot of ice underfoot making everything treacherous!" I'm puffing as I talk.

"You're not in real good shape, are you, dear?" she says.

When we get to the next corner, I confront her.

"Ethel," I say, "I admire your spirit, not to mention your legs, but you're not as young as you used to be. A fall at your age could be a very bad thing!"

"Pshaw!" she says. "I think I'll look for blouses."

"I had an aunt like you, Ethel," I warn, "and it would be better, I think, if you didn't know what happened to her hip because of a fall."

"Let's go across," she says.

"And when we slow down," I say, panting, "I'm going to tell you, for your own sake . . . about . . . my . . . aunt."

"She was probably old," says Ethel.

We shop in several stores for most of the hour, and then there is trouble. I feel just awful. Afterwards, I help a weary Ethel into a chair at the restaurant and we wait for Miriam. I meet her at the door.

"Miriam," I whisper, "your mother is fine, but she gave me an awful scare."

"Oh no!" says Miriam.

"You're really going to have to slow that lady down! She thinks she can do anything."

"Well, usually she can," says Miriam. "It was just the icy streets."

"Exactly. And that was the only reason for the fall."

"Oh no!" Miriam is horrified. "Fall?"

"In the middle of the street in the traffic."

"Oh my God! Is she all right?"

"Just a little shaky, I think. Just let her sit and rest."

My friend looks over at her mother with an agonized smile of concern. Her mother waves back.

"**My grandmother started walking five miles a day when she was sixty. She's ninety-three today and we don't know where the hell she is.**"

Ellen Degeneres

"Tell me what happened," says Miriam.

"Well," I say, "she was so brave . . . really wonderful. Right after the fall, the first thing she does . . . she's got a head on her shoulders . . . is throw up both of her arms!"

"To show she was all right?"

"Oh no! To hold the traffic back."

"Mother has always had a cool head," says Miriam.

"And fast feet. Because after that, Miriam—and it's not easy at her age—your mother, single-handedly, bent down and dragged me out of the street."

(From *Russell Baker, Erma Bombeck & Me*, © 1987 by Lance Tapley, Publisher [Yankee Books].)

Illustration by Peter Farrow

MY MAN BOVANNE

Toni Cade Bambara

Blind people got a hummin jones if you notice. Which is understandable completely once you been around one and notice what no eyes will force you into to see people, and you get past the first time, which seems to come out of nowhere, and it's like you in church again with fat-chest ladies and old gents gruntin a hum low in the throat to whatever the preacher be saying. Shakey Bee bottom lip all swole up with Sweet Peach and me explainin how come the sweet-potato bread was a dollar-quarter this time stead of dollar regular and he say uh hunh he understand, then he break into this *thizzin* kind of hum which is quiet, but fiercesome just the same, if you ain't ready for it. Which I wasn't. But I got used to it and the onliest time I had to say somethin bout it was when he was playin checkers on the stoop one time and he commenst to hummin quite churchy seem to me. So I says, "Look here Shakey Bee, I can't beat you and Jesus too." He stop.

So that's how come I asked My Man Bovanne to dance. He ain't my man mind you, just a nice ole gent from the block that we all know cause he fixes things and the kids like him. Or used to fore Black Power got hold their minds and mess em around till they can't be civil to ole folks. So we at this benefit for my niece's cousin who's runnin for somethin with this Black party somethin or other behind her. And I press up close to dance with Bovanne who blind and I'm hummin and he hummin, chest to chest like talkin. Not jammin my breasts into the man. Wasn't bout tits. Was bout vibrations. And he dug it and asked me what color dress I had on and how my hair was fixed and how I was doin without a man, not nosy but nice-like, and who was at this affair and was the canapés dainty-stingy or healthy enough to get hold of proper. Comfy and cheery is what I'm tryin to get across. Touch talkin like the heel of the hand on the tambourine or on a drum.

But right away Joe Lee come up on us and frown for dancin so close to the man. My own son who knows what kind of warm I am about; and don't grown men call me long distance and in the middle of the night for a little Mama comfort? But he frown. Which ain't right since Bovanne can't see and defend himself. Just a nice old man who fixes toasters and busted irons and bicycles and things and changes the lock on my door when my men friends get messy. Nice man. Which is not why they invited him. Grass roots you see. Me and Sister Taylor and the woman who does heads at Mamies and the man from the barber shop, we all there on account of we grass roots. And I ain't never been souther than Brooklyn Battery and no more country than the window box on my fire escape. And just yesterday my kids tellin me to take them countrified rags off my head and be cool. And now can't get Black enough to suit em. So everybody passin sayin My Man Bovanne. Big deal, keep steppin and don't even stop a minute to get the man a drink or one of them cute sandwiches or tell him what's goin on. And him standin there with a smile ready case someone do speak he want to be ready. So that's how come I pull him on the dance floor and we dance squeezin past the tables and chairs and all them coats and people standin round up in each other face talkin bout this and that but got no use for this blind man who mostly fixed skates and skooters for all these folks when they was just kids. So I'm pressed up close and we touch talkin with the hum. And here come my daughter cuttin

"No matter what your fight, don't be ladylike. God Almighty made woman and the Rockefeller gang of thieves made the ladies!"

Mother Jones

her eye at me like she do when she tell me about my "apolitical" self like I got hoof and mouf disease and there ain't no hope at all. And I don't pay her no mind and just look up in Bovanne shadow face and tell him his stomach like a drum and he laugh. Laugh real loud. And here come my youngest, Task, with a tap on my elbow like he the third grade monitor and I'm cuttin up on the line to assembly.

"I was just talkin on the drums," I explained when they hauled me into the kitchen. I figured drums was my best defense. They can get ready for drums what with all this heritage business. And Bovanne stomach just like that drum Task give me when he come back from Africa. You just touch it and it hum thizzm, thizzm. So I stuck to the drum story. "Just drummin that's all."

"Mama, what are you talkin about?"

"She had too much to drink," say Elo to Task cause she don't hardly say nuthin to me direct no more since that ugly argument about my wigs.

"Look here Mama," say Task, the gentle one. "We just tryin to pull your coat. You were makin a spectacle of yourself out there dancing like that."

"Dancin like what?"

Task run a hand over his left ear like his father for the world and his father before that.

"Like a bitch in heat," say Elo.

"Well uhh, I was goin to say like one of them sex-starved ladies gettin on in years and not too discriminating. Know what I mean?"

I don't answer cause I'll cry. Terrible thing when your own children talk to you like that. Pullin me out the party and hustlin me into some stranger's kitchen in the back of a bar just like the damn police. And ain't like I'm old old. I can still wear me some sleeveless dresses without the meat hangin off my arm. And I keep up with some thangs through my kids. Who ain't kids no more. To hear them tell it. So I don't say nuthin.

"Dancin with that tom," say Elo to Joe Lee, who leanin on the folks' freezer. "His feet can smell a cracker a mile away and go into their shuffle number post haste. And them eyes. He could be a little considerate and put on some shades. Who wants to look into them blown-out fuses that—"

"Is this what they call the generation gap?" I say.

"Generation gap," spits Elo, like I suggested castor oil and fricassee possum in the milk-shakes or somethin. "That's a white concept for a white phenomenon. There's no generation gap among Black people. We are a col—"

"Yeh, well never mind," says Joe Lee. "The point is Mama . . . well, it's pride. You embarrass yourself and us too dancin like that."

"I wasn't shame." Then nobody say nuthin. Them standin there in they pretty clothes with drinks in they hands and gangin up on me, and me in the third-degree chair and nary a olive to my name. Felt just like the police got hold to me.

"First of all," Task say, holdin up his hand and tickin off the offenses, "the dress. Now that dress is too short, Mama, and too low-cut for a woman your age. And Tamu's going to make a speech tonight to kick off the campaign and will be introducin you and expecting you to organize the council of elders—"

"Me? Didn nobody ask me nuthin. You mean Nisi? She change

her name?"

"Well, Norton was supposed to tell you about it. Nisi wants to introduce you and then encourage the older folks to form a Council of the Elders to act as an advisory—"

"And you going to be standing there with your boobs out and that wig on your head and that hem up to your ass. And people'll say, 'Ain't that the horny bitch that was grindin with the blind dude?'"

"Elo, be cool a minute," say Task, gettin to the next finger. "And then there's the drinkin. Mama, you know you can't drink cause next thing you know you be laughin loud and carryin on," and he grab another finger for the loudness. "And then there's the dancin. You been tattooed on the man for four records straight and slow draggin even on the fast number. How you think that look for a woman your age?"

"What's my age?"

"What?"

"I'm axin you all a simple question. You keep talkin bout what's proper for a woman my age. How old am I anyhow?" And Joe Lee slams his eyes shut and squinches up his face to figure. And Task run a hand over his ear and stare into his glass like the ice cubes goin calculate for him. And Elo just starin at the top of my head like she goin rip the wig off any minute now.

"Is your hair braided up under that thing? If so, why don't you take it off? You always did so neat a cornroll."

"Uh huh," cause I'm thinkin how she couldn't undo her hair fast enough talking bout cornroll so countrified. None of which was the subject. "How old, I say?"

"Sixtee-one or—"

"You a damn lie Joe Lee Peoples."

"And that's another thing," say Task on the fingers.

"You know what you all can kiss," I say, gettin up and brushin the wrinkles out my lap.

You Gotta Have Art. 1981

(Reprinted from *Through the Looking Glass: Drawings by Elizabeth Layton.* © 1984 by Mid-America Arts Alliance.)

"Oh, Mama," Elo say, puttin a hand on my shoulder like she hasn't done since she left home and the hand landin light and not sure it supposed to be there. Which hurt me to my heart. Cause this was the child in our happiness fore Mr. Peoples die. And I carried that child strapped to my chest till she was nearly two. We was close is what I'm tryin to tell you. Cause it was more me in the child than the others. And even after Task it was the girlchild I covered in the night and wept over for no reason at all less it was she was a chub-chub like me and not very pretty, but a warm child. And how did things get to this, that she can't put a sure hand on me and say Mama we love you and care about you and you entitled to enjoy yourself cause you a good woman?

"And then there's Reverend Trent," say Task, glancin from left to right like they hatchin a plot and just now lettin me in on it. "You were suppose to be talking with him tonight, Mama, about giving us his basement for campaign headquarters and—"

"Didn nobody tell me nuthin. If grass roots mean you kept in the dark I can't use it. I really can't. And Reven Trent a fool anyway the way he tore into the widow man up there on Edgecomb cause he wouldn't take in three of them foster children and the woman not even comfy in the ground yet and the man's mind messed up and—"

"Look here," say Task. "What we need is a family conference so we can get all this stuff cleared up and laid out on the table. In the meantime I think we better get back into the other room and tend to business. And in the meantime, Mama, see if you can't get to Reverend Trent and—"

"You want me to belly rub with the Reven, that it?"

"Oh damn," Elo say and go through the swingin door.

"We'll talk about all this at dinner. How's tomorrow night, Joe Lee?" While Joe Lee being self-important I'm wonderin who's doin the cookin and how come no body ax me if I'm free and do I get a corsage and things like that. Then Joe nod that it's O.K. and he go through the swingin door and just a little hubbub come through from the other room. Then Task smile his smile, lookin just like his daddy and he leave. And it just me in this stranger's kitchen, which was a mess I wouldn't never let my kitchen look like. Poison you just to look at the pots. Then the door swing the other way and it's My Man Bovanne standin there sayin Miss Hazel but lookin at the deep fry and then at the steam table, and most surprised when I come up on him from the other direction and take him on out of there. Pass the folks pushin up towards the stage where Nisi and some other people settin and ready to talk, and folks gettin to the last of the sandwiches and the booze fore they settle down in one spot and listen serious. And I'm thinkin bout tellin Bovanne what a lovely long dress Nisi got on and the earrings and her hair piled up in a cone and the people bout to hear how we all gettin screwed and gotta form our own party and everybody there listenin and lookin. But instead I just haul the man on out of there, and Joe Lee and his wife look at me like I'm terrible, but they ain't said boo to the man yet. Cause he blind and old and don't nobody there need him since they growin up and don't need they skates fixed no more.

"Where we goin, Miss Hazel?" Him knowin all the time.

"First we gonna buy you some dark sunglasses. Then you comin with me to the supermarket so I can pick up tomorrow's dinner, which is goin to be a grand thing proper and you invited. Then we goin to my house.''

"That be fine. I surely would like to rest my feet." Bein cute, but you got to let men play out they little show, blind or not. So he chat on bout how tired he is and how he appreciate me takin him in hand this way. And I'm thinkin I'll have him change the lock on my door first thing. Then I'll give the man a nice warm bath with jasmine leaves in the water and a little Epsom salt on the sponge to do his back. And then a good rubdown with rose water and olive oil. Then a cup of lemon tea with a taste in it. And a little talcum, some of that fancy stuff Nisi mother sent over last Christmas. And then a massage, a good face massage round the forehead which is the worryin part. Cause you gots to take care of the older folks. And let them know they still needed to run the mimeo machine and keep the spark plugs clean and fix the mailboxes for folks who might help us get the breakfast program goin, and the school for the little kids and the campaign and all. Cause old folks is the nation. That what Nisi was sayin and I mean to do my part.

"I imagine you are a very pretty woman, Miss Hazel."

"I surely am," I say just like the hussy my daughter always say I was.

TRUDY ON GOING CRAZY

Jane Wagner

~~~~~~

. . . goin' crazy was the *best* thing ever happened to me.
I don't say it's for everybody;
some people couldn't cope.

But for me it came at a time when nothing else seemed to be
working. I got the kind of madness Socrates talked about,
"A divine release of the soul from the yoke of
custom and convention." I refuse to be intimidated by
reality anymore.
After all, what is reality anyway? Nothin' but a
collective hunch. My space chums think reality was once a
primitive method of
crowd control that got out of hand.
In my view, it's absurdity dressed up
in a three-piece business suit.

I made some studies, and
reality is the leading cause of stress amongst those in
touch with it. I can take it in small doses, but as a lifestyle
I found it too confining.
It was just too needful;
it expected me to be there for it *all* the time, and with all

I have to do—
I had to let something go.

Now, since I put reality on a back burner, my days are
jam-packed and fun-filled.

SOCIAL SECURITY

Barbara Bolz

She knows a cashier who
blushes and lets her use
food stamps to buy tulip
bulbs and rose bushes.

We smile each morning as I
pass her—her hand always
married to some stick
or hoe, or rake.

One morning I shout,
"I'm not skinny like
you so I've gotta run
two miles each day."

She begs me closer, whispers
to my flesh, "All you need,
honey, is to be on welfare
and love roses."

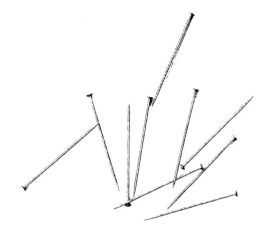

" I'm tired of all this business about beauty being only skin deep. That's deep enough. What do you want—an adorable pancreas?"

Jean Kerr

YOUTH AND BEAUTY, AGE AND WISDOM

Mary Kay Blakely

The man in my TV set was warning me about the dreadful effects "looking my age" could have on my happiness. There is certainly plenty of evidence which supports the notion that, while age may have a positive effect on wine and cheese, it will cause a woman to become invisible. She will disappear from the culture. She won't be offered starring roles in movies or be needed to sell any cars/tools/luggage/etc.

She won't be featured on runways, or billboards, or posters, and what possible reason could an older woman have for showing up on a beach? Youth and beauty, the voice in my TV cautioned me, are about all that men can really appreciate in women. That's why it is important not to let yourself go, he said, "because you don't want to look like your mother."

I could not see the face of the man speaking—his voice came from behind scenes of beautiful young women he admired, all smiling demurely with eyes at half mast. I imagined he was fat. Perhaps bald. He was not a man, in my imagination, who would be at all appealing to the women he admired. But these revengeful fantasies quickly subsided, because I also thought the man was wrong.

What he didn't know, apparently, was that many women, myself included, are actually looking forward to life on the other side of youth and beauty. Reports filtering back from friends who have already begun looking like their mothers are very favorable. Reports from the mothers themselves are enthusiastic. These women are discovering that age and wisdom can be very appealing alternatives. A woman interested in achieving wisdom, in fact, may find that youth and beauty, and the attention of men can be very mixed blessings. Its hard to think during the age of youth and beauty.

I first discovered how incompatible thinking was with youth and beauty when I was in Sister Theresa's sixth grade math class. I was engrossed in the problem of getting Driver A to Minneapolis before Driver B. Before I could ever get Driver A to Duluth, however, I felt a distraction from the race; I became aware of an intrusive presence. My face felt warm, and, without even looking up, I knew it was Danny Pascelli again. Danny Pascelli was the first boy in the class to grow the faint hint of a mustache, which he thought entitled him to the privileges of manhood. That is, while I never tried to look particularly alluring in my saddle shoes and uniform skirt, Danny Pascelli considered it his duty to give me daily reports on my developing puberty. I felt my concentration slip away, the answer escape me, under the pressure of an oncoming comment.

"You know," Danny said. looking up from my anklets, "you would be a really pretty girl if you would only shave your legs."

I had not been thinking about my legs, but for the rest of the afternoon I thought almost exclusively about them. The experience taught me one indisputable fact: A girl's progress on a difficult math problem could be interrupted at any moment by the hair on her legs.

Youth and beauty, I learned, cannot have a mind of its own—it takes its direction from the voices behind the scenes. It must be thoughtless, because thought, as it moves across a face, changes it. If the thought is complex, it will furrow her brow, leaving the lines of reflection there. If the thought is painful, it will leave a shadow around the eyes, invoking a mood of seriousness. If it's a stimulating or exciting thought, it will alert the eyelids, and shatter the illusion of vulnerability and passivity.

But youth and beauty are not all that will waylay a woman trying to solve her own puzzles. Youth and beauty lead, invariably, to housework, not math. The role of "wife and mother," she will soon perceive, is unlike "husband and father" in that it is assumed to be incompatible with other titles, like surgeon, or politician, or attorney. While the position of "wife and mother" will not require all of her attention all the time, it does require half of her attention all the

" Not that I am complaining, but I'll be relieved when you and your kids find a place of your own."

time. She may have only a few minutes to let herself go into her own thoughts between the pressing questions, "Who took my library book?" and "Where are my socks?" She may still wear an unconscious smile and her eyes half opened, not because she's trying to imitate youth and beauty, but because she hasn't had eight hours of sleep since those days.

You can begin to imagine why the threats of age and the dire results of "letting yourself go" might not be so alarming for a woman who still has a math problem to solve. During the first twenty years, she learned about life from the perspective of men, and for the next twenty, through the eyes and the needs of her children. It is only in her forties that a woman might begin to see things for herself. As the visions of men and children merge with her own, there is the dawning of wisdom in the face of a woman. The lines of thought leave a sense of power and confidence that's not easily distracted. That's why the man in my TV set is not crazy about having women look like their mothers. It isn't easy to fool a mother.

If the man in my TV could come out and face a woman the age of his mother, he would encounter a face that knows some things. She might know, for example, that at age three, he had an accident on the way to the bathroom or that, at age eight, he only got to the end of the block when he ran away from home or, age fifteen, he feared no woman would marry a man whose voice hadn't changed or, age twenty-one, he had no idea what he wanted to be when he grew up. There's no limit to the things a woman who looks like your mother might know, and she is not likely to regard the young man with perfect seriousness.

By the time a woman has passed through youth and beauty and wife and mother, there is, perhaps for the first time in her life, the possibility of a peer relationship with men. The men who populate her life, if they are honest men, no longer entertain the notion that they are her superiors in intellect, in strength, in character. They have been startled, too many times, by the examples of her "intuition"—the depth of perception, the uncanny insight, the complex connections that come with her triple vision of men and children and herself.

Nor are women who have seen much of life likely to believe anymore in men's infallibility. Men and women, wise with years and experience, have learned the truth about each other. The illusions are gone. As one woman I know has put it, "By the time you are my age, you've seen what men look like in their boxer shorts. It's hard to intimidate a woman once she knows what you look like in boxer shorts."

The prospect of looking like my mother doesn't frighten me. I see in her face, and in the faces of other women I admire, a remarkable beauty. Their expressions reflect a genuine enthusiam, an enviable self-confidence, an expanding wisdom that only years and experience can leave there. The face of an older woman is truthful—it smiles when it is amused, not because it aims to please. It's both humbled by the compromise and struggle of life and proud of its history. It brings the lines of intelligence together with the lines of compassion, suggesting multiple layers of understanding.

There's a photograph I look to frequently, to learn what age might do for a woman, a portrait of a writer in her fifties. She is sitting at her desk, her chin on her hands, a few wisps of hair neglectfully falling from the bun at the back of her neck. She is lost in thought, her eyes staring intently on some vision outside the range of the camera. She seems to be unconscious of the requirements of her gender—she is not smiling or looking demure. Her posture is confident, there is a certainty about her—it's impossible to imagine anyone's barging in to ask that she please do something with her hair. It's unthinkable that anyone would want to interrupt the beauty that thought is weaving on the woman's face.

(From *Vogue*, November 1981. Reprinted by permission of Mary Kay Blakely.)

WHAT'S THIS "EMPTY NEST" BUSINESS?

Margery Eliscu

Whatever happened to the empty-nest syndrome? You know, when the kids leave home? Does it exist anymore? Seven grandchildren later, I'm still wondering when it's safe to turn the bedrooms into dens.

I thought I had dumped the nest out back in 1970 when our youngest daughter, Kathy, went off to college. True, college was only forty minutes away, but she was going to be living in the dormitory. "Don't think," she warned me as she packed all of her belongings and many of mine, "that I'll be home a lot. Especially don't expect me weekends. I'm planning on being totally on my own."

"An occasional call . . . ?"

"I'll see you Thanksgiving," she said.

So on Monday I drove her the forty minutes away and deposited her with her lamps and posters and independence in her new home with two other girls, Mary and Chris. Then I gave her a brave kiss good-bye and prepared for the long weeks until Thanksgiving.

When I got home, I had two minutes to stare into her lonesome room before the phone rang.

"Hi, Mom, it's Kathy!" she said. "I just wanted to thank you for your help and let you know I'm managing on my own."

"Terrific!" I said. "I miss you al . . ."

"And to tell you there's a wine and cheese party in an hour . . ."

"Oh?"

"And the mothers who are still around are invited."

"Oh, for goodness sakes!"

"Are you around?"

"I thought . . ."

"Wine and cheese," she said. "I could be independent tomorrow."

I got back into the car.

On Tuesday I prepared anew for the empty nest. I started by promising myself I would not call to see how she liked school. "I will not call her," I said to myself as I picked up my ringing phone.

"Hello, Mom," said a cheerful Kathy. "Are you driving anywhere near the school today?"

> " Male theologians, philosophers, and scientists have viewed women's cycles of menstruation, pregnancy, childbirth, lactation, and menopause as manifestations of our carnal nature, while conveniently denying their own bodily processes (such as birth, aging, and death, not to mention the uncontrollability of the penis), which just as definitely mark them as carnal. "
>
> **Carol P. Christ**

"Well, I hadn't . . ."

"Because I completely forgot my trash basket, my laundry bag, and my hangers. But I don't want you to make a special trip unless you're coming this way . . . just because I need them . . . badly."

On Wednesday Kathy's call was not so cheery. "Mom," she said, "remember the medical form you thought you should put in your purse Monday for safekeeping? The one the school requires the first day of gym?"

On Thursday she called to check if there was any mail. "Would you rather forward it or come over and see how I finally got the room decorated?"

On Friday she didn't call. On Friday I spent most of the day adjusting to my empty nest. Friday was a wonderful day.

It was so wonderful that I called my husband's office late in the afternoon and said: "The nest is finally empty. How do you feel about slipping away someplace for the weekend . . . just the two of us?"

"Sounds good to me," said my husband's boss.

"Oh, sorry!" I said. "I thought you were Larry."

"Does that mean we're not going?" said his boss. And then, "He's on another line, but I'll tell him what you want and see that he calls back with an affirmative answer right away."

When the phone rang a few minutes later, I picked it up quickly. "Well," I said, "do we have exciting weekend plans or don't we?"

"We sure do," said Kathy. "I'm bringing Mary and Chris home."

(From *Russell Baker, Erma Bombeck & Me,* ©1987 by Lance Tapley, Publisher [Yankee Books].)

DOES IT SAY WHERE WE CAN JOIN A SUPERMARKET HIT AND RUN SHOPLIFTING COLLECTIVE!

(Reprinted by permission of bulbul—Gen Guracar.)

THERE'S NO SIN ON THIS COUCH

When Alice Neel (age 76) was artist-in-residence during a summer conference at the University of Notre Dame, she was housed on campus in the rector's rooms. The 35-year-old rector met Alice when he returned to his suite for a book.

"I hope you don't mind if I violate your bed," Alice said playfully. The rector's eyes grew large. Alice smiled. He quickly excused himself and went for the door.

"Wait a minute!" Alice said. She tapped the space on the sofa beside her. "Come sit down here, Sonny," she beckoned. "There's no sin on this couch."

The rector squirmed and mumbled inaudibly. He was not up to Alice's patter, and she, hugely amused, went on: "O, this couch is so nice: it's like lying in bed. Of course, it really isn't the same—because if I were lying in bed, I wouldn't be talking to you." And then she pointedly added with all her immense seductive charm, "Or would I now?"

The rector rushed out.

If Clothes MAKE the Man Do Clothes UN-make the Woman?

JOSEPHINE **CRACKS** UNDER THE PRESSURE OF DECIDING WHAT TO WEAR TO MEET MIRIAM'S PARENTS.

(Drawing reprinted from *WomaNews*, 1984, by permission of Alison Bechdel.)

SOME OBSERVATIONS ON THE LANGUAGE OF CLOTHES

Alison Lurie

You can lie in the language of dress just as you can in English, French or Latin, and this sort of deception has the advantage that one cannot usually be accused of doing it deliberately.

Women entered the second decade of the twentieth century shaped like hourglasses, and came out of it shaped like rolls of carpet.

The most striking thing about British dress, both urban and rural, is its tendency to follow the principle of camouflage. City clothes are most often made in colors that echo the hues of stone, cement, soot, cloudy skies and wet pavements. . . .

The American tourist abroad . . . wears clothes suitable for a trip to a disaster area, or for a visit to a museum or zoo: comfortable, casual, brightly colored, relatively cheap: not calculated to arouse envy or pick up dirt.

On Fashionable Labels: . . . it soon became apparent that even obviously inferior merchandise, if clearly labeled and known to be extravagantly priced, would be enthusiastically purchased.

. . . thinking seriously about what we wear is like thinking seriously about what we say: it can only be done occasionally or we should find ourselves tongue-tied, unable to get dressed at all.

More generally, the idea that even when we say nothing our clothes are talking noisily to everyone who sees us, telling them who we are, where we come from, what we like to do in bed and a dozen other intimate things, may be unsettling. To wear what "everyone else" is wearing is no solution. . . . We can lie in the language of dress, or try to tell the truth; but unless we are naked and bald it is impossible to be silent.

(From *The Language of Clothes*, Random, House, copyright © 1981 by Alison Lurie—reprinted by permission of Melanie Jackson Agency.)

PAT OLESZKO

making a spectacle of herself
as Tom Saw-yer
in "The Soiree of O"

Photo by Neil Selkirk

The Soiree of O advances the heART of overt dressing thru sighs,
tries, size and lies. "It is after all, not what you wear but what you
'puts on' that's impo'tent!" This concept, as presented thru myriad
forums of costume, performance, oration and installation tries un-
flailingly (like Dumb Quixote, another comic night) to punch holes
in prime-evil concepts of mythology, modernity and social glaces.

DESIGNER GUNS?

Sandra Willow

What if we looked at guns as an article of *clothing* rather than an instrument of loathing? Suppose guns cease to be a sign of male sexual impotence (that's the reason they just HAVE to keep them legal: if men can't shoot sperm, they settle for bullets). Suppose we make them aesthetically alluring, drape them in a dazzle of delightful color. . . .

Showing once again that the artist can do the outrageous and the unimaginable, Molly (a sculptor) has turned artillery into clothing. Is it her intention to create a new mythos of the stylish crook and to make felony as fashion-conscious as it is fashionable? Hardly. The press release for Molly's striking show in SoHo (Amos Eno Gallery) reads:

> A crime involving a hand gun is committed every two minutes with a death occurring more than once every hour.
>> "Shoot to laugh" not "Shoot to kill."

Molly's guns are loaded with sequins, feathers, beads and baubles, lace and sparkles and spangles. She has given us the definitive answer to crimes of passion. When you're ready to kill, you point your mauve-feather weapon, tastefully trimmed with delicate pearls, at the object of your fury, and you say, "Bang! bang!"

DIRECTION FOR USE
1. Purchase: 1 designer gun per child; 1-2 designer guns per adult.
2. Usage: The designer gun can be used anywhere and everywhere, when angered at those you love or hate. Please choose colors and materials to enhance your *specific* environment.
3. Method: when angry just reach for the designer gun, put finger on trigger and say, "Bang, bang." Join those who "Shoot to Laugh."
4. Warning: This product has been determined to be harmless to your health and those you shoot.

YOUR WEDDING GOWN

Dave Barry

Listen up, brides. You get only one shot in your life at a real wedding gown, and you better not blow it. Because a wedding gown is more than just a dress. It's a dress that costs a whole ton of money. It's a dress that you'll cherish for several decades in a box in a remote closet, perhaps to be taken out one day by your daughter when she's looking for (sniff) a wedding gown of her own. She'll wisely reject yours, of course, because by that time it will have served as the home environment for 60,000 generations of insects. The last thing she wants, when she's up at the altar on her own Very Special Day, is for a millipede to come strolling out of her bodice.

Nevertheless you must have a wonderful gown. This is where you need the expert help of a qualified bridal couturier, who can answer your technical questions:

YOU: What kinds of gowns do you have for under $2,000?
COUTURIER: Well, we have this one right here.
YOU: This is a group of used Handi-Wipes sewn together.
COUTURIER: Yes. By preschool children.

With this kind of guidance, you'll be able to select a truly memorable gown, one that will cause your parents to remark in admiration: *"How much?!* That's more than we spent on our first *house!"* If they don't make this remark, your gown is not memorable enough, and you should take it right back to the couturier to have some more pearls glued on.

(From *Dave Barry's Guide to Marriage and/or Sex,* © 1987, Rodale Press.)

RHODA MOGUL'S LETTER TO HER DAUGHTER

July 25, 1975

Dearest Daughter,

I'm enclosing a check for you for the dress for your brother Mark's wedding [Mark—three years younger and getting married first]. Somehow I'm wondering how appropriate black is. Maybe you could keep looking in Loehmann's for something else and keep the black dress anyway or return it. We are all wearing very light-colored clothes.
Love,
Mom

[Edited by Susan Mogul]

FIVE MONTHS BEFORE THE WEDDING

Dave Barry

Now is the time to select your bridesmaids. This is a very large honor, which you bestow only upon people who meet the following criteria:

1. They should be female.

2. They should be willing to wear bridesmaid's dresses.

This second criterion is the most important, because the whole point of the bridesmaid's dress is to render the person wearing it so profoundly unattractive that she cannot possibly outshine you, the bride. In fact, one of the really fun things a bride gets to do is go to the bridal salon with her mother, and the two of them get drunk and howl with laughter as they consider various comical outfits that they might encase the bridesmaids in. Some of them go so far as to select actual clown suits, but most prefer the traditional look, which is:

> **"I keep my campaign promises, but I never promised to wear stockings."**
>
> **Ella Grasso**

- Long frilly dresses in bright pastel colors reminiscent of Bazooka bubble gum or some experimental and ultimately unsuccessful ice cream flavor with a name like ''Pumpkin Surprise.''
- ''Puffed'' sleeves that make any woman who is larger than Audrey Hepburn look like a Green Bay Packer.
- Large ''fun'' floppy hats that obscure the bridemaid's face so thoroughly that you could use men if you really had to.

(From *Dave Barry's Guide to Marriage and/or Sex,* © 1987, Rodale Press.)

RAY IN HIGH HEELS

Tama Janowitz

A few nights later Ray called to ask if he could drop by. I was surprised to hear from him; though I hadn't felt any elementary particles hopping between us, I decided to go to bed with him. The prospect seemed somewhat boring, but I thought I might as well get it over with. Perhaps I'd be fonder of him if something physical happened between us.

When Ray showed up, he had a carload of furniture from his apartment to give me: two chests of teak, with many tiny drawers and compartments, three chairs, an expensive floor lamp, very modern. ''When will you need this back?'' I said. I assumed he was just lending it to me, or storing it with me for the moment.

''No, it's for you,'' Ray said.

''For keeps?'' I said.

''Yeah, yeah,'' Ray said. ''My father has a whole warehouse of furniture.'' He looked pleased.

After carrying the furniture upstairs we went out to an espresso place a block away. Cappuccino coffee was two dollars, so I had never gone there. I had one of the coffees with whipped cream, and a big piece of carrot cake. I ate the cake eagerly, cramming it into my mouth as if it were a drug, somehow feeling this would give me strength for whatever was to happen with Ray. ''I like to watch you eat,'' Ray said, looking at me dreamy-eyed. I wiped off my chin with a napkin; the cake had abruptly become quite tasteless.

Ray stopped at his car to get a bottle of wine out of the trunk. He put his arm around my shoulder as we walked back to my apartment. It was after midnight. I sat on one of the twin beds; it had no frame, just a mattress and box spring on the floor. Ray sat on a chair, uncorking the wine. I figured either he'd make a move and I'd go to bed with him, or he should go home. I was tired. Once again, I felt we had nothing to say to each other, but Ray told me the plot of a movie he had just seen. This is a symptom. I've noticed how any time a man tells me the plot of a movie, it is a kind of declaration of love.

After about fifteen minutes, just as I was ready to suggest he leave, Ray went over to the closet. He took off his shoes and socks and put on my favorite pair of high heels, red leather pumps. ''How do I look?'' he said.

A wave of rage rose within me. He walked all around the apartment in my shoes. I didn't dare say, ''Listen, Ray, you're going to stretch out my favorite shoes,'' because he had just given me all

''On Astral Travel: When you're out of your body, who's picking out your clothes?''

Linda Moakes

that furniture, and I didn't want to embarrass him. My mother always said, "Lend people your clothes, but don't wear other people's shoes or lend yours, because your shoes conform to your feet and other people's feet are different shapes and will stretch them out." Ray didn't have very large feet, but I just didn't see how he could fit them into my shoes, which were definitely small. I didn't have the money to replace them, anyway.

Then Ray tried on my straw hat. Maybe he was trying to be playful. But it was almost one in the morning, and he was walking around in my straw hat and shoes. I couldn't laugh. I finally said, "Well, I'm tired and I have class in the morning."

At the door Ray kissed me good night. . . .

[Time passes. Ray loses track of Cora but finally finds her and proposes marriage—although they barely know each other.]

My mother was still awake when I went to her room. "Did you have fun?" she said. "I can't believe he brought such expensive bottles of wine. Who drinks that stuff?"

"He wants to get married," I said.

"Go ahead," she said. She turned back to her book. "He has small, eloquent feet and hands," she said to the page.

"He likes to try on my shoes," I said.

"As part of sex?"

"We never slept together," I said. "His feet might be small, but I still don't like him wearing my shoes."

My mother shrugged. "If you like him, maybe you could find him a pair in his size at the thrift store."

THE LEAST-SOUGHT-AFTER UNDERWEAR IN THE WORLD

Alice Kahn

"Judith Sloan as Muriel: If gentlemen prefer Hanes, why don't they wear them?"

The public's right-to-know sank to a new low with the success of the television show *Lifestyles of the Rich and Famous.* I don't know how you spend your Sunday afternoons, but I have been spending mine watching "celebrity interviewer" Robin Leach tell me about "conspicuous consumption, playboys and polo, dowagers and diamonds, pagan proportions" and "the agony and the ecstasy of megabuck realities."

In prose pickled in hyperbole (and alluringly alive with alliteration), Leach travels the world to bring back intimate portraits of the rich, famous and frequently fatuous. The show is a cliche collector's wet dream: We're taken to Hollywood parties "where the stars really come out at night,'' to a famous plastic surgery clinic ''just a samba beat away from Rio'' and to a charity ball where a wealthy philanthropist asks his wife, ''What disease are we celebrating tonight, dear?''

Each week we thrill to the Days and Deeds of the Decadently Disgusting—and anticipation is half the fun. In one of the most heavily promoted segments of the show, we're told that Terry Moore will play, for the first time anywhere, ''the secret tape recordings of (her) midnight love conversations'' with her husband, Howard Hughes. How much, we wonder, will we learn about the legendary reclusive billionaire in this ''extraordinary revelation and confession?''

Finally, Moore plays the love tapes:

HOWARD HUGHES: Did you decide which ring you wanted?
TERRY MOORE: I like the little ring. It's just darling.
HOWARD HUGHES: It is cute. I knew you'd like the little one.

Not quite up there with the ''modified limited hang-out'' of the Watergate tapes, but never fear. Things get spicier when Moore reveals more about Hughes' notorious bra fetish. We already know about the famous cantilever job he engineered for sprucy, goosey Jane Russell. But now Moore confesses—*for the first time anywhere*—that when she and Hughes went horseback riding, the great man insisted she wear two bras ''because he was afraid I would break down.''

Underwear of the Rich and Famous is a recurrent theme on *Lifestyles.* Another show takes us to the London salon that sells ''the most sought-after underwear in the world''—the very stuff that Bianca Jagger, Britt Ekland and Princess Di park it in. In yet another segment we learn that when Tom Jones performs in Las Vegas, ''women throw their room keys at him in lace panties.''

. . . I think the thing that keeps me glued to my set is the ongoing fantasy that some day, some time when I least expect it, Robin Leach will be knocking at my door saying. ''May I and the rest of Televisionland come in and just take a look around?''

''Tonight,'' says Leach, ''on Lifestyles we are visiting the fabulous San Francisco Bay Area (where everyone comes out each night) to see the home of one of the most mediocre writers in America, Alice Kahn. It is here in this house that could certainly use a paint job, situated on a quiet street where real estate values have not kept pace with the market, that Kahn sits knocking out articles on her primitive Olympia typewriter. When she's not hoping to sell out to a high-paying girlie magazine, Kahn is hard at work on a new book about the wine industry, *The Name of the Rosé.*

''Tell us, Alice,'' he asks, poking his microphone into my office as I quickly brush the cherry pits into my top drawer, ''how do you start your day?''

''Well, Pigeon . . .'' I begin.

''Er, Robin,'' he interrupts.

''Yes, well, Robin, I know it's kind of wild and crazy but the first thing I like to get into is some clothes.''

''Fantastic!'' he bellows in his Cockney-but-kissing-his-way-up accent. ''Let's see the underwear collection.''

''Collection? You mean here—now?'' I ask with a shyness bred of obscurity.

''Don't worry,'' he reassures me, ''I don't want you to model

Suzanne McNamara, as Myth Tar Heel, models a ball gown made by artist/activist Nikki Craft and Cookie Teer from ripped up copies of *Penthouse*. As part of the action at a shopping mall in Durham, North Carolina, on September 26, 1985, McNamara also repeatedly struck a porñata with Bob Guccione's face on it as she exclaimed, "He loves it! He loves it!"

anything. Just let us look in your drawers. Come on, now, just a look-see.''

In minutes, the camera crew is squeezed into my bedroom. I'm now regretting the fact that I never got the coffee stains out of the comforter. The husband, of course, has last night's Dos Equis prominently lined up next to his side of the bed. Then, to my horror, I notice the gargantuan dust bunnies in the corner. What will this be labeled—Total Slob Lifestyle?

The director is now cueing in the zoom for a close-up of my underwear drawer. ''Tell us about it,'' Leach insists.

''Well, what you see is what you get, Robin. You're looking at 14 pairs of size 38 briefs, white, 100 percent cotton exclusive of decorations.''

''Camera Three, close up on the label,'' shouts the director as Robin asks me, ''14 pairs, huh? Is there some significance there?''

''As a matter of fact there is, Robin. The reason I have so many of them is so I only have to do my laundry every two weeks. I mean I might do it more often but this way I don't have to.''

''Take another shot of the drawer,'' says the director as Leach adds the voice-over: ''White cotton briefs—the least-sought-after underwear in the world.''

(From *Multiple Sarcasm*, Ten Speed Press, © 1985 by Alice Kahn.)

WHEN UNLACING WAS A PATRIOTIC ACT

Hazel Houlihingle

Of course I'm against war, but when we're in it, all kinds of good things happen to women. Like with no men around, all of a sudden women can do any job and up goes our pay. And in World War I, off came our corsets! I'm not kidding. Alice Roosevelt Longworth said we should sacrifice our steel-boned corsets to the war effort. So with a huge sigh of relief and a huge welling forth of female flesh, millions of women released tons of steel (28,000 tons, to be precise) to the munitions factories—and no one called us corset-burners either.

I DREAMED I WAS LIBERATED IN MY MAIDENFORM BRA

Ellen Goodman

BOSTON—It's not that I'd never seen her before.

Years ago, she'd been photographed outside of her apartment building, dressed in a fur coat and bra and panties. Since then she'd been found in similar attire in the theater and hotel lobbies. Usually, of course, you get used to this sort of thing if you live in a city long enough.

But it was a shock to see her in a hospital room. There she was, hair tied back primly, medical chart in her left hand, pen in her right hand, long white jacket over her shoulders, exposing her lacy magenta bra and panties. What was she doing dressed like that in the hospital?

Was it possible? Why, yes! Stop the presses! The Maidenform Woman Had Become a Doctor! According to the caption under this photograph, she was "making the rounds in her elegant Delectables."

At some point when I wasn't looking, everybody's favorite exhibitionist must have actually gone to medical school. I suppose that I had underestimated her intelligence—this happens so often with attractive women. I always thought she was a candidate for a cold, not a medical degree. I can only imagine the difficulties she had getting accepted, what with her portfolio and all.

But now any number of magazines are featuring her personal success story. On their pages, the Maidenform Woman is willingly displaying her new bedside manner in living color.

Poised, concerned, even prim, young Dr. Maidenform is photographed looking down compassionately at her bedridden patient. We don't know exactly what the patient thinks of all this. Fortunately for her, his leg is in traction and he can't move.

The other doctors in the ad seem quite unconcerned about her outfit. Dr. Maidenform seems to have made it in a world that is entirely nonsexist. They aren't even glancing in the direction of her nonairbrushed belly button!

Quite frankly, I must admit that the Maidenform Woman cured me of a disease. She cured me of creeping complacency.

Until I saw her, I had become virtually numb to the advertising image of that handy creature, "The New Woman." We are now out of the era of housewife-as-airhead. We've even come a long way from the era of coming a long way, baby.

We are plunging into the "successful woman as sex object" syndrome. The more real women break out of the mold, the more advertisers force them back in. We are now told that, for all the talk, the New Woman is just the Total Woman in updated gear.

Under the careful dress-for-success suit of an MBA is a woman buying Office Legs for sex appeal. Around the briefcase of a lawyer is a hand shining with high-color nail gloss. Take away the lab coat, the stethoscope, and syringe, and the doctor is just another set of "elegant Delectables."

Costume Jewelry

(© 1950, *Chicago Sun Times*, reprinted by permission.)

Because "marriage is warfare," artist Glenna Park constructed a Camouflage Wedding Dress (1984–88) made of camouflage netting and beads over taffeta. This gown, she says, "is used in a ceremony for forming a primary combat training unit" (one of her definitions of marriage).

The point in all this isn't especially subtle. As Jean Kilbourne, who has long studied media images of women, said, "It's out of the question that they would ever show a male doctor like that. She is aloof but available. Underneath she is still a sex object."

Kilbourne's favorite entry in this category is a perfume ad that shows the successful woman mixing business with, uh, pleasure. In the first frame we see the busy executive at a business lunch with three men. In the second frame, we see her under the covers with one.

Advertisers have a big investment in this new-old image. I'm not talking about the professional woman market. There are hardly enough women doctors to keep the magenta lace factory in business. But there are now an increasing number of women who see professionals as glamorous and want to identify with them.

The advertisers are betting that these women want, as the Maidenform ad puts it, "just what the doctor ordered." So the doctor is ordered to strip, literally, her professional cover. She is revealed in the flesh, to be—yes, indeed—just another woman insecure about her femininity, just another woman in search of sex appeal, just another woman who needs "silky satin tricot with antique lace scalloping."

Pretty soon, I suppose, she will need it in the Senate, in the Supreme Court, even in the Oval Office. The Maidenform Woman. You never know where she'll turn up.

" How would this hold up to repeated wearings?"

WHY WE OPPOSE POCKETS FOR WOMEN

Alice Duer Miller

1. Because pockets are not a natural right. . . .

5. Because it would make dissension between a husband and a wife as to whose pockets were to be filled.

6. Because it would destroy a man's chivalry toward woman, if he did not have to carry all her things in his pockets. . . .

8. Because pockets have been used by men to carry tobacco, pipes, whiskey flasks, chewing gum and compromising letters. We see no reason to suppose that women would use them more wisely.

(From *Are Women People? A Book of Rhymes for Suffrage Times.* New York: George H. Doran, 1915.)

"**Pocket Envy is women's unfulfilled yearning for practical clothes.**"

Cheris Kramarae and Paula Treichler

STEREOTYPES
ÜBER ALLES

Una Stannard

(From *MS.* magazine, April 1988.
Reprinted by permission of Signe Wilkinson.)

Stereotypes die hard. Remember the seventies, when women wore little or no makeup and flat shoes? Some women even dared to feel that breasts had a right to exist without bras and that legs needn't be shaved. One might have thought that the female sex had acquired sense and felt good enough about themselves to be as nature made them. Apparently not. Except in sports clothes, "feminine" is in again, which at present means blue eyelids, bright red lips, spike heels, and a big bust: breast enlargement has become the most commonly performed cosmetic operation. On the beach and at parties women flaunt their fleshly wares more nakedly than ever.

But men haven't come a long way either, baby. The male body is still in the closet. At business and on formal occasions men continue to wear their modest male uniforms—a dark suit and light shirt, the only hint of their sex the symbol of the tie and the presumptive evidence of the fly. Among birds, males display the peacock feathers, but among humans nowadays men are the drab hens and women the flashers, as good little sex objects ought to be. In dress the feminist revolution might almost not have happened.

But fashion is the hardest taskmaster to disobey. In the twenties when flat breasts were in, women dutifully put on binders. Whether the fashion doctors prescribe heavy padding for posteriors or shoulders, women obediently apply the boluses. Men are no better. Tight breeches or full trousers, wide ties or narrow ones, fashion makes slaves of most of us. From kindergarten onward we are afraid not to look like everyone else. Even when we want to dress differently, it is difficult because what else except the current fashions are in the shops? So why make a fuss? Clothes, after all, aren't even skin deep; it is the inner man and woman that counts.

But the inner woman and man still follow the fashions too; the old male-female stereotypes are alive and flourishing. Men, for example, are still believed to be unemotional and rational, women emotional and intuitive. The only difference between the present and the past is that women have turned what were meant to be downers into uppers. Yes, say women, men may be rational; but intuition is better. Yes, women are emotional, but it is wiser to be in touch with feelings.

No one seems to ask if men really are rational, if a rational sex would have spent virtually every year in recorded history settling quarrels by fighting? Both sexes (except, for example, when they are solving logical puzzles) are rarely rational; their actions almost always spring from emotion, old emotional forces originating in childhood.

Men are no more immune from emotions than women; we think women are more emotional because the culture lets them give free vent to certain feelings, "feminine" ones, that is, no anger, please, but it's okay to turn on the waterworks. We then act as if women were defective, born with leaky tear ducts. But back in the eighteenth century men could weep buckets too. In 1755 the German poet Johann Gellert, while reading about lovers who were forced to part, cried so much that his tears drenched his handkerchief, soaked the book, made a puddle on the table and finally dripped on the floor. How do we know? Because he wrote a letter boasting about it.

Men are as emotional as women, and neither sex is particularly rational; but what about so-called female intuition? The women who boast about it seem unaware that it was conceded to women as a substitute for the brains they were literally not believed to have. The ideas women did have were explained away as flashes from the outside, Jove sending a lightning bolt into their empty heads. It's not that women don't have what we now define as intuition, it's just that it's not an exclusively female trait. Men and women both have it whenever they are able to get in touch with the part of the mind that has remained free of social or intellectual conditioning.

Even if one grants that intuition, reason, and emotions are not sex-based, who would deny that men are aggressive brutes, whereas women are kind and nurturing? Back in the sixties Ashley Montagu asserted that women were the superior sex, naturally more humane than men, more considerate, unselfish, self-sacrificing, altruistic, cooperative. It was no new idea; it was his version of medieval Madonna worship, worship that is well-nigh universal today whether one is a feminist or not. The belief in women's moral superiority is so unquestioned that no one asks why it is so popular now. Dare one suggest that modern Madonna worship is a way of keeping women in their old place, flattering them into staying in the nursery, that is, coming home from work

> **"I do love to shop. I rationalize shop. I buy a dress because I need the change for chewing gum."**
>
> **Rita Rudner**

(From *Do You Hate Your Hips More than Nuclear War?* Penguin Books, © 1988 by Libby Reid.)

and having the extra job of diapering the babies?

Feminists don't go into the domestic implications of their belief in the moral superiority of women. They cannot; it is the chief article of their faith, comparable to Freud's belief in penis envy. Freud anathematized any disciple who dared question this pillar of male faith. Similarly, anyone who dares question the moral superiority of women is excommunicated from the feminist church, whose niches are now filled with female gods, declared to be the original gods of humankind.

That the first gods were female is beyond question, but one might have thought that centuries of oppression by a male god would have cured women of any form of god worship. Who needs almighty authority figures, female or male, whether up in the sky or in the home or in government offices? But one must be realistic; society is power-based, so people do become authority figures who, the feminists feel, should be women, for their moral superiority will insure that they don't behave as badly as men. Books have been written to prove that in a few early societies when women were in charge or female values prevailed, the government was humane, non-violent, based on cooperation. Perhaps so. But Elizabeth I, the Chinese Empress Tsu Hsi, and Indira Ghandi were sometimes good, sometimes bad, just like the next guy, as is Margaret Thatcher. And are the female mayors and governors in the eighties proving to be more immune than men from abusing their power? And what about mothers? That they regularly misuse the power they have over children is so taboo a subject that contemporary Madonna worshipers might well slug you for even hinting at it. Feminists too put on rosy Norman Rockwell glasses when they look at Mom.

Our mind's pantheon is still hung with stereotypes: cartoons of sweet little sugar puffs who grow up to be tartlets; boys who will be boys in baseball caps grow up to be business robots in cloned suits;

"Have you ever noticed, if you leave the laundry in the hamper long enough, it's ready to wear again?"

Elayne Boosler

THE BLOOMER GIRL'S WEDDING.

(From *Life*, 1896. Reprinted by permission of Paul Petticrew.)

blond dolls with empty faces; sweating pinheads flexing their Superman muscles; eternally smiling Moms with cute clean babies. And let's not forget the macho Caveman, who still lives on in our heads, as does his female counterpart, Mama Mia. Stereotypes all, cookie cutters that try to stamp us out.

CLOTHES WORN BY THE EDUCATED MAN

Virginia Woolf

How many, how splendid, how extremely ornate they are—the clothes worn by the educated man in his public capacity! Now you dress in violet; a jewelled crucifix swings on your breast; now your shoulders are covered with lace; now furred with ermine; now slung with many linked chains set with precious stones. Now you wear wigs on your heads; rows of graduated curls descend to your necks. . . . Ribbons of all colours—blue, purple, crimson—cross from shoulder to shoulder. After the comparative simplicity of your dress at home, the splendour of your public attire is dazzling.

Even stranger, however, than the symbolic splendour of your clothes are the ceremonies that take place when you wear them. Here you kneel; there you bow; here you advance in procession behind a man carrying a silver poker; here you mount a carved chair; here you appear to do homage to a piece of painted wood; here you abase yourselves before tables covered with richly worked tapestry. And whatever these ceremonies may mean you perform them always together, always in step, always in the uniform proper to the man and the occasion.

Apart from the ceremonies, such decorative apparel appears to us at first sight strange in the extreme. For dress, as we use it, is comparatively simple. Besides the prime function of covering the body, it has two other offices—that it creates beauty for the eye, and that it attracts the admiration of your sex. Since marriage until the year 1919—less than twenty years ago—was the only profession open to us, the enormous importance of dress to a woman can hardly be exaggerated. It was to her what clients are to you—dress was her chief, perhaps her only, method of becoming Lord Chancellor. But your dress in its immense elaboration has obviously another function. It not only covers nakedness, gratifies vanity, and creates pleasure for the eye, but it serves to advertise the social, professional, or intellectual standing of the wearer. If you will excuse the humble illustration, your dress fulfils the same function as the tickets in a grocer's shop. But, here, instead of saying, "This is margarine; this pure butter; this is the finest butter in the market," it says, "This man is a clever man—he is Master of Arts; this man is a very clever man—he is Doctor of Letters; this man is a most clever

> **"Fashions are born and they die too quickly for anyone to love them."**
>
> **Bettina Ballard**

man—he is a Member of the Order of Merit." It is this function—the advertisement function—of your dress that seems to us most singular. In the opinion of St. Paul, such advertisement, at any rate for our sex, was unbecoming and immodest; until a very few years ago we were denied the use of it. And still the tradition, or belief, lingers among us that to express worth of any kind, whether intellectual or moral, by wearing pieces of metal, or ribbon, coloured hoods or gowns, is a barbarity which deserves the ridicule which we bestow upon the rites of savages.

(From *Three Guineas*, Copyright 1938 by Harcourt Brace Jovanovich, Inc. and renewed 1966 by Leonard Woolf, reprinted by permission of the publisher.)

Photo by Gloria Kaufman

"It occurred to me when I was thirteen and wearing white gloves and Mary Janes and going to dancing school, that no one should have to dance backward all their lives."

Jill Ruckelshaus

CONCEPTION AND CONTRACEPTION

Teresa Bloomingdale

As a service to parents, planned or unplanned, I hereby offer a brief report on the true facts concerning conception and contraception.

First, you must erase from your mind the facts of life as you learned them. They are wrong; all lies. Babies are not caused by . . . well, you know, doing *that*. If doing *that* were all it took, every couple who wanted a child would have one. No, the truth is babies come into being when:

1. The wife finds a fascinating career which she loves and which promises prompt promotion and a brilliant future, providing she doesn't ask for a leave of absence.

2. The husband wins an all-expense paid European Tour-for-Two, with departure date nine months from yesterday.

3. Either husband or wife forgets to pay the premium on the one insurance policy that includes maternity benefits.

4. The wife attends a Spring Fashion Show and spends her entire year's clothing allowance on four darling new outfits, all belted.

5. Husband and wife agree that three children are quite enough, so, on the birth of the third child, they sell the baby furniture and give away the maternity clothes. This is called double indemnity, for it assures the birth of at least two more children. (Who's going to buy a whole new wardrobe and a roomful of nursery furniture for just one baby?)

Those are just a few of the infallible methods for conception. If, however, you wish to avoid having babies, I suggest the following:

1. The wife must resign her well-paying job and announce to all her friends that she and her husband are going to start their family.

2. Promise your mother a grandchild for Christmas.

3. Tell your five-year-old son that he is going to have a baby brother. (This may not prevent pregnancy, but it will guarantee you a girl.)

4. Promise the school principal that, in the event that you are not pregnant by September (though, of *course* you will be), you will serve as First-Grade field-trip supervisor.

5. Spend $5,000 turning your husband's den into a nursery or, better yet, buy a bigger house.

See how easy it is? Who needs the Pill?

(From *I Should Have Seen It Coming When the Rabbit Died*, copyright © 1979 by Teresa Bloomingdale. Used by permission of Doubleday, a division of Bantam, Doubleday, Dell Publishing Group, Inc.)

"That the most intelligent, discerning and learned men of talent and feeling, should finally put all their pride in their crotch, as awed as they are uneasy at the few inches sticking out in front of them, proves how normal it is for the world to be crazy. . . ."

Françoise Parturier

LETTER TO A VERMONT PHARMACY

Kathleen Rockwell Lawrence

Dear Sir:

I say sir because I know you must be a man. I recently visited your store with the object of purchasing contraceptive cream for use with my diaphragm. It was a Sunday. I was quite disturbed to find that you display all manner of male contraceptives, but require that women ask Big Daddy in Prescriptions for their protection. Since Big Daddy wasn't there on Sunday I had to do without. If I get pregnant, I intend to sue you for child support.

Who has more to lose by going without adequate contraception, men or women? So how come you only display things for men? The answer is that you think only men should have sex.

Here's another question. Who else has something to lose? You do, Big Daddy, 'cause I'm telling the local chapter of NOW. Better stock your shelves with more care. I feel morning sickness coming on.

Sincerely,
BIG MOMMA

(Reprinted with permission of Atheneum Publishers, an imprint of Macmillan Publishing Company, from *Maud Gone*. Copyright © 1986 by Kathleen Rockwell Lawrence.)

GENITALES

Una Stannard

I

The penis is the man in little,
It cannot lie,
It talks straight,
It is the infallible divining rod
Of the heart's state—
The trumpet of lust's charge,
The fallen flag of its retreat.
The penis is blunt,
It acts the way it feels,
Pushy when cocky,
Cowering when afraid,
Blood rushing to what it likes,
Or fainting, limp and white,
At the tiniest of slights,
Shrinking at the portal
Like a disappearing turtle,
Or shoving right in
Where it oughtn't to have been.
The penis is a natural brute,
It doesn't have to give a hoot;

"NOT BAD, PHILLIP. CLOUD EIGHT."

It's a child
Who wants its pleasure now.
  The penis can't pretend,
  Its means is its end,
  Its truth is bared,
  It is the soul's talebearer.

II

The vagina is woman belittled,
It's prone to lie,
It needn't speak its mind,
It is the slippery hiding-place
Of the heart's state—
All smiles, though most reluctant,
Tight-lipped, though hot to go.
The vagina is refined,
It likes to bide its time
And be holier than thou.
It grooves on romance,
A song and a dance,
But to get what it wants
It can do what it hates.
It's an actor
Whose rapture can be fake,
Accommodating mates
And giving thrills for a supper.
The vagina is a natural whore:
It can take all comers
Who press upon its doors
And lay itself out to please.
  The vagina can pretend,
  Be a means to an end,
  Its truth can be veiled,
  It is the soul's purdah.

III

Penises are savages
Springing from the bush;
Vaginas can be connivers
Intriguing in the dark.
But the one's damnation
Could be the other's salvation,
If penises learned politics
And vaginas played it straight.

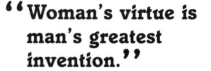

Suzanne Opton, Four Women, Vermont 1980.

TRUDY'S COMMENT ON GENITALIA

Jane Wagner

My space chums say they're learning so much about us
since they've begun to time-share my trances.
They said to me, "Trudy, the human mind is so-o-o strange."
I told 'em, "That's nothin' compared to the human genitals."

(From *The Search for Signs of Intelligent Life.* Copyright © 1986 by Jane Wagner Inc. Reprinted by permission of Harper & Row.)

SOME DEFINITIONS

Nancy Linn-Desmond

APHRODISIAC refers to something that turns a man on; this varies from man to man, though, in general, anything works if the woman is someone he barely knows, shouldn't be with, and will probably never see again.

EASY is an adjective used to describe a woman who has the sexual morals of a man.

FOREPLAY 1. activity that precedes sexual intercourse. While methods vary, most males prefer to limit themselves to the basic three-step approach . . . , consisting of (1) taking off their pants, (2) crawling into bed, and (3) turning out the light. 2. a man's interpretation of any touch from a woman.

NYMPHOMANIAC is a man's term for any woman who wants to have sex more often than he does.

Z-Z-Z-Z is the male part of the conversation between a man and a woman, following sex.

(From *Dating,* © 1988, Citadel Press.)

ANSWERS TO COMMON SEXUAL QUESTIONS

Dave Barry

Q. How long should sexual intercourse last?
A. This is an area of some disagreement between the sexes. As a

"**Roseanne Barr to Her Audience: On the Donahue show I saw that many men were impotent. . . . How many men HERE are impotent? [Pause.] Oh, you can't get your arms up either?**"

rule, women would like to devote as much time to foreplay and the sex act as men would like to devote to foreplay, the sex act, and building a garage. This tends to lead to dissatisfaction on the part of the woman, who is often just beginning to feel pleasantly sensuous when the man is off rooting around in the refrigerator to see if there's any Jell-O left.

Q. Well, isn't there some sensitive and caring and loving technique that a couple can use to slow the man down?

A. Yes. When the woman senses that the man is nearing climax, she can whisper: "'The Internal Revenue Service called again today, but don't worry, I hung up on them.''

(From *Dave Barry's Guide to Marriage and/or Sex*, © 1987, Rodale Press.)

CRABS

Marge Piercy

They are light as flakes of dandruff with scrawny legs.
Like limpets they cling to the base of each curly hair,
go lurching among the underbrush for cover.
Our passions are their weathers.
Coitus is the Santa Maria hitting on virgin land,
an immigrant ship coming into harbor,
free homesteads for all.
Or native crabs vs. conquistadors wrestle and nip.
Or maybe they too mingle.
As the boat glides in, there they are, the native crabs
with mandolins and bouquets of bougainvillaea
swaying on the dock singing Aloha.
For three generations we haven't seen a new face.
O the boredom, the stale genes, the incest.
Or perhaps when the two shores approach
the crabs line up to leap the gap like monkeys,
the hair always lusher on the other side.
They travel as fast as gossip.
They multiply like troubles.
They cling and persist through poison and poking and picking,
dirt and soap, torrents and drought,
like love or any other stubborn itch.

(Copyright © 1969 by Marge Piercy. Reprinted from *Hard Loving* by permission of Wesleyan University Press.)

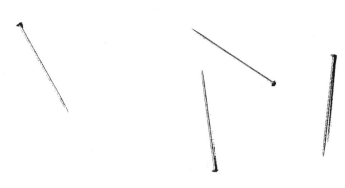

(From *Lyrics from Life*, copyright © 1980 by Nicole Hollander, St. Martin's Press.)

DID I CLIMAX DURING *PSYCHO* (AND WILL I EVER AGAIN)?

Cathy N. Davidson

> **"I've started a new group for Slightly Older Sexual Objects—SOSOs. Our motto is, 'You can be young once, but you can be soso forever.'"**
>
> **Linda Moakes**

For weeks now Sarah and her husband, Tim, have been trying to fix me up with Dan. Married people have this compulsion to see the rest of us paired off. Like Noah preparing for the Flood. Don't get me wrong—I'm happy for Sarah, really I am. After one whole year of wedlock, she and Tim still act like newlyweds. They're always celebrating some anniversary—the day they met, the first time they slept together, the day she admitted she loved him, the day he asked her son's consent, their wedding day. Sarah's a history teacher, "pulling forty," she likes to say. Tim's a motorcycle mechanic, twenty-six come February. He has a tattoo of an anchor on his right arm from the Navy, and he brags to his friends about his brilliant wife.

"She has a *Master's* degree," Tim says, "from Columbia University—in New York."

She brags to us about how he can fix anything, "Even the garbage disposal. Shit, my ex couldn't change a lightbulb!"

Five or six of us crowd around Sarah's kitchen table every Thursday, Tim's bowling night with the guys, for coffee, conversation, and Sarah's casual descriptions of the sinewy contours of Tim's body or how they make love three or four times in a row sometimes. We call ourselves OINKS, One Income, No Kid Support (when is *Time* going to do a cover story on us?). Sarah calls us DPs, Divorced and Pitiful, and passes around her latest catalogue from "Eve's Garden," a mail order place that specializes in "feminist erotica." She writes down the address so we can send away.

I flip past African Sex Balm, Korean ginseng, French ticklers, Japanese Ben-wa balls; multi-colored condoms with brushes, ridges, bumps, extenders; a rainbow assortment of panties—zippered, lacy, crotchless, leather, edible.

"Now this is more my speed," I point to an ad for a book called *Sex for One.*

"If you weren't so hostile about Dan . . ." Sarah wags a finger in my face.

Sarah's started giving elaborate dinner parties. Tim hates them—new jeans, a clean T-shirt, Sarah in the kitchen the whole Saturday when he'd just as soon have spoonburgers. But he presides munificently over every dinner, and directs Dan to the place across from me.

"It's collusion," I tell them. "Just because you're getting it regularly, you think everyone has to."

Sarah doesn't even answer. She looks at me over her glasses and cocks one eyebrow, her patented Now-Tell-Me-Again-Why-You-Didn't-Finish-Your-Assignment look.

"It's not that I *dislike* Dan," I try again. "It's just at this stage in my life I'm looking for someone a little older, fatter, balder, more secure. Right now a sex symbol, for me, is Charles Kuralt.

Sarah gives me the eyebrow again. She is my best friend. At her dinner parties, I am civil to Dan. When she asks one more time, I even agree to come to her high school class as 1963. It's her latest scheme. She's trying to get ten of her friends to come in period costume, as the Good 'Ol Days, she calls them, the years 1963 to 1972.

"It beats hell out of Betsy Ross or the Statue of Liberty. Think about it, Cory. You can wear a flip like Leslie Gore, a pillbox hat, a little polka dot shift-dress, white patent leather T-straps with squash heels. I'll even lend you the marvy pink bucket bag I picked up at the Salvation Army. Besides," she winks at me (they must award teacher's certificates for eyebrow-raises and knowing winks), "Dan's coming as '64."

Mention 1963 to most people my age and they immediately go all serious: the Kennedy assassination, "I know exactly where I was . . ." Yes, yes, I was there too. But, if I'm going to be honest about it, I have to admit that the most traumatic death of 1963 for me wasn't JFK's. It was Janet Leigh's.

I saw *Psycho* three times in three nights in September of my Freshman year in high school, and I'm inclined to attribute my subsequent career as a feminist and a revolutionary to that drive-in weekend in '63. I don't want to get too heavy about this, but I suspect *Psycho* served as an allegory for much of my generation, especially the women. At a tender age, it taught us to be suspicious of solicitous, sweet-faced men and never to trust anyone over thirty—especially grandmotherly ladies with white hair and skin shriveled like a jack-o-lantern in December.

The first lesson is still easy to remember (there aren't very many young men in my life). It's the second that's a problem, especially on those mornings, under the scrupulous blue light from the fluorescent tube, when I pluck out the day's grey hairs and try not to notice the new lines invading my thinning face. It was easy, sitting there in the dark, to see yourself as Norman's victim. I never dreamed I would one day feel like his mother.

> "If men really knew how to do it, they wouldn't have to pay for it."
>
> **Roseanne Barr**

(Reprinted from *Dykes to Watch Out For*, © 1986 by Alison Bechdel, Firebrand Books.)

Friday night's *Psycho* partner was Gary Martino, the weight lifter. I remember settling against the fuzzy leopard-print seatcover in his '57 turquoise-and-white Chevy, Gary's huge hand caressing the back of my neck, stroking my hair, both of us ignoring the other preview of coming attractions, the one on the screen. With his free hand, Gary removed the unfiltered Marlboros from his T-shirt pocket, tapped the bottom of the pack once with his forefinger. A cigarette rose, he took it between his lips. He struck a match one-handed (try it sometime: it's harder than it looks), lit his cigarette, and inhaled deeply. Then he smiled, leaned forward, and breathed slowly into my waiting mouth. French Smoking, 1963: open mouth kisses as innocent as nicotine.

Gary was the best kisser I ever dated. He had this way of encircling your back with his hands, his thumbs slowly stroking the sides of your blouse, numbering your ribs as his tongue worked moist magic in your mouth (a full-bodied brew of Winto'green Lifesavers blushed with hot buttered popcorn and a flinty aftertaste of Marlboro). Four stars in the Mobil guide.

It promised to be a perfect night. Freshman year of high school, my very first car-date, *Psycho*, the drive-in movie everyone wanted to see, a balmy September night like a promise that summer would never end. All this and Gary Martino—the kind of guy my daughter calls an HP, Hunk Personified. The kind of guy parents hate.

"When we told you that you could car-date," my mother carefully inserted the brush into the Revlon Fire-and-Ice bottle, "it was because we thought you were mature and responsible enough to exercise sound judgment."

"I am, Mom. You haven't even met Gary yet. He's one of the nicest guys I know."

"We're familiar with the family," mother sighed. She pouted her full perfect Fire-and-Ice lips and blew evenly over cool, scarlet talons.

"Meaning?"

"Well, they're just not our class, Caroline." She glanced over at my father, "And he's Italian."

"So am I!" I protested.

My father joined in, "Caroline, honey, they're *Southerners*. Our family comes from the North. Florence wasn't even part of Italy until a hundred years ago."

"Besides," my mother added, "you're only half Italian."

My father shot her a look. She shrugged her shoulders, beautifully. My mother could do all kinds of nasty things beautifully.

"Well, can I go or can't I?"

They exchanged glances. My father answered. "You can go this time, but you tell him if he tries anything, I'll break his neck."

"Thank you, Daddy," I threw my arms around his neck and gave him a long, wet kiss on the cheek. "Thanks, Mom." She leaned toward me and made a kissing noise in the air about a half-inch away from my forehead. My mother does not like to be smudged.

Gary Martino, Gary Martino: I ran home from school that Friday so I'd have plenty of time to get ready. But I discovered soon enough there was no getting ready for *Psycho*. Terror set in right from the opening credits, the jagged slash through the word "Psycho," creepy in black and white. And the music was jagged too: staccato and shrill like a scream after the throat's been cut.

Gary kept his arm tight around me the whole movie. No more

"After getting a diaphragm in, I don't want to make love: I want a certificate of achievement!"

Elayne Boosler

sexy ciggy tricks, no more French kisses, no more hands trespassing against adolescent bosom.

"Hey, Cory, you can look," he consoled at one point. "It's okay, nothing's happening now." I slowly removed my fingers from my eyes as the music calmed to silence, only to have a full view of an arm slashing forward into Janet Leigh's naked body, in the shower, the slashing over before I could shut my eyes.

This provided irrefutable evidence to support my case against overly solicitous men. Never trust the guy who says, "It's all right, baby. I won't ever let anything happen to you. Trust me. Everything's gonna be fine from now on." If you believe a line like that, don't blame me if you end up with a knife in your heart.

Our timing was off the whole movie. At one point some guy jumped out of nowhere, and we both screamed. Gary tried to stifle his but it came out thin and high-pitched, nothing at all like his normal sandpapery Aldo Ray bass. It surprised him, the squeal, and we looked at each other and I burst out laughing and so did he.

"Damn!" he exclaimed, relieved he could stop pretending to be brave.

After the movie, Gary drove me straight home. He gave me a perfunctory kiss at the door. "I need a beer," he said. "Bad," and got back into his car and sped away.

Men weren't supposed to be scared in 1963. Ever. But Gary didn't worry about things like that. He was a senior, the oldest guy in Algebra I, and we all looked up to him. Most of the kids in there were VT students, Vocational Training, trying, again, to pass algebra so they could finally graduate. They worked in the afternoons as mechanics or plumbers, beauticians or secretaries. I was the only freshman in the class, the only one in the College Prep track, and the only girl who didn't wear cat-eyed black glasses or rat her hair. Thank God I smoked. I wasn't all bad. Besides, I found algebra a snap and was good at leaning back far enough in my chair that Babs could copy all my answers and pass them on to the other Greasers in the class.

It drove my parents wild that I was taking Algebra I, with "those kind of people," as mother used to say. She even called the school about it.

"But, Mrs. Aligheri, your daughter's test scores . . ."

"My daughter is bright enough," my mother answered archly (my mother can do arch better than anyone I know), "to *insure* that her test scores would be low enough."

"But why would anyone purposely test into the remedial class?"

"Clearly, Miss Jones, if you had a child of your own, you wouldn't have to ask that question. Caroline's father *is* a mathematician, after all."

If Miss Jones had asked me, I could have told her why I took VT algebra. I hated the kids in the accelerated classes, simple as that: rich suburban WASP girls and boys with their baby blue sweaters, their baby blue cars, their baby blue bedrooms, their baby blue minds. But mother wasn't completely wrong about the kids in Algebra I. I didn't really fit in with them. Like on the Monday morning after *Psycho,* a quick smoke in the john before class, Babs and Nancy quizzing me about my date with Gary, *kidding* about it. I mean, you weren't supposed to joke about sex. So as far as most of the girls at my school were concerned, sex, boys: there was no more serious subject in the entire universe.

"If questions make the holy penis unhappy, who could survive what answers might do?"

Andrea Dworkin

"It ain't only Gary's biceps that're big," Babs smirked.

I couldn't think of a come-back, but I knew enough to inhale deeply, allowing a significant haze of Marlboro to escape from beneath what I hoped looked like a lasciviously curling upper lip, Dietrich-style, Brando-style, butch.

"Nice thing about Gar," Nancy laughed, "he can pump iron and keep it up there too."

"You're telling me," I inhaled again. "I'd snatch and jerk with Gar any time."

"How about you come with us to the Whitecastle for lunch, Cory?" Nancy smiled at me. "I got pa's car today."

Sitting in Nancy's car, fifteen-cent hamburgers, a jumbo coke, fries. I liked the way Nancy's eyeliner looked almost exactly like her cat-glasses when she took them off, and the way she breathed in the cigarette smoke a second time and let it drift lazily out her nose.

"Gary's cool," Nancy said reverently, her head back, the smoke flowing in two white streams over her mouth and down her chin. "I climax with Gary faster than with any guy I've known," she said, watching me.

"Me, too," Babs chimed in, smiling. I saw her return Nancy's wink.

"Ditto," I added, trying to sound knowing, the Marlboro balanced moistly on my lower lip, wondering what in hell "climax" meant, positive I would not be able to find it in the Thorndike-Barnhart Dictionary my grandmother gave me for Christmas, seal on the endpapers certifying it had been "Approved by the Archdiocese of Chicago." This climax thing had something to do with sex, obviously. All of the important tests in high school had something to do with sex. And for all I knew, maybe I *had* had a climax with Gary: how could a girl tell? Tongue waggling, blouse rumpling, thigh rubbing. The Forest Gardens High Rule of Thumb: if it's above the knee, he likes you; if it's above the panty line, he doesn't respect you.

"All that guy has to do is touch me," I exhaled, "and I climax."

"Really?" Babs was impressed.

"How about another Coke?" Nancy offered, "On me."

As I expected, my dictionary didn't tell me anything I didn't already know about sex ("Climax, n., from the Greek *klimax*, ladder; *cf.* Latin *clinare*, to bend, recline, decline"), and it was becoming clear that I had better find out fast or my new status with the Greasers might be lost forever. I couldn't ask any of the other Greaser girls without admitting I'd lied to Babs and Nancy, and one thing Greasers didn't do was lie to one another. Especially the women. It was the closest thing to sisterhood I'd ever encountered. The Collegiate girls would sell you short in a second if it meant a chance at a date with Kent or Trent or Brent. But the Greaser girls learned early that men weren't the solution to anything, most times they were the problem, and there was an implacable code of honor that ruled all they did. The Greasers made up a close-knit community, despised by school principals, probation officers, and the local police. But within the clan, they were as loyal as Boy Scouts, mobsters, or nuns.

How many women in 1963 knew what a climax was anyway? I remember my mother telling me once (it was the closest we ever came to a Mother-Daughter Chat) not to have sex too young be-

"Men reach their sexual peak at 18. Women reach theirs at 35. Do you get the feeling that God is playing a practical joke?"

Rita Rudner

96

WHATS SEX?

ITS THE THING **THEY** DO TO GET US.

DO WE HAVE TO DO IT?

IF WE GROW UP INTO THE REAL WORLD. ITS LIKE GOING TO WAR. OR WORK. OR INCOME TAX.

DOES ANYONE LIKE IT?

YOU MAKE YOURSELF. ITS LIKE PRETENDING TO LIKE ORGANIC VEGETABLES BECAUSE THEY'RE GOOD FOR YOU.

IS IT GOOD FOR YOU?

NO ONE'S SURE THEY'RE STILL INVESTIGATING

DOES IT HURT?

I THINK A LOT.

THE WHOLE IDEA MAKES ME SICK.

I THINK IT MAKES EVERYONE SICK.

THEN WHY DO PEOPLE TALK ABOUT IT SO MUCH?

WHY DO PEOPLE SMOKE CIGARETS?

YOU MEAN IT GIVES CANCER TOO?

NO ONE'S SURE. THEY'RE STILL INVESTIGATING.

(Reprinted by permission of Jules Feiffer.)

cause I might as well put off the disillusionment as long as possible. She said it in front of my father. In the books on reproduction we sneaked out of the town library, sex was ovulation, implantation, fertilization, gestation, about as seductive as a VT textbook. And the dirty novel I swiped from mom's lingerie drawer wasn't any help at all. Throbbing passion, lust incarnate, "I want you," he breathed into her ear, his hard manhood insistent against her warm thigh." Sex, in 1963, was something men *did* to women. It was years after I finally lost my virginity that I discovered there might be something in it for us girls.

Cory Aligheri, Cub Reporter, painfully aware that my status with the Greasers hinged on the nuances of a word. Where to find out? I was already a member of Philosophy Club (we thought of ourselves as Free Thinkers) who sat around every Thursday, 8th hour, discussing *Das Kapital* or *The Fountainhead* or *The Interpretation of Dreams*. Our teacher was finishing up a Ph.D. at the University of Chicago, and he affected all of the careful mannerisms of the incipient philosopher: mismatched socks, dirty hair and fingernails, a pipe, long pauses between sentences as he gazed off into space searching for the precise words with which to formulate his views on Platonic Idealism or Aristotelean causes. Climax? Ask Mr. Halpern? It would take a half hour for his response, a brief survey of the philosophical attitude toward the subject ("If a climax occurs in a forest and there's . . ."). I knew I'd leave with no more information than I came with. This was one problem with intellectuals, I was finding. They didn't know very much.

Climax, climax, climax, climax. Had I or hadn't I climaxed with Gary Martino during *Psycho*? The solution to the problem was obvious, though not one I relished. I'd have to ask him.

Another drive-in, the fur-lined Chevy, a boring movie this time.

"Whatsa matter, Cory?" Gary asked, pressing a thick forefinger into the furrow at the bridge of my nose.

"This is embarrassing," I stalled.

'You know you can talk to me," he said, a lie. The sum total of our previous conversations amounted to one terse exchange about

> **"When men stay at *your* place and wake up, they want things like toast. I don't have these recipes."**
>
> **Elayne Boosler**

Psycho ("Do you think Norman's a homo?" I had asked him on the drive home. "Is the Pope Italian?" Gary had answered) and to shared curses at Mr. Percy during Algebra I ("That guy is such a prick, pardon my French," as close to a complex sentence as Gary ever came).

"It's, well, it's a word I don't understand. I thought you could tell me."

Gary beamed. "You mean there's a *word* I know that you don't?"

"I think you know it. They said it about you. *Climax.*"

"What?"

"*Climax.* Nancy and Babs were joking the other day that they climaxed with you faster than anyone and I was too embarrassed to admit I didn't know what it meant. I said I did too. During *Psycho.*"

Gary bent forward, laughing until the tears ran, his forehead pressed against the fur-covered steering wheel, gigantic fists pummeling the padded dash.

"Great!" I said. "Just great, I'm glad you think I'm so funny. Here I thought I was only stupid."

Gary stopped then, suddenly. He gazed at my face. Before I knew what was happening, he scooped me up and placed me gently in his lap. He curved one hand around my chin. With the other hand, he stroked my hair. He made little kisses on my forehead and told me I was the nicest girl he had ever known. Like most Greasers, Gary had a sentimental streak that I found very touching. But he hadn't exactly answered my question.

When I asked a second time, he invited me to the Senior Prom. I forgot all about climaxes then because I knew it was a big deal if Gary Martino asked a freshman to the Prom and in September. Greasers didn't go to the Prom, wouldn't be caught dead at the Prom, and it cost a lot too, so when he asked me, I said if my parents agreed, I would be honored to go with him. "Honored," that was the word I used, and I held up my face to be kissed, but this time he kept his tongue in his mouth. His hand never stopped stroking my hair.

Maybe all my father could see was his skinny daughter standing in the entry hall with this brute, six-foot-two, his huge hand gripping and ungripping my shoulder as he asked my father if he could have the privilege of taking me to the Prom. I could tell Gary was nervous, but my father read the opening and closing hand as obvious evidence of lust. And every parent knew the dangers of Prom night.

Dad refused, flatly refused, without any explanation, and Gary, rejected but dignified, kissed my cheek, then turned and left the house. I listened. Car door. Engine. Backing down the drive. When he hit the street, Gary popped the clutch on his '57 Chev and zoomed away. I glared at my father but he said that the Prom was special, I was only a freshman, I should save something for my senior year.

"What? You saving it for your wedding night?" Sarah succumbs to sarcasm, an occupational hazard of high school teachers. "You're worried Dan's intentions might not be honorable?"

Dan's an unreconstructed Greaser. He rolls his T-shirt sleeves, slicks back his hair. The night Tim introduced us, Dan even called me "ma'am."

He's in the living room now watching a video called "Return of the Monster Trucks'' with Tim and the kids.

"This is so *rad*!'' my son shouts.

Dan's on his feet. "Holy shii-iit!'' he cheers as Big Foot, Awesome Kong, Rollin' Thunder, and Monster Vett crush rows of Toyotas, Hondas, and Datsuns. "Get those mothers!'' he cries out again, then notices me watching from the doorway, clears his throat, and sits down. "Pardon my French,'' he mutters, downright sheepishly.

"He's perfect,'' Sarah jabs an elbow into my ribs. "I mean he's got everything—even the golden egg.'' It's her word for that signature faded place, about an inch to the left and down from the fly on Dan's favorite jeans.

"What does that make me? The goose that gets to lay it?''

Sarah cocks her left eyebrow.

(From an unpublished novel, "Canton County, Mon Amour.'')

THEORY AND PRACTICE

Kate Clinton

〜〜〜〜〜〜〜〜〜〜〜〜〜〜〜〜〜〜〜〜〜〜〜

This year the pressure for having children is on. I went to a workshop called "So You Want To Have A Baby.'' It was great; it was real different from the workshop I had gone to on S & M, I mean S-slash-M. I really did go. I thought, I'm a happening kind of woman, I have to find out what's going on. So I went to this workshop.

The woman in charge—notice I didn't say "the woman who was facilitating'' because at S/M workshops you don't have facilitators, you have a sergeant-at-arms maybe. The woman in charge made it very clear at the beginning that *no one* was going to talk about theory. We were just going to talk about practice—what you do, what you use, where you get it.

I was sitting there pretending I was at a Tupperware party, when the woman in charge turns to my side of the group and says, "Now we're going to go around the room and everyone is going to tell what they do.'' Well, Lord knows I've had more women than most people have noses . . . but even I knew I was in trouble. Because a week before the workshop I'd seen my first vibrator and I thought it was a Mr. Microphone. My turn comes.

What do I do? Well, here's something. "Sometimes when my lover and I are in bed—and we're eating, *each* of us is eating . . . OK, Popcorn . . . sometimes, I get a little crazy with the salt shaker . . . and salt flies all around the bed, and later when we turn over, it scratches us.''

Bomb. And I tried so hard.

But at the So-You-Want-a-Baby Workshop, it was different. There they didn't want to talk about practice. They only wanted to talk about THEORY. Now why do I think something is reversed about that?

(Adapted from a recording, copyright © 1985 by Kate Clinton and WhysCrack Records.)

"Aren't women prudes if they don't and prostitutes if they do?''

Kate Millet

THE MONTHLY EGG

Susie Day

Every month, a horrible thing happens. A little round egg, that never caused anyone any harm, is released from one of my lesbian feminist ovaries and rolls down my lesbian feminist Fallopian tube until it comes to my lesbian feminist uterus, where it lies around expecting to get laid. I can imagine it at first wistfully humming to itself "Some Day My Prince Will Come." Then, a few days later, with no sweaty ol' prince having come anywhere *near* its premises, it becomes a tad more assertive; belting out "I Wanna a Hotdog for My Roll" with increasingly feeble bumps and grinds. Finally realizing its life a sham, its dream impossible, it flushes itself down the tubes. Perhaps it goes out whistling "Is That All There Is?" I don't know. I don't want to know. You pay a high price in this world for being a dried-up selfish old maid.

Don't mind me. I get this way—periodically. Being a full-time lesbian with political convictions and a part-time job, I can get pretty moody during my "woman's time." It is then that my personal/political outlook can resemble a jackal's dinner, upchucked on a plaid pant suit. Somehow, it all makes me wonder what Snow White did when she got *her* period. Did the dwarves get on her nerves? Was she rude to Mr. Disney?

"Well, frankly, Susie—yes. I guess I do get a little cross." Snow White rolled her lovely dark eyes up toward heaven. She folded her little apron and gracefully sat down on the rustic milking stool that decorated her Hollywood bungalow. "But I just chalk it up to Female Destiny. 'Moody, thy name is Woman,' I tell myself."

"But you've never had a moody day in your life," I exclaimed. "You've tinkled and sparkled and sang through the worst of times. And I've always loved you for it."

"Lies, Susie. All lies. I mean, sure, I sang for my prince to come. But when he finally came, it was no big deal, you know?" Snow White absent-mindedly toyed with a strand of lustrous black hair. "Everybody else thought that goodness had prevailed; virtue had its reward; my roll had its hot-dog. But inside, I died a little. I remember asking myself, 'Is *that* all there is?'"

"You mean—your life has been just—just another media distortion?"

"You betcha."

Fighting back tears of rage and frustration, I was able to stammer, "But—but what do you do to overcome monthly moodiness? America wants to know."

"Why, I wouldn't overcome them if I could!" Snow White cried, clapping her hands together in helpless feminine glee. "Moods are a very important part of being a grown-up woman." Snow White's alluring bodice expanded in pride as she went on to say, "You see, Susie, each of our womanly bodies is absolutely overflowing with little X chromosomes."

> **"Sexual congress with heavy machinery is not a special interest. It is a personality defect."**
>
> **Fran Lebowitz**

(Reprinted from *Dykes to Watch Out For*, © 1986 by Alison Bechdel. Firebrand Books.)

"X chromosomes?" I gasped. "That's none of my business."

"Oh, yes it is!" Snow White gave a short whistle. Suddenly, two dainty swallows soared into the room. Twittering merrily, they pulled a movie screen down from the ceiling. A bevy of fluffy squirrels dashed to turn off the lights, then flicked on a nearby projector. As if by magic, winsome Disney X chromosomes started to rollick and prance their way into my heart. Snow White continued to speak, her rippling, musical laugh occasionally punctuating her words.

"These X chromosomes are paired into billions of chromosomal couples. The couples gossip together; they go out on little dates together; and together they live in a cooperative of same-sex cells, one neighbor chromosome borrowing tiny cups of sugar from another neighbor. Gosh, Susie, each woman's body is really nothing more than a gigantic lesbian community, if you think about it. This was a big revelation for me," Snow White added, reaching for my hand. "You see—I used to be a Mormon.

"Oh, look!" Snow white's enthusiasm was contagious. "Here come Connie and Candy Chromosome! They're on their first date. Ooooh, they are starting to give each other teeny backrubs . . . Now see all the little chromosomes getting ready for their period! Some are laughing; some are crying; some are retching . . . Uh-oh. Here is a gang that is fed up with working within the System. See their teensy-weensy rally? They are about to hold a protest march to Miss Uterus, where they intend to kick up some mighty bad cramps.

"So you see," declared Snow White as the film ended and the lights came up, "we women go through thousands of itty-bitty ups and downs in a second. No wonder we are moody! And, apart from living their own lives, our X chromosomes are attuned to the larger rhythms of the cosmos.

"Yes, Susie," Snow White's crystal soprano rang out, "much like the moon, the tides, the international political scene, women are in perpetual change. Unlike the international political scene, however, women tend to change for the better." Snow White and I laughed like sisters.

"When you see the full moon in the sky, you know those little X's are in there, baying at it. And when you see those big, ugly Pershing 2 missiles ready to be deployed, you may be sure that your X's are snarling invisibly, all over your body. Some women are so caught up in their own chromosomes, they have been known to camp outside military bases and act as moodily as they can." Snow White rose. She picked up her floor-length gown and started for the door.

"But Snow White," I whimpered, "I thought this story was going to have a happy ending."

"Well, it's possible." She sighed a sigh both worldly and demure, "Joan of Arc listened to her chromosomes, and *she* saved France."

"You mean—to thine own cells be true?"

"You've got to break eggs to make an omelet, dearie." She turned to go.

"Snow White!" I cried. "Where are you going?"

"It's nearly 8 o'clock," she said with a ladylike wink. "I promised Sleeping Beauty I'd wake her."

And she was gone. Leaving me with much to think about, and no Midol.

SEX VS. COOKING

Karen Williams

〰〰〰〰〰〰〰〰〰〰〰〰〰〰〰〰

My best friend called 976-DATE, got a date, and called me for some advice.

I told her that I don't worry about sex on the first date. But I have my definite do's and don'ts. I don't COOK on the first date . . . I mean to me, that's an intimate act that they definitely come to expect. If you're having sex with someone on a regular basis, you can have a headache and get out of it; but once you start preparing those home-cooked meals—major surgery, they want to hear those pots and pans clattering in your kitchen.

How do I get out of it? Well, first I tell 'em, I won first place in the Top Ramen cookoff: 1½ minutes from stove top to table top. I know it takes 5 minutes and it's still a little crunchy, but once they start picking noodles out of their teeth, they'll take you out to dinner.

Excerpts from

CENSORED EROTICA

Janice Perry

〰〰〰〰〰〰〰〰〰〰〰〰〰〰〰〰

It was lying beside me, verbing quietly. I could hear its steady breathing and the soft sounds of its verbing. I began to get adjective, so I turned to it and put my body part around it. It looked deep into my body part and verbed me with its body part. I began to verb and to verb its body part with mine. It moaned and said, "I emotion it when you verb me like that."

There was the sound of its adjective body part rubbing against my body part and the slow rhythm of our verbing each other. It was adverbly verbing me and I began to verb. I saw its color body part and grew more and more emotioned. I knew I would soon verb. My skin verbed with excitement, and I felt tiny nouns shooting up and down my body part. I said, "Faster, faster my endearment, I'm going to verb! Yes, I'm Verbing, I'm VERBING! VERB me! VERB me! Oh endearment, you are the SUPERLATIVE! I emotion you."

We lay together in silence, and then got up and ate three entire packets of nouns.

JANICE PERRY   a.k.a.   *Gal*

Photo by Erik Borg

ELEANOR KEEPS CONTROL

Molly Hite

I never got to hold out until Frank, and he called me a cock-tease before I could explore the ramifications. Once he had indicated there were names for girls like me I gave in. I think I was a little comforted by the fact that I had finally fallen into a recognizable sexual category. But I suppose I've always wanted to hold out. It seems very powerful to remain the object of a gaze, provoking longing, creating frustration, like sitting in the warmth of a spotlight in sequinned tights with your legs crossed smoking a cigarette. I have, in fact, crossed my legs. There is something about not coming through. The thought of not coming through excites me. I find I'm thinking about taking off my blouse, the nylon one that itches anyway, of pulling my slip top around my waist, unfastening my bra—tricky, there are three little *hook* things Frank could never negotiate without help—of getting it now yes bending slightly from the waist the cups loosening descending and now yes I fling it triumphantly at the wastebasket, turn away from the board, insouciantly now, wipe chalk dust across my nipples yes straighten, arch my back so my alabaster breasts are *thrust* yes toward his questing fingers. But of course his questing fingers don't get anywhere near me.

"Your breasts," he whispered huskily. "They're . . . they're alabaster, they are."

"Silence!" was her imperious command. "You are to gaze. Speech is forbidden you."

He swallowed painfully. Beneath the rough-spun fabric of his nether garment his swollen member arched toward the translucent flesh, veined blue like the marble of Carrara, lightly freckled in an attractive manner. Beneath the simple tunic the firm rod reached, quivering, entreating. "Oh, your breasts," he choked.

"Another word," she commanded, "and they disappear from your sight." He trembled, pressing his chapped lips together with the effort not to cry out his desire. The courtiers stirred behind her, restless.

"You want me, then," she continued languorous, feline.

"Majesty," he gasped, "more than life itself."

"Take heed of what you say," she murmured, the shadow of a smile grazing the perfection of her lips while the tip of her tongue darted over them. "Desires may come to, how shall we say? Fruition?"

"Fruition is good," he agreed. "Oh, it is what I wish!" and his rugged knees began to buckle.

"Stand!" she ordered, and again he struggled to his feet to gaze in spellbound fascination across the chasm of his frustration, the moat of all earthly desire, at the promised end, those palely glimmering globes. "I would—" he began, and then stopped, terrified by his own presumption.

"Go on," she murmured.

"I would taste them," he murmured back.

Her lip curled, almost imperceptibly. "Taste only? Would you go further? Would you . . . bite?"

His lips were trembling. Beads of sweat stood out on his noble brow. "Majesty," he whispered, "I would indeed bite."

"Take him away," she commanded scornfully. "No biters."

"I had always understood—" he called after her, but she was fixing her shoulder straps.

They took him away. It comes to that, finally: power lies in having him dragged off, hard-on throbbing, little rivulets of drool coursing down his manly chin. Any more and you lose. Never mind that there's a sexual revolution going on.

I stare at the page for a while before I slide it into the drawer where I'm keeping my manuscript or the beginnings of my manuscript, my false starts. Even my fantasies only get this far, right up to where he wants you more than life itself. Then he has to do something dumb. Any further and the dynamics change; even in fantasy I draw the line here, where I'm still in control. In a way the real kick is getting him to say he wants you more than life itself. Then he marries you. That's why the stories end there, with the wedding: this is fulfillment; this is the state of the art if you're into female pornography. Afterwards its all *post coitum triste.*

(From *Class Porn,* copyright © 1987 Molly Hite The Crossing Press.)

(From *The Calgary Sun.* Reprinted by permission of Sue Dewar.)

ELEANOR'S PROBLEMS WRITING PORN

Molly Hite

■ ■ ■ I finally decide it's now or never. Same setup. Satin-draped queen, elevated, nipples protruding through the slick fabric like grapes. Burlap-clad adventurer, depressed, tongue flickering over simian lips. Courtiers in attendance. A lot of ogling all around. Some posturing: bulges on both sides. Foreplay. But this isn't what I'm after. What I'm after, I reflect muzzily, is contact, mutually pleasurable contact with the emphasis on mutuality, none of this ramming banging poking prodding sticking drilling screwing violating penetrating invading wounding business; just, you know, intercourse. Surely this is possible, even granting the unfortunate precedents.

(From *Class Porn,* Copyright © 1987 Molly Hite The Crossing Press.)

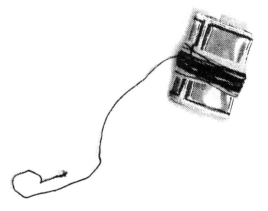

THE MYTH OF THE NINE-MONTH PREGNANCY

Teresa Bloomingdale

The father-to-be expects the doctor to be on call, twenty-four hours a day, seven days a week, for the next nine months, while the doctor expects the father to see to it that the baby arrives after breakfast and before lunch, Wednesdays and weekends being an absolute no-no.

Neither man seems to understand the indisputable facts about any pregnancy. In the first place, there has never been, in the history of motherhood, a nine-month pregnancy. Seven, sometimes; eleven, lots of times. But nine? Never. In the second place, nobody decides when the baby will be born except the baby, who will considerately give you several choices: (a) On the evening you have welcomed twelve guests to dinner and have just opened the wine and put the steaks on; (b) In the middle of the night during a raging blizzard on the day you were supposed to get the gas tank filled up and forgot; (c) During the ninth inning of the seventh game of a tied World Series.

> " Electric flesh-arrows . . . traversing the body. A rainbow of color strikes the eyelids. A foam of music falls over the ears. It is the gong of orgasm."
>
> **Anaïs Nin**

THE HOLY CONDOM

Katherine Rockwell Lawrence

Even though it's all about birthing babies, a traditionally feminine activity, the Vatican's edict of March 11, 1987, "Instruction on Respect for Human Life in Its Origin and on the Dignity of Procreation," which forbids artificial insemination, doesn't consult one real woman in all its forty pages. Actually the only woman referred to by Cardinal Ratzinger and Archbishop Bovone is Holy Mother Church, as in:

> The Church's intervention in this field *[procreation]* is inspired also by the love which she owes to man, helping him to recognize and respect his rights and duties.

(The church is a girl, in the same way boats are and hurricanes used to be. It's confusing, isn't it, the way they blame this stuff on a woman, when really it's all men?) Men, however, are quoted and referred to throughout, from the very first sentence:

> The gift of life which God the Creator and Father has entrusted to man calls him to appreciate the inestimable value of what he has been given.

There are three words that recur with about the same frequency

106

as the male pronoun: dignity, natural, artificial.

The Vatican now says that sex is natural. Within marriage. It used to be sex was only for having children. If you had fun doing it, it couldn't be helped, but it wasn't recommended. Then the Church recognized what it calls the unitive function of sex, and said that pleasure was O.K. too, if you were married. It was an important concession because it allowed a husband and wife to do it all month long without guilt and without contraception. The new edict has taken it a step further by saying that sex, the actual act, is the only way to conceive.

You'd think that the Vatican would welcome artificial means of conception because it could ultimately free everyone from having sex, make procreation purer. Because, even with the unitive function, sex can't be all that great if the men in charge don't indulge, and forbid their clergy to.

It is unnatural and therefore a sin to use artificial means to fertilize a woman's egg with her husband's sperm because the masturbation that precedes it is unnatural. Please note that we're talking about the husband's sperm only here. Anyone else's sperm is unnatural, artificial, and undignified. So if your husband is infertile, do something else right now. Watch television or something. Or go ahead, have sex with him. Just do not consider having a child.

But all is not lost. Catholic medical authorities have suggested an antimasturbatory sperm-collection method! During sex, use a condom deliberately pierced with a hole or two. (These holes are actually loopholes, because an intact condom is a contraceptive and therefore artificial.) There will be plenty of sperm left, and the couple can, with a clear conscience use it for insemination because it was produced naturally, during intercourse.

Rev. John Connery of Loyola, a priest and medical ethics consultant for Catholic hospitals, has another suggestion. "If a couple, let's say, had intercourse, and the doctor then took a syringe and went into the vagina and got the sperm and then injected it farther into the uterus or the Fallopian tube—if that could be done, I think you could justify it." Question, to Father Connery: Where is the doctor during the act? In the room? Just waiting outside? If you had to stand up and take a cab to the doctor's office you'd lose a lot of sperm. Is the proximity of the doctor and the syringe during intercourse all that natural? Wouldn't masturbation have more dignity?

What if the wife waits until her husband is asleep, then sits close by him and reads something really sexy aloud. Maybe he'll have a wet dream! And then she can quick, collect the sperm and shoot it in. Wet dreams aren't a sin because they're unconscious. She wouldn't tell him in advance, so how could he know? And it wouldn't be the wife's fault. She was only reading. Reading trash is only a venial sin, not mortal. Not way up there with masturbation. Anyway, it's worth a shot.

But why is masturbation so terrible, when Ratzinger and Bovone get to do it? This tract they've written is replete with self-reference, including sixty footnotes, citing only Popes and no scientists. The Vatican's entire argument is based on things the Vatican has said before. How come I wasn't allowed to do that in my high school term papers?

Abortion is unnatural . . . masturbation . . . birth control, and now artificial insemination. I do not think the Church should limit itself to matters sexual in its vigilance against the unnatural. There

"The act of sex, gratifying as it may be, is God's joke on humanity. It is man's last desperate stand at superintendency."

Bette Davis

are so many other things that are unnatural:

Penicillin
Indoor Plumbing
Racism and sexism
Clipping one's toenails
Starvation
Blood transfusions (If you can't have sperm that isn't your spouse's, you sure shouldn't have blood that isn't.)
Organ transplants
Hair dye and nose jobs and pacemakers
War
Contact lenses
Carrying a fetus conceived in rape to term

Starvation in a world stripped of its resources by overpopulation. For while the church is keeping people who want children from having them, it's forcing people who don't to have them. Will this world have dignity?

But anyway, I'm glad the Vatican thinks sex is natural. It must be, because a study has shown that people think about sex every sixteen seconds. What's unnatural is the suppression of one's sexuality. Take celibacy; it could cause you to get obsessed. It could cause you to think about sex even more than every sixteen seconds.

(Originally published as "Unnatural Acts and Other Papal Indiscretions," *Ms.* magazine, September 1987; reprinted, with alterations, in Kathleen Rockwell Lawrence, *The Boys I Didn't Kiss*, © 1990, British American Publishing Co.)

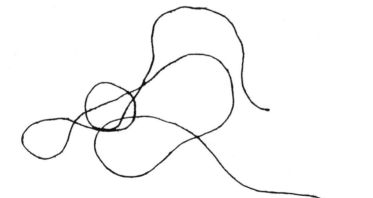

"On Prostitution: How could any woman sleep with a total stranger without having dinner and a movie first?"

Elayne Boosler

© 1980 Light Allusions

(From *The Whole Enchilada,* copyright © 1986 by Nicole Hollander, St. Martin's Press.)

SNOOL, noun. A tame, abject, or mean-spirited person. *Oxford English Dictionary* (O.E.D.). Normal inhabitant of sadosociety, characterized by sadism and masochism combined; stereotypic hero and/or saint of the sadostate. Examples: Adam; Saint Paul; Marquis de Sade. *Wickedary* by Mary Daly with Jane Caputi.

SNOOK, verb. To gesture derisively, to engage in derisive behavior.

SNAFFLE, noun. A simple form of bridle bit. O.E.D.—verb. 1. To put a snaffle on (a horse, etc.); to restrain or guide with a snaffle. 2. slang, to arrest; to seize. O.E.D.

BATHROOMS BY THE MARQUIS DE SADE

Margery Eliscu

I have just returned from a car trip to New York, and I can personally report on a good number of the public women's rest rooms from the Maine Turnpike to the Saw Mill River Parkway. I have concluded that women's rest rooms are designed and supplied by America's most ingenious businesspeople. I am also sure that behind every public bathroom there was an original telephone order that went like this:

"Is this the Marquis de Sade Plumbing Company?"

"Speaking. Simon de Sade here."

"Well, this is Burger McJohnson with an order for a women's bathroom facility for our newest restaurant. What do you have in your fast-service line? Have you come up yet with your proposed drive-through john?"

"Still on the drawing board, Mr. McJohnson. But we can supply you with features that will save you toilet paper, water, soap, and money. We can move your ladies along faster than ever. How many are you seating?"

"Huh?"

"In the dining room. How many does the restaurant serve?"

"Oh! Seating for five hundred."

"Well, checking my chart, that calls for one stall and you should be able to move twenty-five women through in a given minute."

"One stall? Twenty-five a minute?"

"Twenty-four stand in an unheated hallway lined up between the men's and the ladies' room. The desperate ones hop into the men's room, which our market research tells us is always empty and a total waste of space."

"I don't see twenty-five . . ."

"Let me assure you. There's a fast-food place in Connecticut that has sold one hundred billion hamburgers, and they manage with a one-seater combined with a hand dryer over the john, a four-inch sink, and twenty square feet of floor space."

"Amazing!"

"We're proud of it. It has an added efficiency. While the woman washes her hands with cold water, water from a pipe drips on the toilet seat."

"How is that good?"

"Keeps the next gal from lingering. Let me tell you . . . no one carries a book into a de Sade john."

"I'm ready to talk business."

"Well, first, we start with the door locks . . . the ones that slide across but don't catch. They're wonderful. They look like they should catch, so the woman figures she's stupid. Rather than complain, she decides to wait until the next gas station."

"But what if . . ."

"If she can't wait, she holds the door closed with an elbow or a knee and chants rapidly: 'Someone's in here. Someone's in here.'

"Now it's important that we add the door that opens in and has a broken coat hook. That way, you can virtually eliminate anyone with a fur, a large pocketbook, or a weight problem. It's next best to the drive-through john."

"Sounds reasonable."

"But the important thing is the toilet paper. You don't want to be stuck supplying tons of toilet paper year-round, which is why I recommend our top-selling toilet-tissue holder, The Rock 'N Roller.

"Now, you take this same lady who is holding the door closed with her elbow and chanting. She pulls on the tissue, and she gets one square before the rack rocks back. As long as she doesn't figure it out that she can unfold from the top, you get six months' service out of one roll.

"Or, you could go instead with our pasted-shut new roll. This one looks nice and full, but the lady finds she has to tear across the grain with her fingernail to start the paper. Now, if she succeeds, the paper drops off in eensy teensy pieces. You've seen them on the floor."

"How much . . . ?"

"Or maybe you're better off with our least expensive 'Just Used Up' roll . . . a few pieces of paper pasted to a cardboard cylinder with Elmer's glue."

"We'll go with that. Now, what about the sinks?"

"We've got either the faucets that you have to hold down or the double faucet set, in which one side runs icicles and the other boils eggs. We also have a choice of the thin-rimmed sink that dumps the pocketbook into the basin, or the faucet handle that sprays into the purse.

"You also have a choice between the towel rack that hangs at the exact height to guarantee dripping up the sleeves or the ever-popular cloth towel roll permanently stuck—the greasy finger stains are included. There's also the liquid no-soap dispenser with the gooey surface and the pink painted interior. The ladies touch the wet plastic bottom and go away happy."

"Don't you get some women who complain to the . . . ?"

"Solved. On the outside of the john, we stick this report board which lists the hours the bathroom was inspected. Once an hour, the cook runs to the john, chalks the time and some initials. The women blame the teenagers ahead of them in line for messing up the place and stealing the supplies."

"I'm ready to talk money."

"I'm afraid the price is up this year, but you're buying more than

"If nuclear power plants are safe, let the commercial insurance industry insure them. Until those expert judges of risk are willing to gamble their money, I'm not willing to gamble with the health and safety of my family."

Donna Reed

> "It is not true that there is dignity in all work. Some jobs are definitely better than others. It is not hard to tell the good jobs from the bad. People who have good jobs are happy, rich, and well dressed. People who have bad jobs are unhappy, poor, and use meat extenders."
>
> **Fran Lebowitz**

a bathroom, you're buying American ingenuity."

"Which is why I have to ask you now whether you have anything else new that can save us even more money. We don't need all that luxury you described."

"Okay. We do have one further economy model if you want to go for our New Year's Special available all the time. It's a worry-free set-up that meets the requirements and moves traffic at an incredible speed."

"What's that? It sounds good!"

"We cut a door in a wall, add a knob that doesn't turn, and hang an out-of-order sign."

(From *Russell Baker, Erma Bombeck & Me*, © 1987 by Lance Tapley, Publisher [Yankee Books].)

BALLAD OF MALE HEGEMONY

Clare Will von Faulhaber

Ecclesial power remaineth, oremus,
With those who can say, "Testiculos habemus."

Empowering persons whose claim is testiculi
Strikes millions of women as pretty ridiculi.

(Reprinted from *Commonweal*, September 9, 1988.)

ON SANTA'S LAP

Jane Wagner

I took the boys to see Santa Claus. When Santa Claus asked Robert what he wanted for Christmas, Robert said,
"A nuclear freeze."
And then McCord yanked Santa's beard off and said,
"What animal got killed for this?"
I knew you'd be proud.

I mean, for a kid that age to have the spirit to confront Santa Claus on what he thought was a *moral* issue . . . Well . . .

Maybe we did *some* things right, after all.

(From *The Search for Signs of Intelligent Life*. Copyright © 1986 by Jane Wagner Inc. Reprinted by permission of Harper & Row.)

WE HATE TO SEE THEM GO

Words and Music by Malvina Reynolds

INTRO: (freely)

Last night I had a love-ly dream; I saw a big pa-rade with tick-er tape ga-lore, and men were march-ing there the like I'd ne-ver seen be-fore.

VERSE (lively)

1. Oh, the bank-ers and the dip-lo-mats are go-ing in the ar-my, Oh hap-py day! I'd give my pay to see them on pa-rade; Their paunch-es at at-ten-tion & their strip-ed pants at ease, They've got-ten pa-tri-o-tic and they're go-ing o-ver-seas; We'll have to do the best we can and brave-ly car-ry on, So we'll just keep the lad-dies here to man-age while they're gone!

CHORUS

Oh,____ We hate to see them go, The gen-tle-men of dis-tinc-tion in the ar-my.

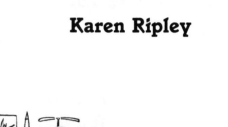

"The truth is the funniest thing around."

Karen Ripley

NO SANTA IT'S NOT OUR TOY WISH LIST IT'S A DISARMAMENT PLAN FOR TOYLAND!

(Reprinted by permission of bulbul—Gen Guracar.)

The bankers and the diplomats are going in the army,
It seemed too bad to keep them from the wars they love to plan.
We're all of us contented that they'll fight a dandy war,
They don't need propaganda, they know what they're fighting for.
They'll march away with dignity and in the best of form,
And we'll just keep the laddies here to keep the lassies warm.
    Chorus

The bankers and the diplomats are going in the army,
We're going to make things easy cause it's all so new and strange;
We'll give them silver shovels when they have to dig a hole,
And they can sing in harmony when answering the roll,
They'll eat their old K-rations from a hand-embroidered box,
And when they die, we'll bring them home, and bury them in Fort Knox.
    Chorus

A LETTER TO THE REVEREND

Susie Day

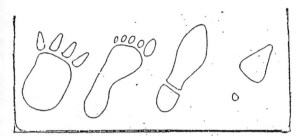

The evolution of authority

"If a woman gets nervous, she'll eat or go shopping. A man will attack a country—it's a whole other way of thinking."

Elayne Boosler

"**Y**ou're much too hostile," my therapist said. "Why don't you—in your own words—try to *thank* the people who cause you momentary grief and frustration? After all, they are the agents of your own personal growth."

"OK," I retorted. I spent all last Friday being thankful:

Dear Reverend Falwell,

I've seen your posters around town for several days now, and would like to show my appreciation for their clear, easy-to-read lettering and correct grammar. That picture of you with the horizon came out really well and is quite flattering. Unfortunately, I will be busy the night of your Rally for a More Righteous Decency, so cannot attend. Thank you, though, for putting your sign in my neighborhood, where a militant homosexual such as myself could read it.

It's little gestures like that that make me doubt you are really anti-gay, Reverend. Anti-gay people are mean and spiteful, and your poster shows you smiling and brave. Yes, you must be very brave, Jerry Falwell, to have had a lifelong primary relationship with a Jewish carpenter who's been dead for over 2,000 years. Doesn't anyone in your family object to the difference in your religions?

Seriously, Jerry. I've been hearing quite a lot about you lately. You see, sometimes I talk to Jesus. Oh, don't get me wrong; we're not even good friends. But we do get together at the 92nd Street Y from time to time and play dominoes.

We gossip. For instance, did you know that God is really a pansexual, multi-ethnic, racially mixed, non-hierarchical collective? Which should prove, once and for all, that God is not a God of Revenge, and that our earthly misfortunes are simply the result of shoddy processing. You might want to emphasize this fact more at your rallies, Reverend.

Jesus also tells me things about your relationship. All about your inability to express vulnerable emotions; the fact that you never take out the garbage; your kinky positions on nuclear missiles and other projectiles; that sordid trip to South Africa, where you made him feel "so cheap."

Jesus is pretty fed up, Jerry. So I thought the Truth might set him free. On my suggestion, he's been writing his memoirs about his life with you. *A Bomb in Gilead, or Even Saviours Get the Blues.* Random House has offered us a generous contract and movie rights, once it's finished.

Please, Jerry. It's never too late if you love someone. Jesus doesn't *want* to write those terrible things. Won't you give him something nice to say about you—while there's still time? Hurry, Jerry. We're proofing the galleys.

Hope you two can work things out—
A Wayfaring Stranger

I admit it's a modest beginning. There are so many more people to thank. But if we *all* pitch in, we can get the job done a lot sooner. And we'll be better people for it.

A-MEN'S RIGHTS

Lydia Sargent

Welcome to Hotel Satire USA, where we gals are SICK and tired of all this talk about gals equal rights because it's upsetting our men. Nobody voted for what's it called? the ERA? Energetic Rush to Annihilation? But libbers persist, forcing our men to join what's it called? the NRA? Need Rifles At-the-ready?

Even commie men have had it. It says so in that gals lib magazine, what's it called? *Nympho?* Some day soon you libbers will realize if you want a man to listen, you're gonna have to say things he wants to hear. Someday you libbers will realize that as a working gal you earn 70% of what he makes, while as a homemaker you could get a full 100%. Just for light housekeeping. When are you libs going to realize that all you get from a lib marriage is extra work and a hyphenated last name?

. . . Our Hotel Satire men want to voice their rights for ONE LAST TIME.

Matthew Speaks

Men.
I like gals. My mother and sister are gals. I want like hell for gals to be equal. If I was God, I would have made them equal. No question. But some other guy got to be God, through no fault of mine because I tried hard to get to be God. The guy that is God, the guy that isn't me, he made guys so they could be Shakespeare and Einstein and Joe Montana and Pat Boone, and gals so they couldn't. God did it, not me. It's not my fault. Right?

Mark Speaks

Bros.
I don't remember picking this God guy but He is aces with me. He made guys to look like Gods and gals to look like Venus on the half-shell. As far as I'm concerned, gals are equal. As long as they're gals doing it. As long as gals look pretty gals can play football for all I care. Just so gals sweat like gals and bounce around on the scrimmage line. Heck, gals can earn a living for all it matters to me. Just shave the legs and show some skin. Gals can even be smart just as long as the mascara doesn't run, the hair stays in place. I'll go even further. Gals can be cops. Just show some gam getting out of the black and white. Hell, let gals be vice president. But no sagging and show cleavage. All right?

> " The more complete the despotism, the more smoothly all things move on the surface. "
>
> **Elizabeth Cady Stanton**

WE'RE NOT PLAYING COPS AND ROBBERS...
WE'RE GIVING SANCTUARY!

(Reprinted by permission of bulbul—Gen Guaracar.)

Luke Speaks

Men 'o mine.

I wish I'd been appointed God. This current bozo who made a mess of it by putting gals on top. Everywhere I go gals are running the show. I get home from work my wife-gal wants me to help out. I go to the office my employee-gal wants a decent salary. I go to the bar and a bartender-gal serves me a brew. I go to church a minister-gal tells me God's a woman. I go to a ballgame, a lesbian-gal wants to clean home plate. When I'm God guys get first dibs on rights. Right?

John Speaks

Fellows.

I voted for women's equality. It's the women who don't want to be equal. And that's their right. My personal woman could have a career and earn enough money to pay for day-care while taking care of the household. As long as it doesn't disrupt my life. She could easily handle the stress of kids who need a psychiatrist because their mother's never home. If she wanted to go to the trouble. What's to stop her? Pas me. Pas this guy. Not moi. But she doesn't want to. Is it my crime? So sue me. How right am I?

Peter Speaks

Best buddys.

I'm not God. But I'm His close buddy, which puts me nearer to God than she. My buddy God decided on equal but special rights. White guys have white guy rights and gals get their share in descending order, cause broads are quite far from God. But my buddy God gave broads some terrific rights so don't get upset. For instance, copy rights (the right to take dictation), water rights (the right to wash windows, toilets, bathtubs), stride rights (the right to wear high heels), animal rights (the right to be called foxes, chicks, heifers, and fillies), and so on. When broads try for guys' rights is when things go wrong. Take your executive broads. Fact is: Boss broads turn guys off. Deduction: Bossy broads are bad for business. Conclusion: No boss broads . . .

Paul Speaks

Associates.

I'm not God, yet. But God looks like me. And He gave gals a choice: go through life perched on pedestals or go through life as pains in the neck. God gave men two tasks in life: lifting gals onto pedestals and punching out gals who are pains in the neck. So I ask you: How can gals be equal when guys can pummel the living daylights out of them? It's not our fault. God made us do it. Leave us alone. Just shut up, gals. Just shut the heck up. All right?

(From the column "Hotel Satire," *Z* magazine, June 1988.)

"I am working for the time when unqualified blacks, browns, and women join the unqualified men in running our government."

Cissy Farenthold

(Reprinted from *Dykes to Watch Out For*, © 1986 by Alison Bechdel, Firebrand Books.)

THE STORY OF ED

Barbara Ehrenreich

> "Social activism is not a question of courage or bravery for me. There's no cheaper way to have fun, is there?"
>
> Flo Kennedy

> "A woman has to be twice as good as a man to go half as far."
>
> Fannie Hurst

Ever since the attorney general declared open season on smut, I've had my work cut out for me. I'm referring, of course, to the Meese commission's report on pornography, which urges groups of private citizens to go out and fight the vile stuff with every means at hand . . . spray paint, acetylene torches, garlic and crucifixes. In the finest spirit of grass roots democracy, the commission is leaving it up to us to decide what to slash and burn and what to leave on the library shelves. Not that we are completely without guidance in this matter, for Commissioner Frederick Schauer (''golden Schauer'' to those wild and crazy boys at *Penthouse*) quotes approvingly a deceased judge's definition of hard-core porn: ''I know it when I see it.''

Well, so do I, thanks to the report's thoughtful assertions that pornography is something that ''hurts women'' and, in particular, ''bears a causal relationship to the incidence of various nonviolent forms of discrimination against or subordination of women in our society.''

I thought my citizens group should start its search for materials damaging to women with the Bible, on the simple theory that anything read by so many people must have something to do with all the evil in the world. ''Gather around,'' I said to my fellow citizens. ''If those brave souls on the Meese commission could wade through the likes of *Fellatio Frolics* and *Fun with Whips and Chains,* we can certainly get through Genesis.''

It was rough going, let me tell you, what with the incest (Lot and his daughters), mass circumcisions, adultery, and various spillings of seed. But duty triumphed over modesty, and we were soon rewarded with examples of sexism so crude and so nasty that they would make *The Story of O* look like suffragist propaganda. There was the part about Eve and her daughters being condemned to bring forth their offspring in sorrow, and numerous hints that the bringing forth of offspring is in fact the only thing women have any business doing. There were injunctions against public speaking by women, and approving descriptions of a patriarchal dynasty extending without the least concern for affirmative action, for countless generations from Isaac on. And then there were the truly kinky passages on the necessity of ''submitting'' to one's husband—an obvious invitation to domestic mayhem.

We wasted no time in calling the newly installed Meese commission hot line to report we had discovered material—widely advertised as ''family'' reading—that would bring a blush to the cheek of dear Dr. Ruth and worry lines to the smooth brow of Gloria Steinem. ''Well, yes,'' said the commissioner who picked up the phone, ''but could this material be used as a masturbatory aid? Is it designed to induce sexual arousal in all but the most priggish Presbyterian? Because it's the arousal, you know, that *reinforces* the sexism, transforming normal, everyday male chauvinism into raging misogyny.''

We argued that we had seen a number of TV preachers in states of arousal induced by this book, and that, furthermore, religious

---

ecstasy might be far more effective at reinforcing sexism than any mere tickle of genital response. But we reluctantly agreed to stop our backyard Bible burnings and to try to focus on material that is more violent, up-to-date, and preferably, with better visuals.

A week later we called the hot line to report we'd seen *Cobra, Raw Deal,* three episodes of *Miami Vice,* and a presidential address on the importance of Star Wars, and felt we now had material that was not only damaging to women but disrespectful of human life in all forms, male and female, born and unborn. "But is it dirty?" asked a weary commissioner. "You know, *sexy?*" And we had to admit that neither the sight of Arnold Schwarzenegger without a shirt nor the president in pancake makeup had ever aroused in us any feeling other than mild gastric distress.

Now I think we're finally getting the hang of it. "The problem, as identified by the Meese commission, isn't violence, sexism, or even sexual violence. The problem is sex, particularly those varieties of sex that might in any way involve women. So in the last few weeks, our citizens antismut group has short-circuited six vibrators, burned 300 of those lurid little inserts found in Tampax boxes, and shredded half the local supply of *Our Bodies, Ourselves.* It's a tough job, believe me, but as Ed Meese keeps telling us, someone's got to do it.

THE FOUNDING OF THE NATIONAL WOMEN'S STUDIES ASSOCIATION

Robin Wright

The last good year of Women's Studies, at least from a student's perspective, may have been 1976. Those were the days of consciousness-raising groups, self-righteousness, and papers for classes that began, "Growing up female in our male-dominated society has made me a second-class citizen. If things are ever going to change, we have to destroy the patriarchy."

San Jose State University was one of the first to offer graduate degrees in Women's Studies, and I was one of the first to sign up. Most students choose classes (after eliminating those before 10:00 A.M.) based upon a professor's background, perspective, and area of expertise. I, on the other hand, developed the Birkenstock Approach. I took classes only from professors who had at least one pair of Birkenstock sandals. You could always count on at least half of the semester discussing how the class should be run and the other half discussing how the structure was oppressive.

Somewhere during the Birkenstock era, a change started taking place. There was a movement to make Women's Studies a real

> **"Ann Richards is smart and tough and funny and pretty, which I notice just confuses the hell out of people."**
>
> **Molly Ivins**

Emily Kirkland Musil, at age ten, displays a homemade rattle of paper plates, ribbons, and rice to celebrate the Tenth Anniversary of the National Women's Studies Association (NWSA).

Inscribed on the rattle:
"Women's lives should rattle with excitement,"
and
"We can shake off 'that' role."

academic discipline. Yep, we are talking seminars in Feminist Theory, dialectic of this, pedagogy of that. The way I heard it, the Women's Caucus of the Modern Language Association met and out popped the National Women's Studies Association. Ah, our founding mothers. A group of brilliant-looking women gathered around a table in some oak-panelled room and signed the NWSA Declaration of Existence.

San Jose State University faculty member Sybil Weir was among the signers, and she agreed to be responsible for the logistics of putting together NWSA's Founding Conference. When Sybil returned to campus, her excitement was truly contagious. Flyers sped around announcing the first planning meeting, and the usual twenty or so students, faculty, and Women's Center groupies gathered together. We pulled up a pillow or two (remember this was 1976) and got started. Since SJSU cold not accommodate the conference, an alternative site, the University of San Francisco, was chosen. We would be putting this thing together some sixty miles away. Doesn't that sound like a good time?

Sybil was brilliant in the way she enlisted our assistance. "An inspirational idea translated into action . . . be a part of history . . . earn class credit." Hands went up as if we were planning a pot-luck dinner. We volunteered for tasks, thinking we could put in a few hours of work and then sit back and watch history being made. As it turned out, I don't think any of us sat down for a whole semester.

My part was the Book Fair and Exhibits. I thought I had gotten off easy—hustle up a few tables, whip up some signs, rent some tablecloths for a classy touch, and I'm out of there. I figured this job could only be topped by being in charge of hospitality for Meg Christian, Holly Near, and Margie Adam. Someone else had nabbed that one.

It took about a day, long enough for my first meeting with Sybil, to burst my bubble. I had never been to an academic conference before. Publishers were paying big bucks, Sybil informed me, and certain standards would have to be maintained. We must present a professional, well-organized image so that they would feel that their money was well spent. (I thought I had covered that with the tablecloths.) Also, she added, some people would want to drop off a few flyers for the conference attendees to pick up. That seemed reasonable—one table ought to do the job.

The planning crew consisted of some dedicated Women's Studies faculty like Fanny Rinn, Ellen Boneparth, and Marilyn Fleener, who always seemed to be in thought, you know, making big decisions. There were also about fifteen students who always seemed to be carrying things. I knew the conference was getting bigger because the faculty members were getting very stressed and the students were getting huge biceps. The work mounted. The excitement grew. A conference with six last names of Freewoman, a handful with names of Greek goddesses, and a full ten percent without any last names, was not going to be dull!

I was full on into this Book Fair stuff, showing incredible flexibility by accommodating publishers' and exhibitors' requests and squeezing more and more tables into a very small space. We loaded truck after truck, and finally, after innumerable trips up what became known as the Sybil Weir Memorial Freeway, we made the last trek up to the University of San Francisco.

Looking back, Sybil's rather large bottle of scotch should have been a clue as to what was going to happen, but we chose to ignore it. When the first exhibitors started arriving, I was the model of graciousness and understanding. "Flyers, no problem. Just put them on that table." "You want a table facing north because Venus is rising? Well, that's understandable, let me switch you." That went on for ten hours straight. I finally checked the conference registration form to see if bringing flyers was a requirement. Had 1977 been declared the International Year of the Flyer? My "one table" had mushroomed to five, to six, to a hundred . . .

About 11 P.M. I sat down for a few minutes. Out of the corner of my eye, I caught sight of a woman slowly dismounting from a Harley Davidson. (She rode that motorcycle right into the Exhibit Hall.) This woman was, no fooling, six-foot-five, in full black leather and boots with a huge black helmet—Steven Spielberg's inspiration for Darth Vader. Well, she sauntered over to me, picked me up by my collar and said, "Where can I put my flyers?"

"Anywhere you'd like."

Then a group of Seattle Radical Women burst in demanding two tables. I tried to explain that people *paid* to exhibit, but after a thirty-minute struggle I gave up. I hunted down the bottle of scotch and decided the Book Fair should be run by consensus. Even so a resolution was proposed to end fascism in the Book Exhibit areas.

There were *a lot* of resolutions put forth during those four conference days. I personally made fifty trips to the printers. With the parking situation in San Francisco you can understand how much I appreciated the opportunity to make all those trips. After the second day, I finally got smart. I found a No Parking barricade and attached a sign that read "RESERVED FOR MEG CHRISTIAN AND HOLLY NEAR." People started hanging out there after a while but I didn't care. I had my private parking stall and there were fewer people in the Delegate Assembly cranking out bizarre resolutions. Since I was spending so much time at the printer, I had a chance to read some of them: A resolution to end hunger in the world? A resolution to pay all travel and lodging expenses of future conferences for

> " . . . no man can any more represent a woman at the polls than he can in a millinery shop."
>
> **Dorothy Dix**

THE ONE WHO VOTES

(From *Life*, 1913. Reprinted by permission of Paul Petticrew.)

any woman who requested it? A resolution that would give the Third World Caucus power to veto any resolution passed by the association?

There was always a group of women in the front of the Delegate Assembly huddled in deep discussion. They were the Coordinating Council members, and they were always huddled. They huddled in the dining room, they huddled in the lobby, they huddled in the elevators. The last I saw of them they were nervously huddled at the airport.

NWSA was an organization that was challenging, stimulating and out-right fun. I was thoroughly hooked. I made an easy transition from the scotch bottle to the North Pacific Region Organizing Committee and, yes, eventually to the Coordinating Council where I huddled with the best of them. Incidentally, I always make it a practice to hold a private moment of silence for the Book Fair and Exhibit Coordinator, and I *never* bring flyers.

MEDICAL LOGIC

Hazel Houlihingle

There's a new trend in the United States. Generals are going to medical conventions. It's because of their interest in Pentagonorrhea—a disease first described by Flo Kennedy. There was a rumor that physicians were classifying Pentagonorrhea with herpes, syphilis, AIDS, and other VD, so the generals wanted to explain that Pentagonorrhea is a *necessary* social disease.

After a few conventions, however, the generals found other reasons to attend. At medical workshops on Profit-Effectiveness, they discovered that medical prices rise even faster than military costs, and they're hanging around to study medical monetary techniques.

The military are not the only outsiders moving in. The Felon's Association has a regular caucus at the AMA. I'm not talking about medical felons. I'm talking about run-of-the-mill, ordinary, all-American crooks. They go to the meetings to study medical logic.

Medical logic? Felony? Let me explain.

The Felon's Association actually got the idea from me.

In 1984 I was mugged on 8th Avenue in New York City, and in 1985 I had an unnecessary hysterectomy—which, by the way, is a lot more common than mugging. Anyhow, on the Phil Donahue show, I said that I enjoyed my mugging much more than my unnecessary surgery.

"Really?" said Phil.

"Yeah," I said. "What does a mugger get? Only what's in your purse. What does a surgeon get? He cleans out your bank account, you sell your house, you *borrow* . . . Did you every hear of a mugger making you *borrow* to insure the best possible mugging?"

"But Hazel, you've *gotta* be frightened by a mugger. He might knock you down, and . . ."

"He did!" I said. "The mugger knocked me down, and the surgeon knocked me out. From the mugger I got a bruised elbow. From Dr. Gooser I got drugged, cut open, ovaries taken out, sick for

months, *still* sick . . .''

''You've *gotta* be kidding.''

''When three gynecologists told me the surgery was uncalled for, I asked for my money back. Ha! Never mind it was fraud. Dr. Gooser performed an operation, so by medical logic, he get's paid.''

Medical logic. That's the key phrase. Someone from the Felon's Association who saw the show picked it up. He figured, if healthy people (using medical logic) pay surgeons for unnecessary surgeries, why can't *banks* (using medical logic) pay robbers for unnecessary robberies? Think about that. The answer, he said, was because banks are not surgeons. So the Felon's Caucus came up with a position paper to expedite bank robberies. First, they argue, since bankers are as respectable as physicians, banks should also be allowed to use medical logic. The paper gets really sophistical (academia has no monopoly on sophistry), so I won't go through it blow by blow. Here's the conclusion:

> When a surgeon performs unnecessary surgery, botches it, and the patient dies, the family not only *pays* the surgeon, they thank him. Using medical logic, banks should *thank* robbers instead of chasing them. And further, they should pay felons for *attempted* robberies (which are like failed surgeries)—with *added* bonuses when nobody dies.

The Felon's Caucus is also interested in medical *language*. They like the way MDs call their customers ''patients,'' and they're adopting the term ''patient'' for victims of crime. Most crime victims, they say, like most medical victims, don't complain or file charges, so their customers are certainly as ''patient'' as medical customers.

Another expression the Felon's Caucus likes is ''Side Effect.'' What is a side effect? When an MD prescribes a drug, everything bad that happens is a side effect. You know the routine. You go to the doctor for a headache, and he prescribes some pills—which you take. Next week your hair's falling out, you're vomiting, and you're so sick you've forgotten the headache. You call the doctor and tell him your new symptoms. He looks at his chart.

''Lovely,'' he says, ''the medicine worked.''

''But my hair . . .''

''Forget it, that's just a side effect.''

''And the vomiting . . .''

''Another side effect. Don't worry.''

What's *good* about a side effect is, it's not important, it doesn't count. The doctor doesn't care about it, so neither should you. In reality, though, you hate the side effects so much that you develop a fondness for your headache, and you stop taking the pills so you can get your headache back. By then you feel so good without the side effects, your headache's gone too. (You don't dream of accusing the physician of poisoning you—because poisoning is a direct effect and you only had side effects.)

The *direct* effect of taking enough poison is, we die. The only time that's not true is when it's prescribed by an MD for a broken toe or something, and then the death is a side effect. You get the picture, anything that happens that the MD doesn't like, he gets to call a side effect. Other people can't do that. For example, housepainters. When they finish painting your living room, they can't call any paint they've dripped on the floor a side effect. (Does

(From ''*Mercy, it's the revolution and I'm in my bathrobe,*'' copyright © 1982 by Nicole Hollander, St. Martin's Press.)

❝Feminism is the radical notion that women are people.❞

Cheris Kramarae and Paula Treichler

that mean our floors are more important than our bodies?)

The Reagan administration, by the way, also likes medical language. They would love to call Ronnie's slips and faux pas a mere *side effective* consequence of the President's press conferences. And the illegal money to the Contras is just a side effect of Congress's failure to vote them additional funds. But the AMA won't let the White House use their language: they want to retain its credibility.

The generals are also thinking side effectively, and they're really excited. They've been depressed ever since Carl Sagan spilled the beans about nuclear winter. Madison Avenue did *not* come up with a good gimmick for their Learning-to-Love-Nuclear-Winter Campaign.

"We should have come here first," General Oiler told me. "Doctor's can sell anything. Think of it," he said, his eyes twinkling with boyish excitement. "The survivors of nuclear war come out into the dark, cold, barren landscape, their Geiger counters clicking away—and they're *happy*, they're cheerful, because they know the Winter doesn't count: it's all just a *side effect*."

I didn't want to deflate Oiler, but no way would physicians let generals use medical logic. "Generals have their own gobble-de-gook," Dr. Puregood told me, "and we're going to stay side-effectively safe."

HOW THE WOMEN MOPPED UP COALDALE

Mary Harris Jones

Not far from Shamokin, in a little mountain town, the priest was holding a meeting when I went in. He was speaking in the church. I spoke in an open field. The priest told the men to go back and obey their masters and their reward would be in Heaven. He denounced the strikers as children of darkness. The miners left the church in a body and marched over to my meeting.

"Boys," I said, "this strike is called in order that you and your wives and your little ones may get a bit of Heaven before you die."

We organized the entire camp.

The fight went on. In Coaldale, in the Hazelton district, the miners were not permitted to assemble in any hall. It was necessary to win the strike in that district that the Coaldale miners be organized.

I went to a nearby mining town that was thoroughly organized and asked the women if they would help me get the Coaldale men out. This was in McAdoo. I told them to leave their men at home to take care of the family. I asked them to put on their kitchen clothes and bring mops and brooms with them and a couple of tin pans. We marched over the mountains fifteen miles, beating on the tin pans as if they were cymbals. At three o'clock in the morning we met the Crack Thirteen of the militia, patroling the roads to Coaldale. The colonel of the regiment said "Halt! Move back!"

I said, "Colonel, the working men of America will not halt nor

(Reprinted from *Dykes to Watch Out For*, © 1986 by Alison Bechdel, Firebrand Books.)

will they ever go back. The working man is going forward!''

"I'll charge bayonets," said he.

"On whom?"

"On your people."

"We are not enemies," said I. "We are just a band of working women whose brothers and husbands are in a battle for bread. We want our brothers in Coaldale to join us in our fight. We are here on the mountain road for our children's sake, for the nation's sake. We are not going to hurt anyone and surely you would not hurt us."

They kept us there till daybreak and when they saw the army of women in kitchen aprons, with dishpans and mops, they laughed and let us pass. An army of strong mining women makes a wonderfully spectacular picture.

Well, when the miners in the Coaldale camp started to go to work they were met by the McAdoo women who were beating on their pans and shouting, "Join the union! Join the union!"

They joined, every last man of them, and we got so enthusiastic that we organized the street car men who promised to haul no scabs for the coal companies. As there were no other groups to organize we marched over the mountains home, beating on our pans and singing patriotic songs.

Meanwhile President Mitchell and all his organizers were sleeping in the Valley Hotel over in Hazelton. They knew nothing of our march into Coaldale until the newspaper men telephoned to him that "Mother Jones was raising hell up in the mountains with a bunch of wild women!"

He, of course, got nervous. He might have gotten more nervous if he had known how we made the mine bosses go home and how we told their wives to clean them up and make decent American citizens out of them. How we went around to the kitchen of the hotel where the militia were quartered and ate the breakfast that was on the table for the soldiers.

When I got back to Hazelton, Mitchell looked at me with surprise. I was worn out. Coaldale had been a strenuous night and morning and its thirty mile tramp. I assured Mitchell that no one had been hurt and no property injured. The military had acted like human beings. They took the matter as a joke. They enjoyed the morning's fun. I told him how scared the sheriff had been. He had been talking to me without knowing who I was.

"Oh Lord," he said, "that Mother Jones is sure a dangerous woman."

"Why don't you arrest her?" I asked him.

"Oh Lord. I couldn't. I'd have that mob of women with their mops and brooms after me and the jail ain't big enough to hold them all. They'd mop the life out of a fellow!"

Mr. Mitchell said, "My God, Mother, did you get home safe? What did you do?"

"I got five thousand men out and organized them. We had time left over so we organized the street car men and they will not haul any scabs into camp."

"Did you get hurt, Mother?"

"No, we did the hurting."

"Didn't the superintendents' bosses get after you?"

"No, we got after them. Their wives and our women were yelling around like cats. It was a great fight."

(From *The Autobiography of Mother Jones*, 1925.)

Grabasket

MOGUL IS MOBIL—a postcard announcement released in 1973 by artist Susan Mogul stating that "after three feminist tries, I was issued my first driver's license. . . ."

THE SUICIDE NOTE

Jane Wagner

Oh, Lonnie, you look drenched, but doesn't the rain feel good?
I've had the most extraordinary evening.
Waiter, two brandies.
Since I've seen you, so much has happened
I feel like a new person.

No, it's not my new fingertip.

Good, though, isn't it?

No, this evening, first this little boy played the violin—
absolute genius!

Before I forget, here's that article I had Xeroxed for you—all
about boredom, remember?

Oh, no, no, no, no. Sorry, that's not it. That's my suicide note.

Well, not *my* suicide note . . .
It's one I've been keeping because,
well, I found it,
and I haven't been able to throw it away, because . . .
well, I don't know exactly, it's the strangest effect . . .
Where shall I start?

When I was in L.A. I found this suicide note in the
street where my exercise class is. I don't know why I
picked it up. You know, it's more my nature to step *over*
things.

But something compelled me . . .

I thought
it could be a sign.
Lately, I seem to look for signs: the closer I get to
menopause, the more metaphysical I'm becoming.

I had no idea who it belonged to. *Anyone* living in *that*
neighborhood had *reason* to want to end it all. I couldn't
bring myself to throw it away. There should be a
service one could use in cases like this, but there isn't.

I was saddened by what she said in the note—
but I felt even worse when I realized that losing the
note could only *add* to her feelings of low self-esteem.
Further evidence she could never do
anything right. I should
imagine there's only one thing more depressing than writing a
suicide note,
and that's *losing* the one you've just written.

Photo by Susan Storch

Evi Seidman, Stand-Up Environmentalist as Groucho Groundhog, an underground activist who works "at the grass roots level."

For a while, I kept it in my wallet. And then I grew concerned.
Well, supposing I got hit by a car, or, in that neighborhood, a
beer bottle, I go unconscious, the paramedics come, they
discover the note, they think it's mine and they give it to
Freddie.

Well, it would seem very strange that I just happened to be
carrying someone else's suicide note.

So I started keeping it at home.
In one of those fireproof boxes with my important papers. Then
the thought, again, what if something happened?

The note would be discovered and be given great importance
because it was with my important papers.

So I began moving it around the house.
Lonnie, I am becoming so forgetful. I was so afraid I would
misplace it. So I wrote myself a note telling me where I'd put
it.

Now I had the suicide note *and* the note telling me *where* the
suicide note was hidden.
So I have decided it is best kept in my purse. But don't
  worry—
I've written a note explaining the whole business.

Go ahead and say it: I am *possessed*. What is it about this
phantom person that is so compelling?
She seemed so fragile and yet courageous, too. Ironically,
there is in this suicide note more feeling, more forgiveness,
more capacity for life . . .
Whatever this person is, or was, she was *not* jaded. She was
not bored. Her only real complaint was something she called
"false hopes."
If she *did* commit suicide, it would be out of feeling too
much—not too little.

There's hardly a trace of bitterness or petty *anything*. That's
really something, don't you think?
I mean, in writing a suicide note, the *real* person must come
out.

There was nothing dramatic—
no big tragedy,
no terminal illness—
it seems, just,
a lifetime of being . . .

dismissed . . . by everyone, apparently . . .
except me.

Lonnie, this experience has had such an effect on me. Made me
aware of just how closed off I've been to people's suffering,
even my own.

"**Why be normal?**"

Z. Budapest

129

This evening, after the concert, I saw these two prostitutes on the corner . . . talking with this street crazy, this bag lady. And I actually stopped to watch them. Even though it had begun to rain.

And I remembered something I think it was Kafka wrote about having been filled with a sense of endless astonishment at simply seeing a group of people cheerfully assembled.

I saw this young man go up, obviously from out of town, and he asked them, "How do I get to Carnegie Hall?" And the bag lady said, "Practice!" And we caught each other's eyes—the prostitutes, the bag lady, the young man and I.
We all burst out laughing.

There we were, laughing together, in the pouring rain, and then the bag lady did the dearest thing—
she offered me her umbrella hat.

She said that I needed it more than she did, because one side of my hair was beginning to
shrink.

And, Lonnie, I did the strangest thing.

I took it!

"We need new curses, like 'Audit you, Buddy!'"

Elayne Boosler

A JOB FOR WILSON TOPAZ

Sheila Ortiz Taylor

'm Wilson Topaz, student of the dance.
Actually I'm a student of a lot more than that. I watch. I'm taking notes. Nothing escapes me.
Scared you, didn't I? You're not scared because I'm six foot three in my stocking feet. You're scared because I'm black, gay, and six foot three in my stocking feet. Right? See, I'm watching.
So you want to know about Arden Benbow. Well, I went to work for Arden right after my little altercation with the University of California. It was about money. They made out it was over a point of honor, but it was really over money, of course. But that's another story.
All summer I had worked at the Hollywood Bowl, sometimes dancing, sometimes hawking opera glasses. Mostly it was opera glasses. Oh, I have talent. It isn't that. But I tend to stand out in a

line of gents in tuxedos, or anywhere else, for that matter. The last choreographer I worked with said I was larger than life. I take that as a compliment.

So I was out of work, the university had declined my loan, as I have said, and I was a month behind in my rent. It looked like my mother's worst fears were about to be realized.

Everybody's mother has a worst fear for her child. I guess mothers worry that their daughters will become whores and that their sons will be gay. Or maybe it's fathers who worry about this last possibility. Anyway, since I had already explored and embraced that worst fear, my mother moved along to the next available worst fear, that I would become a drag queen. Actually I haven't got the mentality of a drag queen, but she doesn't understand that. And because any fear is real to the person that's got it, I try to take hers seriously. You know? So she was the other reason I had to find work in a hurry.

But there just wasn't much work around. Especially not for someone black, six foot three in his stocking feet, with an aversion to violence. Without this last qualification, I could have had plenty of work.

Well, one morning on my way to ballet, I passed the bulletin board next to the drinking fountain and something caught my eye, a blue index card, carefully lettered, saying

> LESBIAN MOTHER
> needs child care in own home.
> Small salary, board, private
> room. Equal opportunity
> employer.

and then her phone number. There was a lot there to mull around. That night I gave her a call.

"Hello," says a kid's voice. Then there are sounds of scuffling and another voice off in the distance asking who is it.

"Who is this?" asks the first voice.

"Wilson Topaz."

"It's Joan Baez," screams the kid's voice to the voice off in the distance.

"Listen, kid," I say, getting pissed, "do I sound like Joan Baez?"

"What?" says the kid. Then the receiver hits the floor, and I am on the point of hanging up, when the voice of reason asks can it help me. I don't need to tell you about Arden Benbow's voice, if you've heard it. Like Ben Gay on a sore muscle. It's the muse in tails.

"Hello," I say, "are you the lesbian mother?" Just testing her, you see. I really knew she was, on account of her voice. It made you think of unicorns in moonlight.

"Yes it is," she answers, so cool, like I had asked if she was Golda Meir, and she was. I figure she has not been around much.

"I saw your ad."

"Yes, I know." There is barking in the background, and scuffing sounds, then the lady issuing directives with her hand over the receiver. Then, "Look, Mr. . . . ."

"Wilson, Topaz Wilson."

"Mr. Wilson. It would be best if you came out here—we live in the Valley—for an interview. Can you do that tomorrow? Late afternoon?"

By now I was beginning to get cold feet. How did I know I even liked children? I had always liked them in the past, but people took them away when I got tired of them. There would be none of that in this situation. When I am panicked my subconscious floods my conscious, like high tide into the streets of Venice, and I am likely to say anything.

"You should know that I'm a drag queen."

There was a pause, one of those brief ones that feels long, and an undertone of barks, laughs, and squeals. Then she says, "Well, Mr. Wilson, I see no reason why we can't arrange your hours around your job schedule."

That pretty much did it. If she was willing to accept me in the costume of my mother's worst fantasy, then I was willing to accept the yelling and barking. At least on a trial basis.

(From *Faultline*, Naiad Press, 1982.)

IS THIS A PIZZA JOINT OR THE FBI?

Margery Eliscu

Illustration by Peter Farrow

Apparently, pizza-to-go is such big business these days you need a Dun and Bradstreet rating to order by phone.

My daughter tells me she called her favorite pizza joint and asked them to get a pepperoni pizza ready for her to pick up in thirty minutes.

"Please spell your full name and give me your address and phone number," said the clerk at the other end.

"I don't want you to mail it out," she said. "I'm coming by for it."

"We need your address and phone number so we can verify who you say you are and that you actually live there."

My daughter thought this over. Then she said, "Is there a pizza raid going on? Is this an undercover pizza ring or have I reached the usual pizzeria I call?"

"New policy," said the clerk. "You want a pizza, we need ID, address and phone number. We'll call right back to confirm it was really you who ordered."

"I'm not home. That's why I'm calling," she explained. "I'm at St. Luke's Cathedral at a rehearsal. I'm going to leave here shortly, call for my daughter at her dance class, stop by the supermarket briefly . . . and pick up my pepperoni pizza.''

"Can you go home first and call us?" asked the clerk.

"You pick up my daughter at dancing class, I'll go home!" she said angrily.

"We don't make any deliveries anymore," he said.

"Then call back here at the church. I don't attend here, but maybe I can find a member of the clergy who will give me a character reference. I'll get him to guarantee that I am drooling for a pepperoni pizza."

"We need to call you at your home," said the pizza clerk. "You have no idea how many people say they want a pizza and then leave us holding the box."

(From *Russell Baker, Erma Bombeck & Me*, © 1987 by Lance Tapley, Publisher [Yankee Books].)

MY LIFE AS A MAN

Alice Kahn

~~~~~~

I can't make it in this man's world. Life would be so much easier if I had a wife. Life would be so much easier if I were a man.

What modern woman hasn't had these thoughts? Those of us struggling to lift ourselves up by our bra straps often feel the deck is stacked against us. Men don't have to "prove" anything. Men can do an OK job; women have to be great.

Men were taught from childhood to be aggressive; we were taught to be nice. Men are encouraged to go for it; we are encouraged to lose weight.

In an attempt to understand what the world looks like to someone who has all these advantages, I decided to be Man for a Day. What would happen, I wondered, if I walked a mile in his big leather shoes? A bit of makeup, a few new items of clothing, a different haircut and—voila—little Alice became Big Al.

The first thing I noticed was the frightened look on my husband's face when he woke up and saw me standing there dousing myself with Stud, the aftershave for men who want to make a stink.

I was about to say, "You get those buns out of bed and make me some breakfast" when I realized I hadn't made him breakfast since our fifth anniversary. Sure, for a few years I cooked, cleaned and was his all-around love slave. But after a while, it became every person for itself.

Later, one of the kids took a look at me in my baggy, pleated pants, felt hat, suspenders and tie and said, "Mom, don't try to be cool. Maybe Diane Keaton can get away with that, but it just isn't you."

As soon as they were all out of the house, instead of my usual routine of not cleaning up and not doing the laundry, I put on my mustache and went out.

As I walked down the street I heard a man who passed me say, "Who was that? Madonna?"

"You've been watching too much Joan Rivers," said his companion. "That was Wayne Newton."

I could pass.

At the office, I introduced myself to the guys as Big Al, the

> "Bread that must be sliced with an ax is bread that is too nourishing."
>
> **Fran Lebowitz**

> "Anonymous is a 'prolific female author.'"
>
> **Cheris Kramarae and Paula Treichler**

new guy.

"Hey, Big Al the New Guy," one of the fellas said, "want to go deer hunting with us after work? We're gonna kill for a couple of hours, then pick up some babes and party."

"Sorry," I said. "Can't make it."

"Whatsa matter, Al? You a sissy?"

As if that weren't enough, the boss called me in at 9:15. "Scotch, Al?" he said, offering me the bottle from the brown paper bag on his desk.

I declined. "Whatsa matter, Al—can't handle it?"

At lunchtime, I went to my favorite bar and grill. Instead of getting the Dieter's Delite, I told the waitress: "Give me the biggest, bloodiest, rawest hunk of meat you've got, a plate of fries, double cole slaw and some chocolate whipped-cream pie."

"No wonder you're so thin," she said. "You eat like a bird."

After lunch I walked over to the bookstore, hoping to find something hard-boiled to carry around but not actually read.

"Where's the men's section?" I asked the clerk.

"We have no men's section," she answered.

"But that's not fair," I said indignantly. "You have a women's section."

"Look, pal," she said to me, her voice dripping with sarcasm. "We consider the rest of the store the men's section."

Back at work, I noticed Marge, the gofer, staring at me. I stared back. I was certain she'd guess my identity.

"Marge, guess what's under here?" I said, smiling at her.

She stood up on her desk and started screaming, "Eek, a pervert."

My sexual-harassment hearing is scheduled for next week.

When the boss heard about the charges, he offered me a raise. And the guys are taking me out to dinner. Phyllis, a gal in the secretarial pool, winked at me and said she would testify on my behalf. Then she asked if I would take her to the annual spring dance.

I think I'll wear a tux.

(Reprinted from *Luncheon at the Cafe Ridiculous*, Simon and Schuster, 1990, by permission of Alice Kahn.)

(Reprinted from *Heresies* no. 18/19, 1985.)

Handy Hints

...for that long, intimate phone call....

① Take one maxi-pad

② Take the paper off the back

③ stick pad onto telephone... Create your own designs with felt pens!

BINGO! you can enjoy your call with EXTRA COMFORT...

How to make a shoulder pad for your telephone...

SOUTHERN CALIFORNIA

Kate Clinton

Before I went to Southern California, the word *relationship* did not bother me at all. But now I would almost rather have a sharp stick in my eye than hear the word "relationship." After living in Southern California, you find you are totally unable to utter a word without adding "ing." Suddenly I was saying things like knowing, growing, showing, caring, sharing, seeing, being. A couple of minutes and I was into networking, nurturing, connecting. Before long I was touching base, giving space, amazing Grace!

I never talked like that before.

(Adapted from a recording, copyright © 1985 by Kate Clinton and WhysCrack Records.)

THE HIGH COST OF NOT BEING A TRANSSEXUAL

Cathy N. Davidson

A few years ago I wrote a novel called *Stet,* a parodic reworking of the Tiresias story in contemporary terms. In the original version Tiresias is turned into a woman for seven years as a punishment for watching two snakes copulate. Later the restored male Tiresias reports, "if parts of love's pleasure . . . be numbered as ten, nine go to women and one goes to men." In *Stet,* Terry Soutenu hates being a boy and as an adult has a sex-change operation. The novel alternates between present-tense female chapters and retrospective past-tense male chapters. In the male chapters, Terry wants to be a woman; in the female chapters, she evolves from sterotypical Schlafly-esque femininity to radical (if always funny) feminism. The novel manages to parody and, at the same time, support a whole range of sexual preferences and behaviors and, as my agent said, it probably offends everyone at one point or another (and especially white male heterosexuals).

One day an editor from a major New York publishing house called my agent's office. The editor had read the first half of *Stet* with great excitement, in one sitting, and thought she wanted to publish it because, she said, it was the first book she'd read by a transsexual that did not buy into the stereotypical notion of femininity.

"It looks like she's going to bid on it, Cathy," one of the assistants at my agent's firm phoned to tell me, equally excited.

"Fantastic! Everyone else is afraid of it and she'll take it! I'm going

to be a real published novelist!'' I gushed and crowed. Then reality set in. ''Wait! Did you say *by* a transsexual?'' I queried.

''Well,'' he stammered, ''at least think about it. You know, *roman à clef*, exposé, nonfiction novel. . . .''

''Hoax,'' I groaned.

It was a pretty fancy way of asking me if I'd pose as a surgically womanized being. I suppose there are worse ways to get a first novel published. Who wouldn't be tempted? Then I envisioned scenes with my friends (''Cathy, we never knew . . .''), my grandmother (''Pink is for girls, blue for boys. Period''), my tenure committee (''Of course this will mean a negative vote from the affirmative action officer''), my son (*''Dad?''*).

''I don't know that I can do it!'' my voice sounded small and tentative.

Sure, rejection slips would be a thing of the past—but did I really want to make the cover of *National Enquirer?* (''Best-selling Transsexual Author Reveals Secret Life as Hetero Assistant Prof!'') My imagination suddenly offered up a vision of my house picketed by high-heeled authentics. ''SHE WANTS THE PERKS BUT NOT THE PAIN!'' one sign read. ''C. N. DAVIDSON, REAL FRAU, TRANSSEXUAL FRAUD!''

And, at last, my writerly principles intervened. ''What kind of editor," I asked imperiously, "mistakes parody for realism? Do I really want to publish my masterpiece with such a . . ."

"Cathy, cut the crap. Yes or no?"

"No. I couldn't pass."

"*Any* woman could pass."

"I'm sorry, the novel has to stand on its own. As is. Stet."

When my agent conveyed my decision to the editor (of course she could publish the novel, but I was a naturally born woman), she was furious. She'd been tricked, betrayed, insulted. It took her six months to read the second half of the novel, and she returned it with a terse rejection slip explicitly offering *not* to read subsequent work. To this day, *Stet* remains unpublished.

PSYCHIC ECONOMICS

Mary Kay Blakely

I used to be an unbeliever. I questioned the integrity of an economic system that valued women's work only half as much as men's. I was—and this seems almost preposterous to admit now—dissatisfied with the lot of women.

Before I reached enlightenment, I suffered from a common form of math anxiety caused by statistics from the Department of Labor. I was easily susceptible to depression whenever the words "supply and demand" came up in conversation. I kept getting lost in the void of the earnings gap. Years of investigation about women revealed many things to me, but didn't make sense of those numbers: Women earn 59 percent of what men earn. Until last week, I was like a haunted woman—devils of injustice chasing me, demons of inequity plaguing me.

My conversion happened unexpectedly, during a business meeting with a highly placed administrator. I had noticed—because skeptics habitually pay attention to damning facts—that the women employed by his prestigious institution were being paid much less money than the men. Like most unbelievers I was there to complain about the inequity. That's the major problem with those who don't have the gift of faith in our economic system. They have their visions trained on the temporal facts of their lives.

The discussion began predictably enough. With benign paternal tolerance, he reviewed the intricate principles of economics, the baffling nuances of budgets, the confounding factors behind the salary schedules. With the monosyllabic vocabulary educators use to address slow learners, he explained the familiar platitudes.

He invoked the dogma of salary surveys—the objective instruments used to determine what "the market will bear." They prove, beyond a shadow of doubt, that women workers are "a dime a dozen." That's reality, he reported almost regretfully, that's how life is outside of Eden. Practitioners of sound business—the members of the faith, so to speak—can in good conscience pay them no more. If he didn't adhere to the precepts of salary surveys, it would cause economic chaos. Other women, in other institutions, would

> "To explain the gaps in my memory from ages five to twenty-seven, I usually say, 'Well, I was married at the time.'"
>
> Nicole Hollander

begin to think they were worth more, too. The brethren in other administrations would expel him from the faith.

"You have to think about what the job is worth, not the person in it," he cautioned me. It always gets you into trouble, thinking about what a person is worth. He warned me against engaging in the fallacy of "comparing apples and oranges," a comparison odious to the members of the faith. It is only the unbelievers, the kumquats, who try to argue for the fruits of their labors. Mixing the categories would produce uncontrollable hybrids on the salary scale. Men are men and women are women and their paychecks are just further evidence of the vast biological differences, the powerful influence of the X and Y chromosomes.

I confess, I had heard these tenets of the faith many times before. It was the kind of conversation that might inspire the vision of a

(From *The Whole Enchilada*, copyright © 1986 by Nicole Hollander, St. Martin's Press.)

lawsuit. So it wasn't with an open heart that I asked the question one more time. How could he accept women's invaluable contributions to the success of his institution, witness their obvious dedication, and withhold their just rewards?

He paused, regarding me carefully, deliberating, apparently, on whether I was prepared to hear the truth, to embrace the amazing mystery of women's wages. Then slowly, respectfully, he revealed the fantastic reason.

Women came seeking positions with an intense longing for work, but with a paucity of credentials and experience. They were filled with gratitude when they were offered a job. They worked in a pleasant environment, doing meaningful work, and had the privilege of writing the name of the prestigious institution on their résumés. They received such an extraordinary sense of well-being, it would be almost a violation of female sensibilities to compensate them with cold, hard cash. Instead, they received something much more valuable; they earned a "psychic income."

I heard my voice becoming hysterical. Hysteria is not at all uncommon during conversions. I was loud—perhaps I was even shouting—when I asked him how much of his income was "psychic." Like many doubters, I didn't immediately see the light. I thought one of us was mad.

But not an hour later, enlightenment came. I was in a car dealership, chatting with the amiable mechanic who had repaired my transmission. He seemed to enjoy his job, especially when he handed me the bill. I gasped, knowing that the balance in my checkbook wouldn't cover the charge. Then I remembered my "psychic income" and that people who love their work, who are dedicated to it, are better paid with congratulations and a pat on the back. I told him what a wonderful job he did, how much I appreciated it. And then I wrote a "psychic check."

Suddenly, I was filled with the spirit. A happiness, a release flooded over me. I realized that every act of spending my "psychic income" was an act of faith. I had so much catching up to do. I worked steadily to increase my state of grace. Immediately, I applied for a loan at the employee credit union at the prestigious institution, authorizing payments through "psychic payroll deductions." I used my "psychic credit cards" to charge two pairs of spiritual Adidas for my kids, whose real toes were poking through their real tennis shoes.

I was filled with a fervor to spread the Word. At a rally of working women, I brought them the message of "psychic incomes," and many converts came into the fold.

Nurses, who had an extraordinary love for their work, felt "psychic bonuses" coming to them. Their sense of self-esteem expanded miraculously, and they no longer bowed down to the false gods in the hospitals.

Clerical workers grasped the theory of "psychic work for psychic pay" and began typing only intangible letters, filing transcendental folders, and making celestial phone calls.

Prior to their conversions, working mothers thought they had to do all the housework, because their earnings were only half of their husbands' salaries. But when they learned how to bank on their "psychic incomes," they never cooked dinner again. They served their families supernatural pot roasts.

Of course, everyone will not accept the gift of the Word. There are those who will try to persecute us for practicing our faith. We must learn to smile serenely at the unfortunate creditors who lack the vision. We must have a charitable attitude toward the bill collectors whose interests are rooted in temporal assets. Beware of the pharisees who pay spiritual salaries but still demand physical work.

And judge not the angry women who file the interminable lawsuits, who still rail against the status quo. Their daily struggle to exist prevents them from accepting the good news. Remember that there, but for the gift of "psychic economics," go we.

(From *The New York Times*, March 19, 1981. Reprinted by permission of Mary Kay Blakely.)

WHAT'S MY LINE?

Teresa Bloomingdale

O ne of my pet peeves is the registration form which asks for "Occupation of Spouse." Since this particular spouse is unoccupied, I never know what to put down. My feminist friends freak out if I admit to being "just a housewife," so I try to enter into the spirit of the thing and claim a profession.

"I got tired of just fixing dinners."

Last week I was faced with another "occupation of spouse" and I cheerfully put down "Plumber." It was not a lie; last week I *was* a plumber. Due to the fact that Patrick had tried to flush his toothbrush down the toilet, our dining room ceiling began to rain, and as it was after 5 P.M. (Naturally it was after 5 P.M.; Section 32 of the Plumbers Code stipulates that plumbing is to be installed in such a manner that it will never break down during working hours), I fixed it myself. It wasn't difficult. Any mother who has spent twenty years retrieving toy trucks from her toilet, and repairing the damage of dozens of teen shampoos to shower drains, qualifies for a plumber's license.

That was last week. This week, when I registered the girls for a drama course, I listed myself as "Waiter." The teacher will undoubtedly assume that I am a waitress who doesn't know her masculine from her feminine, but the truth is, this week I have been, in the literal sense of the word, a waiter.

On Monday, Timmy injured his thumb playing baseball, so I took him to the pediatrician where we waited two hours for the doctor to wiggle Tim's thumb and announce: "This thumb is injured."

"I know the thumb is injured, Doctor," I said, "but is it broken?"

"That is not for me to say," he said. "It must be X-rayed." So I had to take Tim over to the hospital, where we waited another hour for the technician to X-ray the thumb, and another forty-five minutes for the radiologist to read the X-ray and give the results to the technician, who in turn gave them to the pediatrician, who finally informed me, "The thumb is not broken."

Swell. How do you go home and tell your husband that you have just spent three hours and $35 on a thumb that doesn't even have the decency to be broken?

On Tuesday, I went to pick up Danny at his basketball game and had to wait twenty-five minutes while the game went into overtime. If football games can end in a tie, why are basketball games allowed to go on forever?

On Wednesday, I went to pick up Peggy at choir practice and had to wait twenty minutes while Sister Callista convinced the kids that "It's the Real Thing" might be great for Coca-Cola, but it won't do for the Communion hymn.

On Thursday, I went shopping and spent half an afternoon waiting to get waited on, and when I finally did get waited on, I had to wait until the clerk who was waiting on me went to answer the phone. Why is it that when I am a telephone-shopper, I must wait if the clerk has a customer, but if I am the customer, I wait while she answers the phone? I must *look* like a waiter.

On Friday, my husband and I went to a movie where we waited to buy tickets, waited to buy popcorn, waited to get a seat, waited for the feature to start, and then waited (impatiently!) for it to be over. (I can't bring myself to walk out on a movie I paid $4.00 to see.)

On Saturday, I went to pick up the kids at the swimming pool and waited half an hour while one or the other of them ran back to look for towels, sunglasses, sun lotion, transistor radios, and each other. Never send one of your children to look for another; you may be a waiter forever.

NO NOT TRIVIAL PURSUIT OR DUNGEONS AND DRAGONS. HOW ABOUT AFFIRMATIVE ACTION OR DIVESTMENT & DISARMAMENT?

A BRIEF INTERVIEW ON THE SUBJECT OF WOMEN'S HISTORY

Ellen Hawley

Naomi came over last night. It was very important. She wanted to know was I a virgin when I got married. "Was I a virgin? Sure I was a virgin," I told her. "Everybody was a virgin then. In fact, I'm still a virgin. Three kids, I'm three times a virgin." I can't believe that girl. And Frances she calls me. Not Aunt Frances anymore, just Frances.

Was I a virgin. Oh, was I a virgin. Then and for three days afterwards. For a while I was afraid I'd never be anything but a virgin. Not that Sam and I didn't have a good marriage. Things moved slower in those days. We didn't know all about that stuff since we were fourteen like they do today.

No, they gotta know everything now. Like Naomi. "It's history," she says. "What history?" I told her. "If whether I was a virgin is history, I think instead I'll go shoot myself. Enough history for you," I told her, "is you knocked your front teeth out when you were six. You wanted to look older." "I fell off the jungle gym," she says. "You want history?" I told her. "George Washington. Abraham Lincoln. Mayor Wagner. What're you gonna do, write a book about my sex life?"

"It's family history," she says. "I want to interview the women in my family." "Women?" I told her. "Women? What do you think, you've got a family of all women? Whether I was a virgin," I said, "I didn't get three kids from the corner grocer. And to think, I used to say you were so bright. What is it, is this what you learned at Hunter?"

"What did you want to be when you were young?" she asked me. "You're changing the subject," I said. "I know," she says, "but tell me." "I used to think I'd want to be a schoolteacher," I said.

"So when you were young, you didn't think about getting married?" she asked me.

"Sure I thought about getting married. Everyone thought about getting married. What else did a woman do? Get married; be a teacher. In my spare time I thought I'd have babies."

"But what did you dream about?" she wants to know. "Dream," I said. "I used to dream of books, all laid out end to end, and a roast beef on rye to eat while I read each one; an apartment on Riverside Drive and no one to ask me questions. You make me nervous. Do you know that?"

"How'd you feel about the rest of your family? About Bea and Leah and David?" she wants to know. "You think I'll forget who's your mother," I told her, "because you call her Leah like she was someone you met just last week. But I saw you when she brought you home, so tiny you didn't have sense enough to cry. You slept in my bed till they got you a crib. I used to worry I'd roll over and crush you. I can't say I never had the chance, can I? But the crib," I

> **"We are women whose hair is compulsively fried, whose skin is bleached, whose nose is 'too big,' whose mouth is 'too big and loud,' whose behind is 'too big and broad,' whose feet are 'too big and flat,' whose face is 'too black and shiny,' and whose suffering and patience is too long and enduring to be believed."**
>
> **Abbey Lincoln**

told her, "you know where they got it, you with the family history? The junk man. Your father wore a yarmulke till he left home, and he hid it in his pocket when he went off the block. Don't you forget where you come from."

"I don't want to forget where I come from," she said. "I'm trying to find out. You never told me that before, Frances. No one ever told me that."

"We're not a family to complain," I told her. "Not that you didn't have everything any of us could get for you. More than made sense for one kid, I used to say. But you were the first, and I didn't have any better sense than the rest of them, I have to admit it.

"You were the cutest thing. Bright. You talked at a year. Your mother used to call to tell me the things you'd said. And your Dad—he was a good father to you. I don't know why you turned out the way you did. We all thought you'd be something special. And when you went to college, Naomi," I told her, "I don't think I was more proud of my own kids. And what've you made of your life? Three unpublished books and enough poems to fill the holes in the linoleum. And now you want family history. My luck this one you'll publish. That's good. The whole neighborhood's been wanting to know was I a virgin when I got married. The super's wife, you know, she asked me just last week."

(From *The Tribe of Dina*, copyright © 1986, 1989 By Melanie Kaye/Kantrowicz and Irena Klepfisz, eds. Reprinted by permission of Beacon Press.)

THE LAST JEW IN AMERICA

Susan Mogul

Introduction

Jews are famous for being survivors. We have a great capacity to adapt. I would like to suggest that our ability to adapt has become so advanced, particularly here in the United States, that I propose it be considered an official Jewish Fine Art. Take a look at my set. Here is a star of David. Yet it's also a piñata. We can have a Jewish Cinco de Mayo fiesta. And my paper jumpsuit—blue and white stripes. It picks up on the motif of my tallis (a tallis is a Jewish prayer shawl). Now I have a complete ensemble I can wear outside of schul. A fashion statement I've coined—the "observant" look.

Sociologist Charles S. Liebman, is the author of the book *The Ambivalent American Jew*. It's typical of many books that address "Jewish American identity." Liebman always addresses issues in the form of questions (naturally). For example: "Why in 1955, did more Jewish people on Friday night attend an Adlai Stevenson rally than attend all the services in all the synogogues on Long Island?" Liebman became so distressed by questions like this that halfway through writing the book, he emigrated to Israel.

Why Is There No Great Jewish Art?

Liebman's book did not give me any added insight into being Jewish. I'm an artist so I decided to examine great Jewish art. I couldn't find any. There is no great Jewish art. Why? The Second Commandment states: "Thou shalt not make unto thee a graven image." Jewish interpretation: "No figurative art." However there were liberal rabbis in the middle ages who permitted profiles, but no portraits of the full face.

Let me show you how the Second Commandment operates in popular culture today. The irrepressible Jewish urge for the latest thing produced the record album Jewish Aerobics. Although the record is up to date, the album cover is evidence of the Second Commandment in operation. This is an exercise record. Yet, it has no representation of the human form on the cover—just a pair of purple running shoes. Additionally there are no diagrams in the instruction booklet—just words. We learn everything by reading.

Was Columbus Jewish?

The United States of America was founded on a Jewish identity crisis. Are you familiar with the theory that Columbus was Jewish? He is known as the son of a weaver from Genoa, Italy. But according to a number of scholars, it's unclear whether he was actually from Italy or Spain. They say Spanish, not Italian, was his first language and he spoke Italian with a Spanish accent. Columbus was secretive. If anyone asked him where he was from, he immediately changed the subject. This, plus other clues have led scholars to suspect that Columbus was Jewish.

Susan Mogul. "The Last Jew in America." Photo Alan Levinson

> **"Since the Jewish people have so many comics, why doesn't Israel have a laughing wall?"**
>
> **Emily Levine**

> **"One could never accuse this society of being rational."**
>
> **Abbey Lincoln**

During the 15th century in Spain Jews were forced to convert to Christianity. Many Jews converted to save their lives but secretly practiced Judaism. The Christians called these people "marranos." Even the definition of "marrano" is up for debate. Some say it means pig or swine, others say "of darker skin," and fewer suggest "one who changes." Whatever the precise definition, its use was derogatory.

Even if you converted to Christianity you were under suspicion. Plus your weekends were booked. The scholars suspect Columbus was a marrano. Big deal. What difference does it make if Columbus was Jewish or not? Well—what motivated him to come to the states in the first place? Remember, this was the period of the Inquisition—a bad time for the Jews. We had to get out of Spain by August 2, 1492. Short notice. As usual. Doesn't it seem a little more than coincidental that Columbus was way off on the high seas by August 3?

Let's explore the psychology of Columbus. He was a man without a home or a country. Like Jesus, he had messianic tendencies, and like Moses, he was seeking the promised land. Additionally, a theory went that it held the ten lost tribes of Israel. Having an ear for theory, Columbus brought along Hebrew interpreter Luis de Torres. For some unknown reason Luis converted to Christianity the day before the ships sailed off. When they finally arrived in the New World, Luis was the first one off the ship. Assuming the Indians were ancient Hebrews, he greeted them with "Shalom."

Why Advertise?

When I was growing up in the fifties, my mother said, "Intermarriage is for those on the left, Bohemians, or celebrities." But in the eighties, intermarriage is considered normal.

Recently my mother said, "With all your brothers and sisters intermarrying, *you* could be the last Jew in America." That, along with my current Jewish investigations, prompted me to attempt to date a Jewish man for the very first time. So I went to a singles bar in Beverly Hills. I had absolutely no luck. Christian guys would make passes but no Jewish action. I called up my best friend, Carol, and told her: "Jewish men are not interested in Jewish women. I'm convinced."

"Susan, you're paranoid—and neurotic."

"Carol, that's natural."

A number of my friends indicate that I am overemotional and tend to personalize things. So I decided to conduct a rational and scientific experiment to prove my thesis. I went down to Woolworth's and bought a cross. I scratched the words "Not Really" on the back just in case my father saw it. Then I returned to the same singles bar in Beverly Hills, and you would not believe the action! I'd never got so much attention from Jewish men in my life. Or men in general. Boy, what I'd been missing by not wearing a cross.

I finally met Barry. Barry the producer. We began seeing each other on a regular basis. But when he wanted to visit me at my place I got nervous. I put him off for a few days. First I had to hide my mezzuzahs, my menorahs, and my Manischewitz. I went back to Woolworth's and picked up a lovely Mary and hung it over my bed. I invited him over and we had a wonderful evening. He looked at Mary from time to time.

Redecoration is simple. Behavior modification is a struggle. Inflections and gestures are not easy to change. I bought handcuffs so I would stop talking with my hands. There was an unexpected side benefit. These things turned Bernie on. And my "oy vey"'s. Every time I would begin to say "oy . . ." I'd swing my lips into a demure "Oh my."

Bernie still wasn't suspicious of my true identity. It was my birthday and Bernie was taking me out to dinner. I treated myself to a classy white dress from Kamikaze on Melrose Avenue. He walked in my place, looked me over and said: "Susan, you look absolutely elegant! That's some outfit you're wearing."

"You like it? Cacharel! $79.99 including tax. Originally lists for $358.00."

Dead giveaway.

I could give up talking with my hands, I could give up, with a certain reluctance, Yiddish expressions with centuries of European culture behind them. Expressions like schlamazel, schlmiel, schmenderick . . . But, to buy retail?

When I was fourteen years old I remarked to my mother that all my Christian friends wore crosses. I asked, "Why don't we wear the star of David, the symbol of Judaism?" She said, "Honey, why advertise?"

(Excerpted from a performance by Susan Mogul.)

THE TURKEY INCIDENT

Harriet Beecher Stowe

" 'Huldy,' says the minister one day, 'you ain't experienced outdoors; and, when you want to know anything, you must come to me.'

" 'Yes, sir,' says Huldy.

" 'Now, Huldy,' says the parson, 'you must be sure to save the turkey-eggs, so that we can have a lot of turkeys for Thanksgiving.'

" 'Yes, sir,' says Huldy; and she opened the pantry-door, and showed him a nice dishful she'd been a-savin' up. Wal, the very next day the parson's hen-turkey was found killed up to old Jim Scrogg's barn. Folks said Scroggs killed it; though Scroggs he stood to it he did n't: at any rate, the Scroggses they made a meal on 't; and Huldy she felt bad about it, 'cause she'd set her heart on raisin' the turkeys; and says she, 'Oh, dear! I don't know what I shall do. I was just ready to set her.'

" 'Do, Huldy?' says the parson. Why, there's the other turkey, out there by the door; and a fine bird, too, he is.'

"Sure enough, there was the old tom-turkey a-struttin' and a-sidlin' and a-quitterin', and a-floutin' his tail-feathers in the sun, like a lively young widower, all ready to begin life over ag'in.

" 'But,' says Huldy, 'you know *he* can't set on eggs.'

> **"Mental health, like dandruff, crops up when you least expect it."**
>
> **Robin Worthington**

" 'He can't? I'd like to know why,' says the parson. 'He shall set on eggs, and hatch 'em too.'

" 'O doctor!' says Huldy, all in a tremble; 'cause, you know, she didn't want to contradict the minister, and she was afraid she should laugh, 'I never heard that a tom-turkey would set on eggs.'

" 'Why, they ought to,' said the parson, getting quite 'arnest; 'what else be they good for? you just bring out the eggs, now, and put 'em in the nest, and I'll make him set on 'em.'

"So Huldy she thought there weren't no way to convince him but to let him try': so she took the eggs out, and fixed 'em all nice in the nest; and then she come back and found old Tom a-skirmishin' with the parson pretty lively, I tell ye. Ye see, old Tom he didn't take the idee at all; and he flopped and gobbled, and fit the parson; and the parson's wig got round so that his cue stuck straight out over his ear, but he'd got his blood up. Ye see, the old doctor was used to carryin' his p'ints o' doctrine; and he had n't fit the Arminians and Socinians to be beat by a tom-turkey; so finally he made a dive, and ketched him by the neck in spite o' his floppin', and stroked him down, and put Huldy's apron round him.

" 'There, Huldy,' he says, quite red in the face, 'we've got him now;' and he *traveled* off to the barn with Tom as lively as a cricket.

"Huldy came behind jist chokin' with laugh, and afraid the minister would look round and see her.

" 'Now, Huldy, we'll crook his legs, and set him down,' says the parson, when they got him to the nest; 'you see he is getting quiet, and he'll set there all right.'

"And the parson he sot him down; and old Tom he sot there solemn enough, and held his head down all droopin', lookin' like a rail pious old cock, as long as the parson sot by him.

'There! you see how still he sets,' says the parson to Huldy.

"Huldy was 'most dyin' for fear she should laugh. 'I'm afraid he'll get up,' says she, 'when you do.'

" 'Oh no, he won't!' says the parson, quite confident. 'There, there,' says he, layin' his hands on him, as if pronouncin' a blessin'. But when the parson riz up, old Tom he riz up too, and began to march over the eggs.

" 'Stop, now!' " says the parson. 'I'll make him get down ag'in:

hand me that corn-basket; we'll put that over him.'

"So he crooked old Tom's legs, and got him down ag'in; and they put the corn-basket over him, and then they both stood and waited.

" 'That'll do the thing, Huldy,' " said the Parson.

" 'I don't know about it,' " says Huldy.

" 'Oh yes, it will, child! I understand,' " says he.

"Just as he spoke, the basket riz right up and stood, and they could see old Tom's long legs.

" 'I'll make him stay down, confound him,' " says the parson; for, ye see, parsons is men, like the rest on us, and the doctor had got his spunk up.

" 'You just hold him a minute, and I'll get something that'll make him stay, I guess;' and out he went to the fence, and brought in a long, thin, flat stone, and laid it on old Tom's back.

"Old Tom he wilted down considerable under this, and looked railly as if he was goin' to give in. He stayed still there a good long spell, and the minister and Huldy left him there and come up to the house; but they had n't more than got in the door before they see Tom a-hippin' along, as high-steppin' as ever, sayin', 'Talk! talk! and quitter! quitter!' and struttin' and gobblin' as if he'd come through the Red Sea, and got the victory.

" 'Oh, my eggs!' says Huldy. 'I'm afraid he's smashed 'em!'

"And sure enough, there they was, smashed flat enough under the stone.

" 'I'll have him killed,' said the parson: 'we won't have such a critter round.'

"But the parson he slep' on it, and then did n't do it; he only come out next Sunday with a tiptop sermon on the "Riginal Cuss' that was pronounced on things in gineral, when Adam fell, and showed how everything was allowed to go contrary ever since. There was pigweed, and pusley, and Canady thistles, cut-worms, and bag-worms, and canker-worms, to say nothin' of rattlesnakes. The doctor made it very impressive and sort o' improvin'; but Huldy she told me, goin' home, that she hardly could keep from laughin' two or three times in the sermon when she thought of old Tom a-standin' up with the corn-basket on his back.

(From "The Minister's Housekeeper," *Sam Lawson's Oldtown Fireside Stories*, 1872.)

" It's necessary in order to attract attention, to dazzle at all costs, to be disapproved of by serious people and to be quoted by the foolish."

Jill Johnston

AT THE DOCTOR'S

Jane Wagner

~~~~~~~~~~~~~~~~~~~~~~~~~~~~~~~~~~~~~~

You're sure, Doctor?
Pre*men*strual syndrome?
I mean, I'm getting divorced.
My mother's getting divorced.
I'm raising twin boys.
I have a lot of job pressure—
I've got to find one.
The ERA didn't pass,
not long ago I lost a very dear friend, and . . . and
my husband is involved . . .
not just involved, but in love, I'm afraid . . . with this
woman . . .
Who's quite a bit younger than I am.

And you *think* it's my *period*
and *not* my life?

(From *The Search for Signs of Intelligent Life.* Copyright © 1986 by Jane Wagner Inc. Reprinted by permission of Harper & Row.)

> **"Myths make reality more intelligible."**
>
> **Jenny Holzer**

TAYLOR CALLS 1–800–THE–LORD

Barbara Kingsolver

~~~~~~~~~~~~~~~~~~~~~~~~~~~~~~~~~~~~~~

The line rang twice, three times, and then a recording came on. It told me that the Lord helps those that help themselves. Then it said that this was my golden opportunity to help myself and the entire Spiritual Body by making my generous contribution today to the Fountain of Faith missionary fund. If I would please hold the line an operator would be available momentarily to take my pledge. I held the line.

"Thank you for calling," she said. "Would you like to state your name and address and the amount of your pledge?" "No pledge," I said. "I just wanted to let you know you've gotten me through some rough times. I always thought, If I really get desperate I can call 1–800–THE–LORD. I just wanted to tell you, you have been a Fountain of Faith."

She didn't know what to make of this. "So you don't wish to make a pledge at this time?" "No," I said. "Do you want to make a pledge to me at this time? Would you like to send me a hundred dollars, or a hot meal?"

She sounded irritated. "I can't do that ma'am," she said. "Okay, no problem," I said. "I don't need it anyway. Especially now. I've got a whole trunkful of pickles and baloney . . ."

(From *The Bean Trees,* copyright © 1988 by Barbara Kingsolver, Harper & Row.)

ZAP!

Nancy Deutsch as
Aggressiva
(Plutonium Players)

Photo by Gail Ann Williams

"I'm a Guerrilla Girl and I'm not angry. Why should I be angry that only one major New York City museum had an exhibition by a woman artist last year? I'm a Guerrilla Girl and I'm not angry that the art world is administered entirely by middle-aged women for the benefit of very young men. After all, women are accustomed to being wives and mothers. We know how to blow their noses! I'm a Guerrilla Girl and I think that the art

IT ISN'T NICE

Words and Music by Malvina Reynolds

It is-n't nice to block the door-way, It is-n't nice to go to jail; There are ni-cer ways to do it, But the nice ways al-ways fail; It is-n't nice, it is-n't nice, You told us once, you told us twice; But if that is free-dom's price, we don't mind.

It isn't nice to carry banners
Or to sit on the floor,
Or to shout our cry of Freedom
At the hotel and the store,
It isn't nice, it isn't nice,
You told us once, you told us twice,
But if that is Freedom's price,
We don't mind.

We have tried negotiations
And the three-man picket line,
Mr. Charlie didn't see us,
And he might as well be blind.
Now our new ways aren't nice
When we deal with men of ice,
But if that is Freedom's price,
We don't mind.

How about those years of lynchings
And the shot in Evers' back?
Did you say it wasn't proper,
Did you stand out on the track?
You were quiet just like mice,
Now you say we aren't nice,
But if that is Freedom's price,
We don't mind.

It isn't nice to block the doorway,
It isn't nice to go to jail,
There are nicer ways to do it
But the nice ways always fail.
It isn't nice, it isn't nice,
But thanks for your advice,
Cause if that is Freedom's price,
We don't mind.

world is perfect and I would never think of complaining about any of the wonderful people in it. After all, women artists make fully one whole third of what male artists make, so what's there to be mad about? I mean, it's not nice to get angry, nice girls don't get angry. I wouldn't dream of getting angry. Thank you so much for taking time out of your busy day to listen to this."

The Guerrilla Girls, The Conscience of the Art World, 1986.

WOULD YOU MARRY A CHINAMAN?

Hazel Houlihingle

Some things never change: would you marry a Jew? a Black? a Mexican? a Chinaman?

Anna Dickinson was one of the greatest nineteenth-century orators in the United States. When she visited San Francisco in 1869, she was horrified to learn that four Chinese "coolies" with brutally bruised bodies (part of a cargo of a thousand) had arrived dead at the port city. Instead of delivering her prepared speech, she began by lecturing the predominantly male audience on the disgraceful treatment of the Chinese in California. Most of the audience were hearing a woman speak in public for the first time. They hissed her lustily.

"My friends," she said, "you are not used to me. Never before have I had the pleasure of facing you, and you, apparently, never before had the profit of listening to an unpleasant truth. I will then tell you, so as to save time and trouble, that as I have endured a great deal of hissing, some stick-and-stone throwing, diverse odorous eggings, and finally one or two revolver bullets through political campaigns in the East, I am not to be scared by a trifle of goose breath in the West."

Spunky Anna then invited them to do all their hissing at once and let her get on with her talk. She said that California should train the Chinese in citizenship and abandon their racial prejudice.

"Would you *marry* a Chinaman?" a man loudly shouted.

Anna addressed the man directly: "If you were poor and oppressed, wouldn't you like to hear me, or someone else, defend you?"

"Yes," he said.

"And I would defend you," Anna continued, "but oppress you by marrying you? Never! Not if you got down on your knees to me would I marry you!"

Virginia Cholesterol and Mrs. T. "Bill" Banks of L.A.W.
Photo by Norman Millar

REPEAL THE LAW OF EVOLUTION

Gail Ann Williams

Ladies Against Women (LAW) travels around the country enacting right-wing fantasies. Bejeweled, well-heeled, bedecked in pink, polka dots, and furs, the Ladies have marched daintily in parades, passed out tasteful Ladyfestos, and held consciousness-lowering sessions since 1980. They've shown up in tasteful picket-reception lines for "Stop ERA" spokesgal Phyllis Schlafly, the very Right reverends Pat Robertson and Jerry Falwell, and other heart-throbs of the ruling regime. They've confronted the "flatfooted, barefaced, media-manufactured sisterly love conspiracy" by addressing gatherings of groups like NOW and the ACLU. The Ladies have had to keep a stiff upper lip, as well as all other parts of their anatomies, since members of such freethinking groups tend to, well, laugh at them.

Mrs. T. Bill Banks, Lady Chair-man of LAW, and a founding member of the National Association for the Advancement of Rich People, warns uppity women of the signs of consciousness raised too high: "You know who you are. All of your sons play with dolls . . . and all of your daughters play with themselves."

Col. Beauregard Lee assists in the recruitment of male members. The men's auxiliary of LAW—For Ladies Against Women, or FLAW—crusades against the hazards of wimpdom. He advises all real men to be "rough as burlap, tough as chuck steak, hard as steel, and twice as dense."

Virginia Cholesterol, founderette of LAW, works feverishly lobbying for the rights of the unconceived. The Ladies are scandalized by the destruction of perfectly innocent sperm cells (future soldiers) through certain masculine habits, "such as self abuse, or the self-styled 'prophylactic' use of those little rubber penal colonies." Mrs. Banks joins in the reproductive rights crusade with her seminal statement, "We support the paternity rights of those men who choose rape—or incest— as their personal means of perpetuating their family lineage."

LAW maintains that the world is only big enough for one opinion. "We are a right-to-life organization," declares Mrs. Banks. "We believe in the right to make our particular style of life mandatory for everyone." Some of the slogans and chants they use on marches are:

PASSPORTS FOR FETUSES

Blow your whistle! Toot your horn!
We love the people until they're born.

MISTERHOOD IS POWERFUL

Push us back, push us back, waaaaay back!

BAN THE POOR

REPEAL THE LAW OF EVOLUTION

Mommies, mommies, don't be Commies:
stay at home and fold pa-jah-mies!

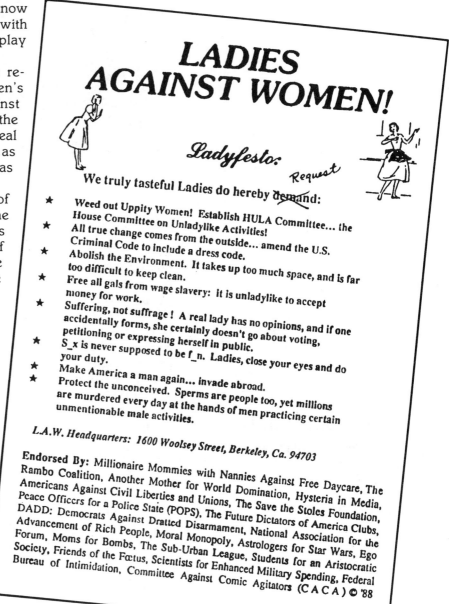

LADIES AGAINST WOMEN!

Ladyfesto:

Request

We truly tasteful Ladies do hereby demand:

★ Weed out Uppity Women! Establish HULA Committee... the House Committee on Unladylike Activities!

★ All true change comes from the outside... amend the U.S. Criminal Code to include a dress code.

★ Abolish the Environment. It takes up too much space, and is far too difficult to keep clean.

★ Free all gals from wage slavery: it is unladylike to accept money for work.

★ Suffering, not suffrage! A real lady has no opinions, and if one accidentally forms, she certainly doesn't go about voting, petitioning or expressing herself in public.

★ S_x is never supposed to be f_n. Ladies, close your eyes and do your duty.

★ Make America a man again... invade abroad.

★ Protect the unconceived. Sperms are people too, yet millions are murdered every day at the hands of men practicing certain unmentionable male activities.

L.A.W. Headquarters: 1600 Woolsey Street, Berkeley, Ca. 94703

Endorsed By: Millionaire Mommies with Nannies Against Free Daycare, The Rambo Coalition, Another Mother for World Domination, Hysteria in Media, Americans Against Civil Liberties and Unions, The Save the Stoles Foundation, Peace Officers for a Police State (POPS), The Future Dictators of America Clubs, DADD: Democrats Against Drafted Disarmament, National Association for the Advancement of Rich People, Moral Monopoly, Astrologers for Star Wars, Ego Forum, Moms for Bombs, The Sub-Urban League, Students for an Aristocratic Society, Friends of the Fœtus, Scientists for Enhanced Military Spending, Federal Bureau of Intimidation, Committee Against Comic Agitators (C A C A) © '88

153

Photo by Donna Marchand

PLUTONIUM PLAYERS

"**Men who teach only men should only get half pay.**"

Dale Spender

At demonstrations they carry lace-bordered signs reading IT'S UN-LADYLIKE TO ACCEPT MONEY FOR WORK and TUPPERWARE PRESERVES THE FAMILY.

New chapters of LAW are springing up all over the country. Pink membership cards—for ladies—have the slogan "I'd Rather Be Ironing," and they have a "permission" blank for the signature of husband, father, or clergyman. Blue cards for FLAW members entitle them to carry heavy luggage, drink more beer, and make other people's decisions for them.

The Ladies have made repeated pilgrimages to the Republican National Convention. In 1980 in Detroit they attempted to get the GOP to call off the election and install Reagan as Shah, on the grounds that "what's good enough for our foreign policy is good enough for our domestic policy." Four years later in Dallas they held a bake sale for the deficit and the Pentagon—but they didn't have much success in moving the Twinkies at $9 billion each. Their recipe for Reagan's budgetary pie was "white sugar, white flour, white power." To angry or befuddled GOP delegates who inquired whether the sale was tongue-in-cheek, the Ladies replied, "We don't use either of those bodily terms in public, and you know that gals don't have a sense of humor."

In 1988, because of the extraordinary shelf life of the Twinkies, LAW was able to bring the same bake sale to the New Orleans convention, and to add Soldier-of-Fortune Cookies to the menu. Delegates opened little cookies and read messages like:

LEADERSHIP IS SKIN DEEP: GIRLS JUST WANNA VOTE CUTE
Baby Boomer Bimbos for Quayle

SECRET GOVERNMENT OUT OF THE WHITE HOUSE BASEMENT
C.I.A. for President

GAY LOVE IS JUST AS EVIL AS TAKING CONTRACEPTIVES
It's the same sin: evading your parental duty again.

Although their bake sales haven't reduced the deficit by a single penny, the men and girls of LAW are convinced that they will get a "God-fearing, patriotic spermie" appointed to the the Supreme Court within the decade.

GLENNA PARK IS TIRED OF WAITING

Virginia Maksymowicz

~~~~~~

Texas artist Glenna Park is tired of waiting. "I waited to be asked out on dates; I waited to be asked to the prom; I waited to be asked to be married; and, after all that waiting, I said 'I'm not waiting for anybody' . . . If you want to be in the parade and it's not coming your way, you make

The Texas Art Band marching in San Antonio

The nude derrieres signify that artists need government backing.

your own goddam parade!'' And so Park has been detouring the parade to San Antonio—sometimes literally. As the leader of the Texas Art Band, she has led kazoo-playing marchers in military-style formation before the San Antonio Museum. She has obtained parade permits to block off that same museum street so that it could be strewn with hundreds of flowers in a graphic visualization of the recurring under-representation of women artists in major museums. . . .

. . . The Texas Art Band grew out of discussions held in a class she was teaching at Trinity University. A New York newspaper had reported that the federal government had allotted more money for military marching bands than for the National Endowment for the Arts. Since in effect it had been ''declared the national aesthetic form,'' it seemed only logical for Park and her students to march. She convinced the Army band director at Ft. Sam Houston to teach her how to march, turn corners, count steps and read paper patterns. At high noon on ''the dullest day in July,'' the Art Band made its debut, decked out with white uniforms and sandwich-board signs, the backs of which were painted with nudes in the style of great artists. Their kazoo version of The Yellow Rose of Texas was followed by a statement directed to the media about the funding cuts at the NEA.

Where Are the Women?

Park orchestrated another performance event in reaction to a San Antonio Museum exhibit of 17 artists from the 1960s, which had been curated by Maurice Tuchman and had travelled from the Los Angeles County Museum. According to Park, it should have been titled ''Seventeen Anglo Saxon Males for the Sixties'' since it did not include a single female or minority artist. Calling a press conference, the artist unloaded barrels of flowers onto the steps of the museum so that visitors had to step over them to enter. She also displayed ten giant bouquets—one for each year of the decade the exhibit was celebrating—tied with ribbons bearing the names of women artists who were missing from the show.

(From *New Directions for Women,* May/June 1988. Reprinted by permission of Virginia Maksymowicz.)

''I've been arrested forty-eight times. I'm going for the women's world record.''

Nikki Craft

A CRAFTY ZAPPER

Nikki Craft

Gas prices went up in 1972, and when I saw how the gas companies manipulated people, I decided I had to do something. I had played several small roles in the Bertolt Brecht Street Theatre in Austin, Texas and had begun to perceive theatre as a political option. So I scrawled DE-STROY THE AUTO BEFORE IT DESTROYS YOU, DEMAND MASS TRANSIT NOW on my 1962 Chevy convertible in indelible paint and planned to blow it up publicly at Lee Park. That was a big deal for someone as poor as I.

My first conscious decision to use theatre was against Rockwell International in 1974. They were having a stockholder's meeting in

Dallas to promote the B-1 bomber. They held it in Dallas to avoid large protest demonstrations. The night before the convention, I went to the Fairmont Hotel, which was under 48-hour top-security guard. A friend and I, dressed as tourists, scoped the place out. We stayed up all night, brainstorming, fixing props, making calls, and we secured press credentials as the Eastfield Junior College Video Collective. If you want to get away with anything, just pose as a junior college student.

The next morning I showed up in a long black dress, wig, and false eyelashes. My friend and I posed as the Eastfield Junior College Video Collective, carrying a suitcase of video equipment. That enabled us to document the event.

The B-1 was called the "Peacemaker." I went to the rear microphone and said in a soft Texas drawl that I had a presentation to make to the Rockwell Board of Directors. Then I walked up to the front microphone and said, "This is what we believe the B-1 will do to world peace." I pulled out armless, legless, bloodied dolls and gave them to five of the stockholders. I gave Rockwell a huge one without a head.

He just said, "Thank you," and took it.

The lights went out immediately for a movie on the glories of the B-1. As I was escorted out into the hall, I put the leftover arms and legs under a three-foot twirling model of the B-1. One of the guards, very upset, hid them under his coat and took them away. The next day the action was reported on the front page of the *Wall Street Journal* under the headline, "Rockwell's B-1 Craft Proves to be Bomb At Annual Meeting."

I later became a volunteer with Dallas Women Against Rape, but I wasn't a very good counselor. I was too angry. I encouraged several furious women to kill their rapists—not that they took my advice.

In 1975 at the University of Texas in Denton, my instructor in a women's studies class gave an assignment to "go out and do anything concerning women you wouldn't ordinarily do." She was shocked when I returned to class with photo-documentation of a defaced Shirley Cothran Miss America billboard that I had enhanced to read MYTH AMERICA.

"Sex sells, and the Dallas Jaycees know it." That was the message we had printed on leaflets and silkscreened on hot pink T-shirts. We dressed in our nicest polyester skirts and leafletted the whole auditorium at Southern Methodist University during the Miss Dallas Pageant. During the bathing suit event, we threw meat on the stage.

The next day, when I saw there was no news coverage, I called the newspaper. I told the woman reporter that my little sister had been to the event and told me some women had thrown meat and did the newspaper have any more details? The reporter asked me a lot of questions, and I told her I happened to get one of the leaflets. She got very excited. "Would you please read it to me?" The article she wrote quoted almost the entire leaflet. There are lots of ways to get news coverage.

Next was the Kitty Genovese Project. I walked into the law office where I worked and said, "What would happen if I published the name of every indicted sex offender?"

Nikki Craft's photo for the marquee of her porn machine

Photo by Bob Marshak

BEAUTY HURTS. Nikki Craft's portable billboard was inspired by the mold of white womanhood line drawing in Andrea Dworkin's *Woman Hating*. The board was one of the many actions at the Myth California beauty pageant protests.

"You can't do that," they said. "You'll be sued."

So I thought we should try it. I always get legal advice but I don't let it stop me from doing anything.

We had no resources, but we had a friend who was a temporary office worker and who told us about a large oil company in a Dallas skyscraper with a room full of Xerox machines. We dressed up as temporary office "girls" and made hundreds of copies of our information forms. Then we went to the Dallas County Records Building and posed as sociology students. It worked. They showed us how to look up indicted sex offenders.

We fished out every indictment from 1958 to 1977. This was before computerization, and it took us nine months to gather our data. The people in the office didn't find out why we were really there until it hit the front page of the Dallas *Times-Herald*. In four days of hand-to-hand leafletting, we distributed 25,000 copies of listed sex offenders. Community women told stories about their rapes on KCHU, a local radio station, on International Women's Day, and they read all the names of indicted sex offenders. The reading took thirteen hours!

The project cost less than $5,000, most of which came from small donations. Because we were dealing with some of the most dangerous men in our community, it was scary asking for donations. One liberal community college instructor said, "I can't give you money. My stepson is on that list." A $1,000 donor's check bounced the day we went to pick up the lists of offenders from the printer. I worked off the $1,000 debt at $3.50 an hour as a maid and dishwasher at Big Sur. It took an entire year.

I moved to Santa Cruz and quietly did ceramics at the University of California until 1980, when I did the "Stack o' Wheats" action. I learned that the university library had photos of murdered women. They were promotional photos for an artist. There were ten black-and-white 3" x 5" prints in a packet that cost $2.50. Each woman appeared to be raped and brutally killed. Chocolate syrup was used as blood—and there was a stack of whole wheat cakes by each body. I couldn't get those photos off my mind. Each woman was posed "erotically," and the pamphlet said, "No police files contain such an array of utterly exquisite corpses," and similarly disturbing things. It was necrophilic pornography.

The Stack o' Wheats action took three months of intensive planning and cost about $2,000. I posed as a journalism student, went into the library, tore up the prints, and poured chocolate syrup on them. I hired a professional photographer to go with me for documentation, which took the action out of the realm of vandalism and into the realm of conceptual art—but I was still arrested for felony, conspiracy, and malicious mischief.

Charges were dropped soon after that, and I was nominated for a Chancellor's award for an "outstanding contribution to campus understanding of ethical principles." I didn't get the award, but my nomination kept the issue under discussion. Three months later I donated copies of the destroyed photos to the library. In a press release I stated that I didn't have the right to decide what was held in the library, and that I only wanted to raise public discussion about individuals' and artists' responsibilities regarding the first amendment. It was a tremendously successful action.

Pornography is a perennial problem. We built a porn machine—a

26" x 26" enameled black box with an exercise machine inside and a 15" golden ceramic dildo ejaculating the American flag. I had seen a cartoon of three men in business suits standing on a nude woman with the sign WE STAND ON OUR FIRST AMENDMENT RIGHT. I recreated the scene, photographed it, and used the photo on the marquee of the porn machine. We took it to *Hustler* headquarters in Los Angeles, where we had a "First Amendment Rights Lie-in" on International Women's Day in 1981. While women were lying under the porn machine, it played patriotic music with a man's voice telling the usual pornographic lies about women. Then, for the benefit of the invited press, we slammed an ax into the porn machine and dismembered it. Our group, Preying Mantis, called for the national destruction of *Hustler* magazines in retaliation for the violence it promotes.

Later that year in Santa Cruz, three of us posed as junior college photography students, entered a Stop-and-Go, and asked if we could photograph some of the product displays. (We wanted to document the destruction of a rack of *Hustlers* for our press-release photo. We thought it laughable that any publication could advocate rape and murder of women and expect to remain unmolested on newsstands, protected by the First Amendment.) The unsuspecting clerk gave us the run of the store. We mutilated the magazines with India ink, and we were never apprehended.

We continued to zap *Hustler*. Within a week, we had destroyed 550 copies. (None of the store owners lost money. They simply returned the magazine covers for credit.) We warned the stores that if we were prosecuted, we would organize a boycott. We gave out a M.U.S.H. Award (Merchants United to Save *Hustler*), which was, again, a huge golden phallus attached to a hand pump that ejaculated cream of wheat and buttermilk. We displayed hundreds of images from *Hustler* in front of the stores, where we read the contents of the magazine aloud. Store owners may be all for the First

GENTLEMEN THIS IS A TEST. CHEMICALS YOU CERTIFIED AS SAFE ARE BEING CIRCULATED IN YOUR AREA!

(Reprinted by permission of bülbül—Gen Guracar.)

The end-product of the Stack o' Wheats Action.

Photo by Bill Reynolds

Amendment, but they prefer that *Hustler* leave their premises in plain brown bags. We also published addresses and telephone numbers of stores selling *Hustler*, and we got 28 stores to remove it.

As another tactic, we encouraged women to take their husband's magazines from under the bed, put them on the coffee table, look at them, read them, discuss them, and if the pornography were violent, to do whatever they thought appropriate. We offered membership in the Preying Mantis Women's Brigade in return for ripped-up pornography mailed to us.

Once I donned a brown Buddhist monk's robe, dropped to my knees at a demonstration, and announced to the media that I was beginning a pilgrimage. I wrote in chalk, VIOLENCE IN THE MEDIA = VIOLENCE IN SOCIETY = VIOLENCE IN THE MEDIA on the sidewalk and streets, continuing from one store that sold *Hustler* to another. I wrote for three days. Several people joined me. Our writing wove 17 miles through Santa Cruz and used up $200 in chalk. Since it's not illegal to write in chalk, there were no arrests. Many people were touched by the message, and we think the action deserves a place in the *Guiness Book of World Records.*

(Freely edited from an interview with tricia lootens and alice henry in *off our backs*, July 1985. Reprinted by permission of Nikki Craft.)

> **"In New York City, The Guerrilla Girls visibly protest the small number of women and nonwhite artists exhibited in galleries and museums and reviewed in art magazines. They list the following Advantages of Being a Woman Artist:**
>
> • **Working without the pressures of success.**
>
> • **Knowing your career might pick up after you're eighty.**

NOT A FORM LETTER

Mary Kay Blakely

While the Growing Girls [ripening feminists] sometimes embarrassed us [Fort Wayne Feminists] in public, they also provided a lot of the fun and just plain goofiness every family needs now and then. One time, a local TV station manager refused to cancel an outrageously sexist game show, "Three's a Crowd." (Points were earned when the women in the boss-secretary-wife "team" guessed the boss's answer to such questions as "Which TV dog most resembles your secretary's bra: Snoopy, Lassie, or Old Yeller?") The station manager dismissed the complaints as "form letters" from organized fanatics. The Growing Girls were incensed, having carefully penned several personal notes themselves. They proposed a Zap Action, a last resort taken when more legitimate means of getting the point across failed.

On this particular occasion, a pickup truck was secured, a half-dozen women donned overalls, rubber boots, and stocking caps, drove to a farm a half hour outside the city, and shoveled what remained after a small herd of well-fed pigs quit the sty. Just after dusk, six barrels of the still steaming stuff were deposited on the lawn in front of the TV station, with this carefully worded explanation:

Dear Mr. Metcalfe:

Here's some feedback, so to speak, on "Three's a Crowd." We hope you don't mistake this for a form letter.

160

The two other networks received anonymous tips about the incident, just in time for the evening news. The show was subsequently canceled. And the next spring, a bright-green patch of grass marked the fertilized spot, an indelible tribute to the spunk and spirit of the Growing Girls.

(From "Growing Girls and Grandmothers," *MS* magazine, June 1987. Reprinted by permission of Mary Kay Blakely.)

RITA'S REVENGE

Crazy Hazel

Yeah, I was in Hollywood when Rita Hayworth was a star. Yeah, they treated her like *merde*—at least Harry Cohn did. He was the head of Columbia pictures. Never asked her how she liked the script or the part, ordered her around like some donkey: "Be there Monday at 10 to fit your costume," he'd say. Never a car to pick her up, never even a "please."

Yeah, she asked for a lot—like some chintz in her dressing room—big expensive item. Ordinary things like that sent Cohn into a hysteria of howl: "What she need chintz in her goddam dressing room for?"

Yeah, she got even. And how. Rita just came down whenever he said, did everything he said, no fuss, sheep-meek for the first two weeks of shooting. By then the studio had a real bundle in the production, and then zap! Rita gets sick and can't continue. All that footage—what can they do with it? Cohn can't even stuff it in his mattress—or the usual place they tell people to stuff things. And I'm thinking, "Remember that, Harry Cohn—$750,000 down the drain because you're too chintzy to give Rita *her* little bit of chintz!"

A ROSE BY ANY OTHER NAME

Evi Seidman

Would *not* smell the same, according to the *Washington Post*. And that conviction, believe it or not, is why the nation at large did not learn about the Minneapolis Women's Patrol. We in the Patrol conceived of ourselves allegorically as the crew of The Good Ship Hope, guided by Captain Mirth of Earth. Crew members were Faith, Charity, Humility, Loyalty, Courage, etc.

On Labor Day 1975, we dressed in Wonder Woman costumes and set up a booth with streamers, helium balloons, gifts, and a birthday cake in front of the *Washington Post* offices in Washington, D.C. Whose birthday was it? Reporters came down from the *Post* to ask. As we sang songs and gave gifts to passersby, we explained to the reporters that we were celebrating Mother Earth, who had given birth to us, so naturally, on Labor Day! Captain Mirth explained that

> - **Being reassured that whatever kind of art you make, it will be labeled feminine.**
>
> - **Being included in revised versions of art history.**
>
> - **Not having to undergo the embarrassment of being called a genius.**
>
> - **Getting your picture in art magazines wearing a gorilla suit."**

Evi Seidman models what the well-dressed M.C. wears on Valentine's Day

"Ginger Rogers did everything that Fred Astaire did, but she had to do it backward in high heels."

Ann Richards

in order to survive the stormy times ahead, we would have to honor the earth and learn to live in harmony with it.

The reporters obviously enjoyed the antics of this ship of virtuous fools, and they wanted to interview each of us. But they insisted upon knowing our "real" names. Mirth, Charity, Faith, Honesty wouldn't do. Our family names, however, placed us in an exact spot in patriarchal lineage. Our names were our fathers' names, which had been *their* fathers' names and so forth, thus perpetuating a tradition we hoped constructively to interrupt. We wouldn't betray the New Order to which we had dedicated ourselves, and the reporters wouldn't bend. Most of our exploits in Washington, DC, thus went unreported by the press.

We did, however, also visit the Pentagon. Dressed impeccably as little old ladies, we called upon the Chairman of the Joint Chiefs of Staff and presented our gift: a beautiful calligraphy of Rudyard Kipling's poem "If," which we recited in a choral reading for the generals. "If you can keep your head when all those about you are losing theirs . . . , you'll be a man, my son."

Dressed in graceful white Grecian-inspired gowns, and singing through the halls, we also visited the Council of Economic Advisers. Our gift to them was a model of a house, each part labeled and symbolizing some part of the new economic order (based not upon gold but upon energy). The currency of the future would be certificates of energy, and the costs of goods would be the amount of energy required to produce and distribute them.

Dressed in ethnic costumes from all over the world, we visited the Senate Foreign Relations Committee. We hand-delivered letters to every member of the House of Representatives and of the Senate, telling them about the 50-Year Plan for the Social Regeneration of the Planet Earth. Singing and bearing gifts, we also visited the U.S. Treasury and the White House.

So even though we had no "real" (read "patriarchal") existence for the *Washington Post,* our gifts were courteously received by several agencies of government—who thereby acknowledged our unrecorded existence.

Back in Minneapolis, the Women's Patrol executed other zap actions. One was a midnight, phantom hit-and-run planting of hundreds of flowering plants at City Hall in downtown Minneapolis. Flower beds were created during the night, and by morning, an entire garden bloomed where there had been none. Small staked signs were also left in the ground. They read: A NEW CIVILIZATION IS COMING INTO BEING. Signed, THE GREAT GODDESS. Another action converted a vacant lot, overgrown with weeds and strewn with trash, broken glass, and old tires, into a park, complete with flower beds, park benches, and fully laid sod. That action was completed in just one weekend. The Great Goddess, once again, left her signature.

Witty Women

I Am, Therefore I Art.
Pat Oleszko

Photo by Neil Selkirk

NORA'S OBSERVATIONS

Clare Boothe Luce

When a man can't explain a woman's actions, the first thing he thinks of is the condition of her uterus.

. . . if God had wanted us to think with our wombs, why did He give us a brain?

Know what Freud wrote in his diary when he was 77? "What do women want? My God, what do they want?" Fifty years this giant brain spends analyzing women. And he still can't find out what they want. So this makes him the world's greatest expert on female psychology?

(From the play *Slam The Door Softly*, Dramatists Play Service, Inc., 1970. Reprinted by permission of International Creative Management, Inc.)

WHITE ENGLISH IN BLACKFACE, OR WHO DO I BE?

Geneva Smitherman

Bin nothin in a long time lit up the English teaching profession like the current hassle over Black English. One finds beaucoup sociolinguistic research studies and language projects for the "disadvantaged" on the scene in nearly every sizable black community in the country.[1] And educators from K-Grad. School bees debating whether: (1) blacks should learn and use only standard white English (hereafter referred to as WE); (2) blacks should command both dialects, i.e., be bidialectal (hereafter BD); (3) blacks should be allowed (??????) to use standard Black English (hereafter BE or BI). The appropriate choice having everything to do with American political reality, which is usually ignored, and nothing to do with the educational process, which is usually claimed. I say without qualification that we cannot talk about the Black Idiom apart from Black Culture and the Black Experience. Nor can we specify educational goals for blacks apart from considerations about the structure of (white) American society.

And we black folks is not gon take all that weight, for no one has empirically demonstrated that linguistic/stylistic features of BE impede educational progress in communication skills, or any other area of cognitive learning. Take reading. It's don been charged, but not actually verified, that BE interferes with mastery of reading skills.[2] Yet beyond pointing out the gap between the young

> **Nice Jewish Girls: A Lesbian Anthology** is, according to Evelyn Torton Beck, a 'book written by people who do not exist.'

brother/sistuh's phonological and syntactical patterns and those of the usually-middle-class-WE-speaking-teacher, this claim has not been validated. The distance between the two systems is, after all, short and is illuminated only by the fact that reading is taught *orally*. (Also get to the fact that preceding generations of BE-speaking folks learned to read, despite the many classrooms in which the teacher spoke a dialect different from that of their students.)

For example, a student who reads *den* for *then* probably pronounces initial /th/ as /d/in most words. Or the one who reads *doing* for *during* probably deletes intervocalic and final /r/ in most words. So it is not that such students can't read, they is simply employing the black phonological system. In the reading classrooms of today, what we bees needin is teachers with the proper attitudinal orientation who thus can distinguish actual reading problems from mere dialect differences. Or take the writing of an essay. The only percentage in writing a paper with WE spelling, punctuation, and usage is in maybe eliciting a positive *attitudinal* response from a prescriptivist middle-class-aspirant-teacher. Dig on the fact that sheer "correctness" does not a good writer make. And is it any point in dealing with the charge of BE speakers being "non-verbal" or "linguistically deficient" in oral communication skills—behind our many Raps who done disproved that in living, vibrant colors?[3]

What linguists and educators need to do at this juncture is to take serious cognizance of the Oral Tradition in Black Culture. The uniqueness of this verbal style requires a language competence/performance model to fit the black scheme of things. Clearly BI speakers possess rich communication skills (i.e., are highly *competent* in using language), but as yet there bees no criteria (evaluative, testing, or other instrument of measurement), based on black communication patterns, wherein BI speakers can demonstrate they competence (i.e., *performance*). Hence brothers and sisters fail on language performance tests and in English classrooms. Like, to amplify on what Nikki said, that's why we always lose, not only cause we don't know the rules, but it ain't even our game.

We can devise a performance model only after an analysis of the components of BI. Now there do be linguists who supposedly done did this categorization and definition of BE.[4] But the descriptions are generally confining, limited as they are to discrete linguistic units. One finds simply ten to fifteen patterns cited, as for example, the most frequently listed one, the use of *be* as finite verb, contrasting with its deletion: (a) *The coffee be cold* contrasts with (b) *The coffee cold,* the former statement denoting a continuing state of affairs, the latter applying to the present moment only. (Like if you the cook, (a) probably get you fired, and (b) only get you talked about.) In WE no comparable grammatical distinction exists and *The coffee is cold* would be used to indicate both meanings.

1. For examples of such programs see *Non-Standard Dialect*, Board of Education of the City of New York (National Council of Teachers of English, 1968); San-Su C. Lin, *Pattern Practices in the Teaching of Standard English to Students with a Non-Standard Dialect* (USOE Project 1339, 1965); Arno Jewett, Joseph Mersand, Doris Gunderson, *Improving English Skills of Culturally Different*

> "When a man in Emily Levine's audience called her a J.A.P. (Jewish American Princess), she responded: 'It so incenses me to hear that, because it denigrates Jews and Japanese, and that means the only people to have come out of World War II smelling like a rose are the Germans.'"

Youth in Large Cities (U.S. Deparment of Health, Education and Welfare, 1964); *Language Programs for the Disadvantaged* (NCTE, 1965).

2. See, for example, Joan Baratz and Roger Shuy, ed., *Teaching Black Children to Read* (Center for Applied Linguistics, 1969); A. L. Davis, ed., *On the Dialects of Children* (NCTE, 1968); Eldonna L. Evertts, ed., *Dimensions of Dialect* (NCTE, 1967).

3. For the most racist and glaring of these charges, see Fred Hechinger, ed., *Pre-School Education Today* (Doubleday, 1966); for an excellent rebuttal, see William Labov, *Nonstandard English* (NCTE 1970); for a complete overview of the controversy and issues involved as well as historical perspective and rebuttal to the non-verbal claim, see my "Black Idiom and White Institutions," *Negro American Literature Forum*, Fall 1971.

4. The most thorough and scholarly of these, though a bit overly technical, is Walter Wolfram, *Detroit Negro Speech* (Center for Applied Linguistics, 1969).

(From *The Black Scholar*, 1973.)

> "It is characteristic of great thinkers to come up with a number of bizarrely ridiculous ideas. By this criterion we can see that Sigmund Freud is a truly great thinker."
>
> **Crazy Hazel**

A BIOGRAPHER'S PROBLEM

Virginia Woolf

...Orlando was a woman—Lord Palmerston had just proved it. And when we are writing the life of a woman, we may, it is agreed, waive our demand for action, and substitute love instead. Love, the poet has said, is woman's whole existence. And if we look for a moment at Orlando writing at her table, we must admit that never was there a woman more fitted for that calling. Surely, since she is a woman, and a beautiful woman, and a woman in the prime of life, she will soon give over this pretence of writing and thinking and begin at least to think of a gamekeeper (and as long as she thinks of a man, nobody objects to a woman thinking). And then she will write him a little note (and as long as she writes little notes nobody objects to a woman writing either) and make an assignation for Sunday dusk and Sunday dusk will come; and the gamekeeper will whistle under the window—all of which is, of course, the very stuff of life and the only possible subject for fiction. Surely Orlando must have done one of these things? Alas—a thousand times, alas, Orlando did none of them. Must it then be admitted that Orlando was one of those monsters of iniquity who do not love? She was kind to dogs, faithful to friends, generosity itself to a dozen starving poets, had a passion for poetry. But love—as the male novelists define it—and who, after all, speak with greater authority?—has nothing whatever to do with kindness, fidelity, generosity, or poetry. Love is slipping off one's petticoat and—But we all know what love is. Did Orlando do that? Truth compels us to say no, she did not. If then, the subject of one's biography will neither love nor kill, but will only think and imagine, we may conclude that he or she is no better than a corpse and so leave her.

THE LIFE OF A PLAYWRIGHT?

Julie Jensen

I never knew what a playwright's life would be like. I never heard of a playwright when I was a kid. And I didn't grow up answering playwright to those questions aunts and uncles asked about my future. In fact, I never knew any playwrights until I was one myself. And so it's hard to say whether my life is or is not what it should be, given that I turned out to be a playwright instead of a nurse or a postal worker.

I've seen some movies with playwrights in them. I remember Jane Fonda as Lillian Hellman tossing pages into the trash and her typewriter out the window in the movie *Julia.* But my life isn't much like that. It's also not much like the opening nights we've all seen in lots of other movies. I've had four plays in New York. I've never arrived in furs, never seen the inside of a limousine, and never hung around in the lobby under chandeliers.

My first play in New York was at the Negro Ensemble Theatre. I actually saw it for the first time three weeks into the run and a few days before it closed. I remember sitting in a bar before I went to the theatre because I was not sure the director and actors knew I was white. And I didn't want to disappoint them. I told some older woman sitting next to me at the bar that I was going to see one of my plays at the Negro Ensemble that night, "Is that right," she said. "I just put my mother in a nursing home today."

My second play in New York was a part of a New Year's Marathon at the Quaigh Theatre. As some kind of fund-raising gimmick, the theatre had decided to produce one-act plays non-stop beginning the morning of December 31 until the evening of January 1. My play was scheduled at 7:00 A.M. New Year's morning. There isn't a single person on the streets of New York at 7:00 A.M. New Year's morning. There are only broken bottles, smashed cans, bent noise makers and trampled hats. I trudged up the street feeling very much like the last person alive. When I got to the, theatre, I walked right on by. I simply could not go inside. I knew I would be the only person in the audience. And somehow the threat of that humiliation just surpassed my tolerance. And so I never found out until much later that my play was actually done at noon before a generous house which received it warmly. Instead I walked on back to my hotel, a tragic picture of theatrical embarrassment.

The last play I had produced was done at the Arena Stage in Washington, D.C. last summer. That play had won a big prize and the production promised to be top drawer all the way. In fact, the reviews were all good, and we sold out the run after the first preview. In response to all that, I invited my parents to come from Utah to see the play. They dutifully showed up and took their seats down front. As soon as the play began, my mother began to fidget and twitch. Then she started to sigh and moan. Finally by the midway point, she was whispering loudly to my sister. "I'm leaving. I can't stand this." My sister was heard to say back to her, "Then go, but just shut up!" She didn't leave, however. She stayed on through till the end, flinching and bobbing all the way. After it was all over,

> " **Antifeminist refers to the woman who claims the only place for a woman is in the home and who has come out of the home to prove it.** "
>
> **Cheris Kramarae and Paula Treichler**

she pinned me to the wall with her dark angry eyes, ''Don't you ever bring us to another play like this,'' she said. And I promised not to.

And that's what it's like to be a playwright. Clearly fame is the reason I do it. Fame and money. Although the money is actually worse than the fame. But that's another story . . .

(© 1987 by Julie Jensen)

MRS. SELWYN'S SWIFT PUT-DOWN

Fanny Burney

'But I'm a sad creature,—don't you think I am, my Lord?' [said Lady Louisa.]

'O, by no means,' answered [Lord Merton], 'your Ladyship is merely delicate,—and devil take me if ever I had the least passion for an Amazon.'

'I have the honour to be quite of your Lordship's opinion,' said Mr. Lovel, looking maliciously at Mrs. Selwyn, 'for I have an insuperable aversion to strength, either of body or mind, in a female.'

'Faith, and so have I,' said Mr. Coverley; 'for egad I'd as soon see a woman chop wood, as hear her chop logic.'

'So would every man in his senses,' said Lord Merton; 'for a woman wants nothing to recommend her but beauty and good-nature; in every thing else she is either impertinent or unnatural. For my part, deuce take me if ever I wish to hear a word of sense from a woman as long as I live!'

'It has always been agreed,' said Mrs. Selwyn, looking round her with the utmost contempt, 'that no man ought to be connected with a woman whose understanding is superior to his own. Now I very much fear, that to accommodate all this good company, according to such a rule, would be utterly impracticable, unless we should chuse subjects from Swift's hospital of idiots.'

(From *Evelina*, 1778.)

STAND BY YOUR FLAG

Barbara Ehrenreich

If you live, as I do, near one of the great scenic spots of this great nation—say, the Grand Canyon, the Statue of Liberty, or the World's Largest Peanut in Ashburn, Georgia—then you've probably had some run-ins with foreign tourists. First they offer your kids a stick of gum for agreeing to be photographed in front of the scenic spot. Then they flash a few kronen or yen and ask if you know of a place to eat where the entree is not served inside a

Photos by Blaise Tobia

biscuit, bun, or pita bread. Finally, when the conversation warms up, they offer to buy you a cup of coffee if you'll sit down with them for a few minutes and explain U.S. foreign policy.

Now I always figure that if you're old enough to be drinking coffee in the first place, you ought to be able to explain your country's foreign policy to any foreigner who comes along—particularly if they're from some two-bit place like England or West Germany that doesn't have a foreign policy of its own and is always having to borrow ours. So I say, sure, just throw in a cruller and I'll tell you anything you want to know, so long as it isn't about Vietnam, which is already available as a movie genre, a videocassette industry, a mini-series, and a sitcom for anybody willing to just sit back and enjoy it.

Sometimes they'll start way back in history and ask, why, other than to provide a plausible plot line for *Heartbreak Ridge*, did we ever invade Grenada. I am pretty sick of this question, but I just take a deep breath and tell them the truth: "Because they were building an airport, of course. And you know what that could have led to."

"Well, what," they ask, "a Holiday Inn?" "That's right," I tell them, lowering my voice. "Possibly an Avis dealership, a Marriott, who knows? We stopped them just in time."

That's probably the easiest question you'll get, though, because next they're likely to get into something more intricate, like the Persian Gulf. I must have had a half-dozen Norwegian backpackers and vacationing English nannies ask me that tiresome old question of why, if it was the Iraqis who hit the Stark, we decided to go after the Iranians. "Well," I say, just as patient as could be, "because the Iranians are fundamentalists, and we hate fundamentalists, except the kind that believe in nuclear war as the Second Coming and the eternal torture in hell of Jews, atheists, and unbaptized baby sinners. So we figured that while we were in the neighborhood . . ."

Yes, of course, they say, or *mais oui* or some such, but just a short time ago weren't you giving those same Iranians discount Hawks and day-old cakes? "Don't you read the papers?" I ask in exasperation. "We gave the cake to the moderates. They're the ones who, while everyone else is chanting 'Death to America,' are chanting sotto voce, as it were, 'A Wasting Disease to America,' or 'The Intolerable Itch of Hemorrhoids to America,' or something moderate like that."

Sooner or later they always bring up that old canard about U.S support for right-wing dictators, to which I just say, "Whoa there! That was then, this is now. Now we just let revolution, free elections, etc., take their course, then we move in to help the local right-wing malcontents mount a little low-intensity harassment. These days, we're proud to be on the side of the underdog—UNITA, the contras, Renamo, plus any other exotic fellows you may have seen modeling combat fatigues in *Soldier of Fortune*."

Of course, this always leads us to Nicaragua. "Do you Americans really believe," I've had a bevy of Belgian schoolteachers ask me, "that the Sandinistas are planning a human wave assault on Fort Lauderdale?" "It's not that simple," I have to say. "There are 3 million Nicaraguans, which is more people than we have in the great cities of Altoona, Pennsylvania, and Bozeman, Montana, combined. They are all hard-core Marxist-Leninists except for the overwhelming majority who are eagerly awaiting liberation at the hands

"**Affirmations? That's where you lie to yourself until it's true.**"

Linda Moakes

of William Webster and his band of Freedom Fighters. So, you see, it's the least we can do.''

Some foreigners give up at this point, figuring that the language barrier is a little steeper than they'd realized, but the really hard-nosed ones just order another round of crullers and hit me with some trick question they must have been practicing all the way from Gander. Like this one: ''Look, the Iranians support terrorists who actually torture and kill American hostages. But the Nicaraguans captured two Americans engaged in acts of war—Hasenfus and Hall—and released them unharmed, with a free psychiatric consultation thrown in in the case of Hall. So the United States sells arms to the Iranians and uses the profits to overthrow the Nicaraguans. I mean, maybe I missed something, but . . .''

At this point you have several options. The first, which I call the ''Ronald Reagan,'' is to duck your head down toward your right shoulder and say, ''Jeez, just because I live here doesn't mean they tell me everything, you know.'' The second, known around town as the ''George Shultz,'' consists of pounding the table and saying, ''By God, you've got a point there. In fact I've said the very same thing myself, in no uncertain terms and on numerous occasions, to that waitress right over there.''

Then there's always the ''Ollie North,'' by which I don't mean the well-known sandwich (bologna and shredded lettuce hero, on a roll, ha ha) but the equally famous speech: ''All right, so maybe it doesn't sound like a foreign policy. Maybe it sounds like the deranged rumblings of a loose cannon rolling around on the gun decks of the ship of state. Well, it's the only foreign policy we have, and this All-American gal is here to tell you that she's proud of it. Darn proud!''

Or just tell these Euro-trash busybodies to cram their crullers and go back to Russia, where they obviously came from.

(Reprinted with permission from *Mother Jones* magazine, © 1987, Foundation for National Progress.)

BAMAMA GOES TO COLLEGE

Ellen Goodman

Boston—My friend received another degree this month. She became a B.A., M.A., M.A., or as we fondly call her, a Bamama.

This latest degree raised her academic temperature and the quality of her resume. In fact, my friend Bamama officially became qualified to be unemployed in yet a better class of jobs.

Let me explain. When she got a B.A. in philosophy four years ago at the cost of $12,000 (them was the bargain basement days), Bamama had the choice between becoming an overeducated waitress or an overeducated office worker. So she became an overeducated day-camp counselor and went back to school.

The next year, for $4,000, she got a degree in library science. Now, qualified as a librarian, she won a job as an overeducated part-time library assistant. In her off-hours, she became an overqualified clerk at a cheese counter. Rumors that she arranged the cheddar according to the Dewey Decimal system were greatly exaggerated.

In any case, her course was clear. Before she entirely coated her brain as well as her arteries with brie, she went back to school. Now, $5,000 later, she is qualified not only as a librarian, but as a school librarian, teacher, administrator, etc., for a school system in need of an efficient, caring, well-educated Bamama. No such luck or, rather, no such system.

So, Bamama has done the only logical thing: applied for and been accepted for a Ph.D. program. With that degree, Bamamaphd, three years older and deeper in debt, would be qualified as a college professor and might therefore be able to find a job as an overqualified school librarian.

THE REAL MOTHER'S DAY

Una Stannard

Mother's Day is not the day when we celebrate motherhood, woman's ability to give birth. That day in May isn't much of a celebration; rather, a universal guilt spreads across the land, guilt we ease by phone calls and flowers. The real Mother's Day, the day when we joyously celebrate birth, fertility, children, has nothing to do with women. It is that day in late December when we mark the birth of a male child who has the power to give us what religion says we can't get by natural birth—immortal life, a divine child who is the son of a male god by a woman who remained a virgin before and after birth, as if she hadn't had a baby at all. Moreover, that holiday's chief lay figure is also a man, whose huge red belly stretches across the world and who, encumbered by a bulging sack, labors down the chimney. The greatest holiday in our year celebrates male maternity, men's unconscious desire to be the real mothers of us all.

N: A PERFORMANCE

Deborah Margolin

Pleased to meet you . . . I'm silent N . . . I'm the letter N in the word CONDEMN . . . NNNNN . . . Jesus! A man said me the other day . . . it was strange . . . First I was floating on the lips of a French woman who was using a lot of plural verbs . . . PLEUR . . . *Elles pleur* . . . ENT . . . I was stuck all day between E and T, and wishing they would just phone home . . . when a strange man said me . . . he said me so

> **"Men who teach only men are called scholars. Women who teach only women are called political agitators."**
>
> **Dale Spender**

beautifully . . . he tongued me . . . He said, This painting of a woman looks like it's all one stroke . . . just one line . . . I feel that I could pick the line up off the canvas at her fingertips and pull 'til she's completely dislimNed. He was a handsome and sexy man . . . I turned to smoke on his soft palate, perched on the tip of his tongue, and I floated out his nostrils and around to where his hair touched his collar. I love that area of a person . . . the Nape of the Neck . . . I spend a lot of time in people's nostrils . . . you know, people with colds, that kind of thing . . . I figure prominently in the sneeze . . . I come roaring out like one of Bob Fosse's dancers split right down the middle in a crash of jazz . . .

But this man . . . mmmmmmNNNNNNNN . . . I wanted to get him mad enough to curse because I wanted him to say me really sweet . . . so I went through his nostrils into his sinus cavity and created a rite-of-spring sort of disturbance . . . the kind bees make in honeysuckle . . . He was flirting with someone at the museum. And he made this pretentious remark about the nude painting being so DISLIMNABLE . . . I think he was about to kiss her . . .

Yeah . . . so he was about to kiss her when I altered his senses completely . . . his eyes filled with water and he said it, O, he said it, O, he said, GODDAMNNNNNNNNNNNNNNNN!

I flew back to his uvula and shook with the air . . . and the woman left . . . she was too good for him anyway . . . she didn't buy that bullshit . . . it saved her slapping his face . . .

When I'm silent, I'm undressed, y'know . . . but when I get voiced I get dressed . . . when the going gets tough, the tough get going . . . SOLEMN becomes soleMNNNity . . . And I go from nude to dressed in a moment . . . like that woman in the painting . . . I bet she wanted to grab a bathrobe real fast in front of a lech like that . . .

You know, when letters meet in words it's not a simple thing . . . a word is a whole show made up of active letters . . . and the energy between letters is . . . physical, you know . . . like actors on the stage. When you say a word you see it, don't you? . . . you lick it . . . and when you write a word down you paint portraits of these actors . . . for example, the word MISOGYNIST is like a Chekhov play because all the letters just stand around wondering how to relate to each other, the Greek roots stick out all over the place, and when it's said and done, the meaning is very sad . . .

So. I was in a relationship . . . that didn't work out. You see me at a depressed and unfocused moment in my life, rushing around people's mouths and nostrils . . . I didn't used to do that so much . . . and I . . . I had everything I ever wanted but I didn't know it . . . you may already have heard . . . I was living with silent G. When he's lower case he is so well HUNGNG, down below the baseline, the floor of the letter, and when he's upper case his form is so beautiful, curving around and back in toward himself like self-recrimination . . . like remorse . . . like GUILT!

I first met him when we were both in the word IMPUGN, and then we started hanging around together in formal words like CONDIGN . . . or in words where I was voiced, and cuddled myself on either side of him while he stayed silent . . . women do that shit for men all the time . . .

Then we moved toward a more mutual relationship . . . we were INDIGNANT! both voiced and full of bristle . . . and I was . . . in love, I think . . . and found I was PREGNANT . . . my body was

Flo Kennedy with Ti-Grace Atkinson

"At a campus lecture, a male questioner to Ti-Grace Atkinson asked: 'Are you a lesbian?' Her response: 'Are you my alternative?'"

changing ... then things deepened ... we became POIGNant ...

I had baby YYY and he went silent again ... I don't know ... he took a traveling job ... he's a lug nut on the wheel of a truck that's moving, moving, moving all night ... the way he used to move me ... I feel it when he gets knocked out of ALIGNment ... one of the places where we lived together for so long ... so long ...

So what's left for me? The ballet of my upper case, the yoga of my lower case, my little place in the dictionary upstate. Come visit me there, if you want, unvoiced, on the tip of some word. Whoever you are, we'll find a way to be together, or at least on either side of a vowel.

Of, if you want, just write me a letter ...

ON THE COMPLEXION OF A ROSE

Fanny Burney

"Your ladyship," said Mr. Lovel [to Lady Louisa], "so well becomes the lilies, that the roses might blush to see themselves so excelled."

"Pray, Mr. Lovel," said Mrs. Selwyn, "if the roses should blush, how would you find it out?"

(From *Evelina*, 1778.)

"In the United States we devote one day a year to mothers and a whole week to pickles. But who would want a pickle for a parent?"

Hazel Houlihingle

ACKNOWLEDGMENTS

The most obvious and most important acknowledgment goes to the many contributors to this volume. Artful humor involves perhaps the rarest and the most difficult of skills. *In Stitches* is a salute to the exciting talents of its contributors.

In another sense, compiling such a collection was a complex and difficult task, for which I received much needed help. First and foremost, I am grateful to Leslie Viktora, whose laughter (upon her reading of the first draft) convinced me that this collection was worth the labor of editing. Leslie read all the subsequent drafts, introduced me to the work of many contributors, and assisted me in making selections. She also compiled our working index without which the manuscript could not have gone forward. Her input was major and essential, and it went far beyond the help that I as Leslie's mother might have expected from my talented daughter.

Eileen Bender generously read early drafts and also made valuable suggestions about particular selections. More significantly, she was of major assistance, along with Mary Kay Blakely, in criticizing an early draft of the Introduction. Eileen's comment led me to focus on humor and power as the main subject of the essay. Mary Kay Blakely's criticism of a close-to-final draft is largely responsible for whatever coherence the Introduction has.

Virginia Maksymowicz went out of her way to help me with many of my initial contacts with women artists. Much that is excellent in these pages reflect Virginia's knowledge, good taste, and generosity. Her talent (see p. 169) speaks for itself.

It was a special delight to work with Jackie Urbanovic, contributor and book designer. Because of her flexibility, good nature, and talent, I was able to make design requests that would otherwise be impossible. Many of Jackie's contributions are happily identifiable. It is perhaps less obvious that she designed every handsome page.

I am indebted to the work of other feminist scholars and researchers whose publications made my gathering tasks much easier. Hilde E. Wenner and Elizabeth Frelicher's *Here's to the Women: One Hundred Songs for and about American Women* (1987) contains a wealth of witty compositions and is a good source for people interested in musical feminist humor. *IN/SIGHTS* (1978), a collection of self-portraits of women photographers compiled by Joyce Tenneson Cohen, with its profusion of witty work, confirmed my intention to include women visual artists in this volume. Elaine Partnow's *The Quotable Woman* (2 vols., 1977) was a convenient source for me to comb, as was *The Feminist Dictionary* (1985) by Cheris Kramarae and Paula Treichler. *Make Way! 20 years of American Women in Cartoons* by Monika Franzen and Nancy Ethiel was another useful source (although the majority of cartoons and strips in the present collection are not reprints but originals). Many publications (such as *Women and the Comics* [1985] by Trina Robbins and Catherine Yronwode) which I did not directly use were nevertheless extremely helpful in making decisions about selections. I have tried to present material that is not printed elsewhere or not easily available. This publication is designed to supplement rather that repeat other materials on feminist humor.

A collection such as this takes years in its compilation, and it is

> "Motherhood—instinctive? Biological destiny? Forget biology! If it were biology, people would die from not doing it."
>
> **Jessie Bernard**

sometimes difficult to invest so much time in editing others' fine work rather than creating one's own. For that reason, I am especially grateful to the encouragement I have received at various times from colleagues and friends. Although some of them may not even remember their kind remarks, I want to acknowledge valued encouragement from Cathryn Adamsky, Eileen Bender, Mary Kay Blakely, Zsuzsanna Budapest, Carol P. Christ, Kate Clinton, Tee Corrine, Cathy N. Davidson, Deidre English, Elizabeth Schuessler Fiorenza, Naomi Goldenberg, Suzanne Hyers, Julie Jensen, Eleanor Kaufman, Flo Kennedy, Madonna Kolbenschlag, Susan Koppelman, Audrey McCluskey, Caryn McTighe Musil, Dale Spender, Una Stannard, Emily Toth, Leslie Kanes Weisman, and the Jewish Women's Caucus of the National Women's Studies Association.

A number of people helped me in a variety of ways. David Shapiro (my son) sent me selected Shary Flenniken cartoon strips. I received sundry assistance from Shirley Carlson, Smiljka Cubelic, Denise Collins, Abbe Dallek, Judy Kelly, Marcy Levine, Sharon McEndarfer, Dora J. Reynolds, Linda Schultz, Claire Sweet, and Sandra Winicur. I am also deeply grateful for the constant support from my husband, Samuel Shapiro, who (whenever my schedule required it) dependably and cheerfully did *all* the housework in lieu of his customary half, and who did not have to be asked for such heroic aid.

For doing their job so superbly, the staff of Indiana University Press have my deep gratitude.

Finally, the enthusiasm of many contributors was deeply encouraging. Their names are listed in the Index. The quality of this collection is wholly due to the compelling artistry of their work.

" There's no reason to repeat bad history."

Eleanor Holmes Norton

INDEX OF CONTRIBUTORS

The following is a complete list of contributors to this volume and their contact addresses, if available.

"On the Low Fertility Rate in the 19th Century U.S.: I am not being entirely facetious . . . when I suggest that, with its double focus on improving female literacy and controlling sexuality, the sentimental novel may well have been the most effective means of birth control of the time."

Cathy N. Davidson

"If all the people at OSHA had ovaries, they might do things a little differently."

Dr. Eula Bingham

> " [If] reformed rakes make the best husbands, might it not be said with equal justice, that if a certain description of females were reformed, they would make the best wives?"
>
> **Sukey Vickery (in *Emily Hamilton*, 1803)**

> "A loaf of bread that is more comfortable than a sofa cannot help but be unpalatable."
>
> **Fran Lebowitz**

> "Women can't have an honest exchange in front of men without having it called a cat fight."
>
> **Clare Boothe Luce**

© 1991 Jm. Urbanovic.

" A man is never so honest as when he speaks well of himself."

Ouida

" On Literary Critics: [The] literary world is infested with a kind of loathsome reptile [that] has lately crawled over the volumes, which I have had the temerity to submit to the public eye. I say *crawled* because I am certain it has never penetrated beyond the title of any."

Susanna Rowson

" The earth's our bank and we're overdrawn."

Evi Seidman

Our readers comment

"All of our voices are here—wicked, sardonic, gently humorous. The wide range of feminist humor is delightfully represented. I have only one problem. The table of contents is so tantalizing; what do I read first?—**Linda Bubon**, *Women and Children First* (Chicago)

"***In Stitches*** made me laugh out loud again and again. A wonderful collection of feminist humor and a true testimonial to our ability to laugh at our foibles." —**Barb Wieser**, *Amazon Bookstore* (Minneapolis)

"***In Stitches*** is a wonderfully diverse collection of amusing, biting and satiric observations on the impact of classism and sexism in our society, not just on its victims, but on its perpetrators as well. From the image of the leaders of the military/industrial complex going off to fight their own war, rather than sending young proxies, to a young black child's first understanding that the American Pie may not be divided fairly or evenly, the pieces provide a very funny, feminist view of our relationships, institutions and culture." —**Carol N. Levin**, *Judith's Room* (New York)

"Diverse, expansive, and consistently funny, ***In Stitches*** is the best collection of feminist humor since its predecessor, ***Pulling Our Own Strings***, was published in the '70's. But this is richer, fuller, more complex. It reveals the extraordinary breadth of the subjects feminists find fit to exercise their wit about and also the sophisticated range of styles for expressing it. What's funny here is instantly recognizable: we might not be able to define exactly what feminist humor is, but we know it when we see it, and there's a healthy dose of it in this collection." —**Ann Christophersen**, *Women and Children First* (Chicago)

GLORIA KAUFMAN, Director of Women's Studies at Indiana University South Bend, has published poetry and fiction (under pseudonyms) and was the editor (with Mary Kay Blakely) of the first collection of feminist humor, ***Pulling Our Own Strings.*** She is an energetic supporter of peace, environmental, and feminist causes, a music-lover, and a dolphin fan (the aquatic variety, that is).